Political Alignment in the
French National Assembly, 1789–1791

Harriet B. Applewhite

Political Alignment in the French National Assembly, 1789–1791

LOUISIANA STATE UNIVERSITY PRESS   Baton Rouge and London

Designer: *Glynnis Phoebe*
Typeface: *Garamond # 3*
Typesetter: *G &S Typesetters, Inc.*
Printer and binder: *Thomson-Shore, Inc.*

Library of Congress Cataloging-in-Publication Data

Applewhite, Harriet Branson.
    Political alignment in the French National Assembly, 1789–1791 /
Harriet B. Applewhite.
        p.   cm.
    Includes bibliographical references and index.
    ISBN 0-8071-1751-x (cloth)
        1. France. Assemblée nationale constituante (1789–1791)—History.
2. France. Etats généraux—History.   3. Legislators—France—
History—18th century.   4. France—Politics and government—
Revolution, 1789–1799.   I. Title.
JN2775.A67   1993
328.44'09'033—dc20   92-32493
                                                                      CIP

Earlier versions of some findings in this book were published in the *Journal of Interdisciplinary History*, IX (1978), 245–73, © 1978 by the Massachusetts Institute of Technology and the editors of the *Journal of Interdisciplinary History*. Revised material is presented here with the permission of the editors of the *Journal of Interdisciplinary History* and the MIT Press, Cambridge, Massachusetts. Additional material was published in *Proceedings of the Eighth Annual Meeting of the Western Society for French History* (Las Cruces, 1981), 265–75, © 1981 by the Western Society for French History. Revised material used here with the permission of the editor, Edgar Leon Newman.

The paper in this book meets the guidelines for permanence and durability of the Committee on Production Guidelines for Book Longevity of the Council on Library Resources. ∞

For Philip B. Applewhite

Contents

Figures and Tables

Figures

Tables

Acknowledgments

This book began with a year of research supported by a Younger Humanist Fellowship from the National Endowment for the Humanities, for which I am most grateful. In addition, my research has been supported by a sabbatical year and release time from Southern Connecticut State University. Most especially I would like to thank Anthony V. Pinciaro, vice president for Academic Affairs, J. Philip Smith, dean of Arts and Sciences, and James D. Newman, director of Faculty Development, for a stipend from Southern Connecticut State University that contributed toward the publication of this book.

Gabriel A. Almond first introduced me to the concept of political culture and its relevance to the political history of revolutionary France, and I thank him for his continuing interest in my work over several decades. Philip Dawson guided me into the study of the French Revolution, and I would like to express my very specific thanks for his assistance in working out the coding for some of the biographical information on deputies. I also appreciate his continuing encouragement and commentary at several of my recent paper presentations. At an early stage of the research on this project, I received some invaluable research assistance from Mme. Jill Bourdais de Charbonnière at Paris Research Associates. She and her team of researchers supplied me with some vital information at a key stage of the research design process.

My colleagues in the Political Science Department at Southern Connecticut State University have encouraged my endeavors for many years. I am particularly grateful for critical reading and technical advice from

John Critzer, Edward C. Harris, John O. Iatrides, Arthur Paulson, and Kul B. Rai. Joseph A. Polka helped me convert from one statistical data-processing package to another, and his patience was never-ending.

I would also like to thank the anonymous readers for the Louisiana State University Press, whose judicious criticisms were stimulating and helpful. The editors at the Press have been the best kind of professionals to work with in transforming a manuscript into a book. Margaret Fisher Dalrymple shepherded the manuscript and revisions through the review process. My editor, Gerry Anders, has a fine ear, a sharp eye, and a ready wit; I am grateful for his patience, his energy, and above all, his intelligent criticism. For errors of fact and interpretation, I alone am responsible.

Jean Polka provided innumerable refills of coffee, lots of wit and good cheer, and countless small services along the way. Donna Aitoro and Mary Ann Coughlin expertly typed earlier versions of the manuscript. Susana Martins helped with great efficiency in putting the final product together. I would like to thank Eleanor V. Applewhite and Kate M. Applewhite for sorting notecards and bibliography, and for being my best cheering section. Douglas R. Applewhite drew the figures and assisted with most of the tables and was endlessly generous with his computer expertise.

This book would not exist without Darline Gay Levy, who has been my friend, colleague, and collaborator for a quarter century. Her critical comments on an earlier version of this study were invaluable. It is a rare thing to find complete intellectual rapport and personal friendship, and I cherish it.

Philip B. Applewhite, to whom this book is dedicated, can do at least three things at once, which is fortunate since in between his own research and writing he has acted as data processor, methodological critic, stylistic consultant, and general life-support system. He has kept me most of the time good-humored, and all of the time well-cared-for.

Methods and Sources

This book combines a systematic study of the political attitudes of a selected number of deputies to the Estates General/National Assembly of revolutionary France, as gleaned from their pamphlets, with an analysis of the alignment and role of all the deputies, as defined by their political behavior. This section explains the pamphlet sources, the technical details of the coding system for attitudes, and the sources for biographical information used to generate measures of behavior.

Attitudinal Sources and Measures

Political culture combines the study of people's political attitudes with analysis of their political behavior. The approach does not assume that attitudes determine behavior or that behavior forms attitudes, but rather that the two are part of the mosaic of people's lives at the points where state and society intersect. Certain sets of attitudes expressed by deputies did tend to cluster and form patterns distinct from other sets of attitudes, as did certain kinds of behavior; and clusters of certain attitudes were associated with clusters of specific behaviors. Just like most people, deputies tended to act in ways congruent with their political viewpoints.

In order to map the attitudes expressed by a large number of deputies, I first needed sources and methods of selection. I sought sources that would allow me to determine systematically and rigorously both the range of opinions that deputies were expressing on current issues and the more general attitudes that underlay those views. I rejected total reliance on the texts of debates within the Estates General/National Assembly for two reasons: first, debates would yield no information on those deputies who never addressed the Assembly; second, debates would not yield any data for the period before the Estates General began to sit.

Pamphlets seemed to be the best sources for the attitudes of deputies. They were public and political communications, and their topics were tied to broad questions of participation in government and the legitimacy of rulers. They may be considered a roughly coessential category of writing, thus meeting a central assumption of systematic content analysis. Deputies' pamphlets varied considerably in style and length, but they were all printed as political briefs to express and win support for their authors' political views. They were the major organ of public opinion in France until the upsurge of political journals after June, 1789. After that, pamphlets were still frequently used by deputies to counter attacks upon them from journals, to express opinions they had not been able to deliver at the bar of the Assembly, to clarify and expand upon certain issues for their constituents, and to persuade others to support their positions or to defend their views against attacks within the Assembly.

It would have been a virtually endless project to locate, read, and analyze as many pamphlets as I could find that were written by the 1,318 deputies. Rather than randomly select a sample of deputy authors, it made more sense to draw up a geographically based sample that would enable me to look closely at Tocqueville's hypothesis about the impact of centralization. If Tocqueville was correct, men from those central provinces administered from Paris and included in the jurisdiction of the Paris Parlement should have exhibited the most hostility between the privileged and the nonprivileged, the greatest resentment of absolutism, and the most radical positions on issues relating to legitimacy and participation; deputies from autonomous provinces that had retained provincial parlements and provincial estates should have been more moderate.

To see whether these expectations were borne out, I selected a sample of deputies from seven localities: the city of Paris within the walls; the provinces of Brittany, Dauphiné, Orléanais, Berry, and Bourbonnais; and the bailliage of Auxerre, in Burgundy. Paris, of course, was the center of eighteenth-century French political, cultural, and economic life. Brittany and Dauphiné had been able to maintain the most significant spheres of independence from the centralizing monarchy, and events in those provinces in 1788 and early 1789 received national publicity as radically innovative prototypes for what articulate Frenchmen supporting the Third Estate hoped to accomplish nationally. The central provinces had a less uniform provincial consciousness and a less distinct political culture, and they had long been closely controlled by royal tax administration and judicial procedures.

Altogether, these seven areas sent 247 deputies—19 percent of the total membership—to the National Assembly. To locate pamphlets written by any of those 247 men, I checked their names against catalogs of printed revolutionary documents in the Bibliothèque Nationale in Paris and in major French revolutionary collections in American libraries.[1] I found that 114 of the 247, or 46 percent, had been authors of pamphlets published between May 8, 1788 (the date of the promulgation of the May Edicts removing from the Parlement of Paris the power to register laws), and September 30, 1791 (the close of the National Assembly).

For the entire period from 1788 to 1791, the 114 authors produced 370 pamphlets. Ninety of the pamphlets were published between May 8, 1789, and June 17, 1789; these have been treated separately in order to analyze the polarization in deputies' attitudes that was already apparent at the beginning of the National Assembly. All 370 pamphlets, however, were coded and analyzed in order to assess systematically the range of opinions on issues involving political legitimacy and participation. In addition

---

1. My main sources for pamphlets were: the holdings of Widener Library, Harvard University, and Sterling Library, Yale University; André Martin and Gérard Walter, *Catalogue de l'histoire de la Révolution française* (3 vols.; Paris, 1936); Maurice Tourneux, *Bibliographie de l'histoire de Paris pendant la Révolution française* (5 vols.; Paris, 1890–1913); Alexandre Tuetey, *Les Papiers des assemblées révolutionnaires aux Archives nationales: Inventaire de la Série C: Constituante* (Paris, 1908); Marcel Blanchard, "Une Campagne de brochures dans l'agitation dauphinoise de l'été 1788," *La Révolution française*, LXV (1913), 225–41; Mitchell B. Garrett, *The Estates General of 1789* (New York, 1935); Ralph W. Greenlaw, "Pamphlet Literature in France During the Period of the Aristocratic Revolt," *Journal of Modern History*, XXIX (1957), 349–54; M. G. Hutt, "The Curés and the Third Estate: The Ideas of Reform in the Pamphlets of the French Lower Clergy in the Period 1787–1789," *Journal of Ecclesiastical History*, VIII (1957), 74–92; and Kenneth Margerison, "History, Representative Institutions, and Political Rights in the French Pre-Revolution (1787–1789)," *French Historical Studies*, XV (1987), 68–98.

to reading and analyzing the pamphlets, I followed the authors' political careers, from their first activities until their deaths, in order to find out whether any particular alignment, as expressed in the pamphlets, was associated with any particular career trajectory.

I defined two key concepts operationally to guide my reading of the pamphlets. *Legitimacy* is used here to mean the conviction that a particular political institution is the right one out of available alternatives. Legitimacy became a key concept once work on a written constitution was under way and the deputies had to define and locate national sovereignty, executive and legislative authority, and political representation. *Participation* has to do with broadening the base of political engagement: involving more people in the connections between governing authority and society, and expanding the meaning of that involvement. Deputies had to concern themselves with declaring civil and political rights, fixing the categories of citizenship, and defining or redefining political responsibilities such as tax obligations and military conscription. They cast their votes on these matters in the context of their views on the political capacities of ordinary people and their reactions to revolutionary violence.

In defining the variables subsumed under legitimacy and participation, I sought to treat the contents of deputy pamphlets systematically, in order to generate information on the range of opinion on issues treated in them.[2] To compute frequencies, scale them, and compare deputies' opinions, I drew up a code with sixteen variables that tabulates authors' opinions on sources of legitimacy, the nature of royal authority, the nature and limits of popular participation in politics, the meaning of the word *revolution,* and attitudes about the political process inside the Estates General/National Assembly. The code "asks" each pamphlet author what he thinks about these issues and then codes his answer according to a range of possible

2. See, for example, the following discussions and applications of content analysis: A. Burguière, "Société et culture à Reims à la fin du XVIIIᵉ siècle: La Diffusion des Lumières analysée à travers les cahiers de doléances," *Annales: Economies, Sociétés, Civilisations,* XXII (1967), 303–33; George Gerbner et al., eds., *The Analysis of Communication Content* (New York, 1969); Albert Kientz, *Pour analyser les media: L'Analyse de contenu* (Tours, 1971); Ole R. Holsti, *Content Analysis for the Social Sciences and Humanities* (Reading, Mass., 1969); Philip J. Stone et al., *The General Inquirer: A Computer Approach to Content Analysis* (Cambridge, Mass., 1966); and Marie-Christine d'Unrug, *Analyse de contenu et acte de parole: De l'énoncé à l'énonciation* (Paris, 1974).

responses. Ordinal scales were constructed in order to rank the responses from one extreme to the other. Each position on the scale was assigned a numeric value and the pamphlet coded according to the nature of its statements on the issue. The legitimacy variable "attitudes toward the king" can be used to illustrate the coding process. If a given statement concerned the king, it was matched with one of five responses: traditional ruler, supporter of liberty, center of authority, weak or misled, and untrustworthy. If a pamphlet did not mention the king, the "attitudes toward the king" variable was coded "not mentioned." Because of the extreme variation in pamphlet length, no record was made of the frequency with which coded opinions were stated within one document. Once all 370 pamphlets were read and coded, the data set was entered into a VAX mainframe computer, frequencies were tabulated, and tables generated that cross-tabulated one variable with one or more other variables.

Ensuring reliability is one of the main challenges in statistical content analysis. At worst, purely subjective coding decisions can yield a false appearance of rigor, objectivity, and quantification. My first concern was to establish simple and clear coding rules. A pamphlet had to mention specifically ·the topic in question before it was coded; no inferences were made beyond the text. If the intensity of the author's opinion was at all ambiguous, I coded the weaker rather than the stronger category.

This method of studying opinion admittedly sacrifices certain advantages of close textual evaluation of a few written documents in order to gain systematic comparison of a large number of documents. My method does not judge or rank the political influence of each pamphlet. I assessed political influence by examining the roles of deputies within the Assembly, not by any inference from what a deputy wrote.

This form of content analysis covered the entire range of published deputy opinion in the geographic regions under study. It facilitated a systematic review of stated opinions on issues of legitimacy and participation. Because other behavioral measures of leadership and alignment were derived from deputies' actions rather than their attitudes, I could investigate the relationship between behavior and opinion, compare authors and nonauthors, and compare the deputies from the sample regions with all of the others.

The relationship between opinions in pamphlets and the background and careers of their authors is complex because many authors wrote more than one pamphlet. If we are cross-tabulating two opinion variables observed in the pamphlets, we are simply examining the distribution of those opinions in the total number of pamphlets, and the individual pamphlet is therefore the unit of analysis. However, if we want to cross-tabulate one opinion variable with a biographical variable about the authors, such as occupation or estate, we have a dilemma because there are more pamphlets than there are authors. When we try to determine whether opinions varied according to their authors' backgrounds and careers, do we choose the 114 authors or the 370 pamphlets as units of analysis? I chose the pamphlets because the prolific authors' views on a given issue varied from pamphlet to pamphlet: each writer did not express one uniform opinion.

Out of a total of 114 authors and 370 pamphlets analyzed in this study, 54 authors (47 percent) wrote one pamphlet; 35 (31 percent) wrote two to four; 15 (13 percent) wrote five to nine; and 10 (9 percent) wrote 10 or more. Thus, 53 percent of the authors have facts about their background (their occupation or province, for example) overrepresented when these are cross-tabulated with their expressed opinions.

To estimate the effects of this overweighting, I took as an example the variable "attitudes toward the king" and determined that 183 of the total of 370 pamphlets could be coded on that variable. These 183 pamphlets were written by 54 different authors, 28 of whom wrote one pamphlet each, 14 of whom wrote from two to four, 9 of whom wrote from five to nine, and three of whom wrote ten or more. This breakdown shows us that 28 of the 54 authors were not overweighted (one author/one pamphlet) and 26 were overweighted by factors from two to sixteen. I then took the three most prolific authors on the issue of the king, Antoine Pierre Joseph Marie Barnave, Jean Joseph Mounier, and Trophime Gérard Lally-Tolendal, and investigated the range of opinion they expressed in their sets of pamphlets.

Barnave addressed the question of the king in eleven pamphlets; five spoke of the king as a traditional ruler, one said the king supported liberty, one called him the center of authority, one said he was well-intentioned but weak, and three said he was untrustworthy. Barnave's opinions on the king became progressively more negative from 1788 to 1791. His eleven pamphlets, when cross-tabulated with his occupation as lawyer, give him the weight of eleven lawyers but do present the full range of his opinions. A somewhat narrower spread of opinions, but still a spread, shows up in the pamphlets by Jean Joseph Mounier, who addressed the question of the king in fifteen pamphlets, calling him a traditional ruler two times, the center of authority ten times, and well-intentioned but weak three times. Lally-Tolendal wrote sixteen pamphlets treating this issue; one said the king was a traditional ruler, three claimed he supported liberty, eleven referred to him as the center of authority, one called him well-intentioned but weak, and one said he was untrustworthy. In short, two-thirds of the pamphlets by each of these authors take the same stand on this issue, and the remaining third express other opinions.

This example confirms that weighting biographical information about the authors (by attaching it to every expressed opinion on any given issue) distorts the influence of pamphlet writing less than trying to reduce to a single category the whole range of an author's expressed views on any given issue. My underlying assumptions are that pamphlets were a central means of political communication during the period of the National Assembly, and that most of the prolific authors expressed different views on broad issues as they played a part in the unfolding of revolutionary events. An author could not change his prerevolutionary occupation or province or estate; he often changed his opinions.

Behavioral Measures

This book also presents systematically collected biographical information on all of the 1,138 deputies who sat in the National Assembly at any time between May 3, 1789, and September 30, 1791. One set of biographical information concerns deputies before their election. I collected and recorded information on each deputy's estate and electoral circumscription, occupation, membership in any prerevolutionary political assembly (such as a provincial estates or the Assembly of Notables), association with any other institution (such as the royal court or an administrative jurisdiction), and kind of mandate given upon election. A second set of measures pertains to alignment, and a third set to roles within the Assembly; both of these are explained fully below. Finally, there are variables that concern deputies' careers after the close of the National Assembly, such as election to the National Convention. For the 247 deputies in the sample drawn up to select the pamphlets, I tabulated information on their political careers until their deaths.

The central variable in this study is a scale measuring the left-to-right political alignment of all of the 1,318 members of the National Assembly. Had the deputies decided to record their names on roll-call votes, we would have an objective way to group them by shared opinions and to arrange them on a continuum from left to right. But two weeks after the formation of the National Assembly, they rejected a proposal to record their roll calls. It took a month of jockeying to establish voting procedures. On June 12, the deputies in the Third Estate had formed twenty bureaus to examine the minutes of electoral assemblies as the first step in the process of verifying credentials. They added ten more bureaus on July 1 to accommodate the full membership of the unified Assembly. Three crucial votes were taken by roll call within these bureaus: a vote on July 4 deciding which delegation to admit to represent St. Domingue, and two votes on July 8, one to excuse deputies from adhering to imperative mandates and another to ask the king to remove troops surrounding Versailles.[3] On July 9, noble deputies from Beaucaire and Nîmes proposed that a register be set up to record the votes of deputies on each motion; their proposal was voted down.[4] Procedures established in the *règlement* of July 29 were followed throughout the life of the Assembly. "Votes shall be taken by sitting and standing; and if there is any doubt, there will be a vote by roll call, following the alphabetical list [of deputies] by bailliages, completed, verified and signed by the members of the bureau."[5]

Roll-call voting records facilitate longitudinal studies of political alignments; shifts in the size and characteristics of majorities, minorities, and coalitions can be followed for the life of a legislature. Without such lists, there is no way to determine the alignment of deputies at one moment and then to trace subsequent shifts in that alignment. Consequently, such measures of alignment as can be devised for the entire membership of the National Assembly tend to be static because they cannot be replicated for an earlier or later time. A moving picture of alignment shifts is possible only for those deputies whose activities and opinions can be traced through

3. *Procès-verbal de l'Assemblée nationale* (77 vols.; Paris, 1789–1791), Vol. I: "Procès-verbal des séances des députés des communes depuis le 12 juin jusqu'au 17 juin, jour de la Constitution en Assemblée nationale" (June 12), 2; *Procès-verbal,* No. 11 (July 1), 21; No. 15 (July 4), 4, 5; No. 18 (July 8), 2.

4. *Procès verbal,* Vol. I, No. 19 (July 9, 1789), 2, 3.

5. *Procès verbal,* Vol. I, No. 35 (July 29, 1789), "Règlement" (follows p. 23 of the minutes, separately paginated), 11.

sources such as journals, diaries, *mémoires,* and speeches. Timothy Tackett has used such sources to reconstruct the dynamics of political struggles within the National Assembly.[6] My approach, instead, has been to specify measures that could be applied to all of the deputies in attendance at any particular date. Because protest lists compiled from April, 1790, through September, 1791, provide the most extensive and reliable means of classifying deputies, I devised a scale of left-to-right alignment for the National Assembly between those dates. I then correlated this scale with other measures of alignment from 1789 and 1790. Finally, I investigated the connection between alignment and other aspects of deputies' political careers before and after the Assembly.

Although a few dozen totals for roll calls are recorded in the *Archives parlementaires,* names are listed for only one, the vote on May 12, 1791, on the rights of free blacks in the colonies.[7] Other means must be found to classify deputies into categories representing points on an ideological continuum from left to right. Such classifications are often made on the basis of patterns of leadership—that is, by determining the beliefs of those who spoke frequently in the Assembly and by identifying their followers.[8] This method will not work for the entire 1,318 deputies, many of whom did not debate and whose views cannot be determined. Other studies present evidence based on deputies' behavior but cover only part of the total membership. Recently, however, Edna Hindie Lemay and her team of collaborators have produced a definitive prosopography of the total membership of the National Assembly, containing personal biographies and full accounts of deputies' political careers. Exhaustively researched, this work is the most thorough modern source for the deputies. It appeared after the research and writing for this book had been completed. The biographical sketches do contain information on positions taken by individual deputies in debates, but Lemay and her team did not attempt to classify the deputies according to a rigorous measure of alignment.[9] My scale, based mostly on measures

6. Timothy Tackett, "Nobles and Third Estate in the Revolutionary Dynamic of the National Assembly, 1789–1790," *American Historical Review,* XCIV (1989), 271–301.

7. *Archives parlementaires,* XXVI (May 12, 1791), 25, 26.

8. For a fine example of this method, see Eric Thompson, *Popular Sovereignty and the French Constituent Assembly, 1789–1791* (Manchester, Eng., 1952), 8–21.

9. The new work is Edna Hindie Lemay, *Dictionnaire des Constituants, 1789–1791* (2 vols.; Paris, 1991). Among the other studies are Lemay, "La Composition de l'Assemblée

dated after April, 1790, classifies deputies whenever possible according to their own decisions and actions, as traced through signatures on protest lists, club membership lists, and resignations from the National Assembly. I also used three anonymous classifications made by contemporary observers, most probably men who were themselves deputies.

Men farthest to the right on the ten-point alignment scale are labeled "consistent right"; they signed four different protest lists. The first is dated April 19, 1790, and includes names of those who protested the Assembly's refusal to declare Catholicism the state religion.[10] On July 9, 1791, a second list was signed by those who protested the suspension of royal executive authority after the king's flight to Varennes on June 21.[11] The third list accompanied Jean Jacques du Val d'Eprémesnil's declaration of August 31, 1791, protesting the required oath of loyalty to the Constitution.[12] The final list asserted that the king's acceptance of the Constitution of 1791 was not a free act. It was drawn up and signed on September 15, 1791.[13]

Deputies categorized as "moderate right" signed two or three of the four protests and/or were unambiguously perceived as sitting on the right

---

nationale constituante: Les Hommes de la continuité?" *Revue d'histoire moderne et contemporaine,* XXIV (July–September, 1977), 341–63; Lemay, *La Vie quotidienne des députés aux Etats généraux, 1789* (Paris, 1987), 181–93; Patrice Higonnet, *Class, Ideology, and the Rights of Nobles During the French Revolution* (New York, 1981); James Murphy and Patrice Higonnet, "Les Députés de la noblesse aux Etats généraux de 1789," *Revue d'histoire moderne et contemporaine.* XX (1973), 230–47; James Murphy, Bernard Higonnet, and Patrice Higonnet, "Notes sur la composition de l'Assemblée constituante," *Annales historiques de la Révolution française,* XLVI (1974), 321–26; and M. G. Hutt, "The Role of the Curés in the Estates-General," *Journal of Ecclesiastical History,* VI (1955), 190–220. Timothy Tackett is working on a study of internal politics in the National Assembly; see Tackett, "Nobles and Third Estate," 271–301.

10. *Déclaration d'une partie de l'Assemblée nationale sur la décret rendu le 13 avril 1790, concernant la religion* (Paris, 1790).

11. "Déclaration de 293 députés sur les décrets qui suspendent l'exercice de l'authorité royale et qui portent atteinte à l'inviolabilité de la personne sacrée du roi," *Archives parlementaires,* XXVIII (July 9, 1791), 91–96.

12. Jean Jacques du Val d'Eprémesnil, *Déclaration d'une partie des députés aux Etats-Généraux, touchant l'Acte constitutionnel et l'état du Royaume* (Paris, 1791).

13. "Déclaration d'une partie des députés aux Etats-Généraux de France, sur l'acceptation donnée par le roi à l'acte constitutionnel, 15 septembre 1791," *Archives parlementaires,* XXX (September 15, 1791), 674–76.

by two different observers who drew up lists of deputies' names, printed in 1791. One list was made by a sympathizer with the right wing and one by a sympathizer with the left. The first is entitled *Liste par ordre alphabétique de bailliage et sénéchaussée de MM. les députés de la majorité de l'Assemblée nationale, vulgairement appelés le côté gauche ou les enragés se disant patriotes.* An attack on left-wing deputies, it does not contain the names of right-wing deputies and (probably accidentally) omits nine electoral circumscriptions. Since moderates *are* on the list, it is best used to determine the names of those omitted, whom a clearly right-wing sympathizer knew to have voted with the right.[14] The other list is entitled *Liste par lettres alphabétiques des députés du côté droit aux Etats généraux, au mois de septembre 1791.* Its compiler supported the left wing, and the names on it are nearly identical to the names omitted from the "enragés de la gauche" list.[15]

Deputies classified as "center right" signed one of the protest lists and/ or were perceived as right-wing by only the right-wing sympathizer (the author of the *Liste par ordre*). The "resigning right" includes deputies who resigned early from the National Assembly but who did not sign protests or appear on either of the two observers' lists just described. Some deputies known to have resigned are assigned another alignment category on the basis of additional evidence; there is no other information available on those classified as "resigning right."

Deputies considered to be centrists did not sign protest lists, did not join the Jacobins or Feuillants, and were not uniformly classified by observers. The "right center" is represented by a short list of deputies who signed no protests and were called right-wing by only the left-wing sympathizer (the author of the *Liste par lettres*). Included in the "contradictory" category are deputies presumed to have been centrist because evidence for their alignment is contradictory. Deputies for whom there is no evidence for

14. The *Liste par ordre alphabétique* is dated Paris, 1791, Bibliothèque nationale, Lb[39].4582. I have followed Philip Dawson's interpretation of the list in his *Provincial Magistrates and Revolutionary Politics in France, 1789–1795* (Cambridge, Mass., 1972), 234, 235. Robert R. Palmer had used it earlier to identify the left; see his article "Sur la composition sociale de la gauche à la Constituante," *Annales historiques de la Révolution française,* XXXI (1959), 154–56; see also correspondence concerning the list between Alfred Cobban and Palmer, *ibid.,* 389–91.

15. The *Liste par lettres alphabétiques* is dated Paris, September, 1791, Bibliothéque nationale, Lb[39].10185.

either right or left alignment are labeled "unclassifiable"; they too are presumed to have been centrist. Chapter 5 contains discussion of the probable alignments of some of the 173 men designated as "unclassifiable."

The three left-wing subdivisions are based on one additional observer's list and on membership lists for the Jacobin Club and the Feuillants. The attributional source, *Le Véritable Portrait de nos législateurs,* is a long pamphlet written in December, 1791, to evaluate the political positions of the deputies who had sat in the National Assembly. The document categorized deputies as "important patriots," "unvarying patriots," and "important ministerials"—the latter signifying moderates who supported Lafayette and the royal ministers.[16] Membership lists for the Feuillant Club were drawn up in July, 1791, just after the moderate Jacobins split off from the parent society and formed the Feuillants. A shorter list was published in September after some members had returned to the Jacobins. Both lists were published by Augustin Challamel in 1895.[17] The Jacobin Club had made a membership list in December, 1790. A century after the Revolution, F. A. Aulard published that list and, in the index to his six-volume study of the Jacobins, added the names of men known to have been members of the club but omitted from the list.[18]

I combined these three sources to create measures for left-wing alignment. Deputies called "ministerials, or monarchical left" were listed by *Le Véritable Portrait* as important ministerials and/or were members of the Feuillants in 1791, but were never Jacobins. The "shifting left" includes those on the Feuillant lists who had been Jacobin members and/or were listed as important or unvarying patriots. The label "consistent left" designates Jacobin members and/or important or unvarying patriots who never joined the Feuillants.

16. *Le Véritable Portrait de nos législateurs; ou, Galerie des tableaux exposé à la vue du public depuis le 5 mai 1789, jusqu'au 1er octobre 1791* (Paris, 1792). Barbier listed this work as written by Dubois de Crancé, but Philip Dawson attributed it to Alquier, who probably wrote it as a campaign document when he sought election as a judge. See Dawson, *Provincial Magistrates,* 239.

17. Augustin Challamel, *Les Clubs contre-révolutionnaires: Cercles, comités, sociétés, salons, réunions, cafés, restaurants, et libraries* (1895; rpr. New York, 1974), 150–58.

18. Aulard, *La Société des Jacobins: Recueil de documents pour l'histoire du club des Jacobins de Paris* (6 vols.; Paris, 1889–97), I, xxxiv–lxxvi. The index is in Vol. VI.

This scale is the foundation for most of the analysis in this study. All 1,318 deputies' names have been placed somewhere on it; the full list is in the Appendix. Except for the April, 1790, protest list and the December, 1790, Jacobin list, all of the measures date from 1791. I have relied upon measures that capture as many deputies as possible, and have rejected those (such as positions taken in debate) that would eliminate most of the deputies.

Several different approaches can be used to determine the distance between deputies' positions on specific substantive issues. For example, one can look at the duration and intensity of debate on constitutional questions, compare vocabulary and rhetorical style, analyze the impact of constitutional decisions (who gained and who lost), or map reactions in the various journals across the political spectrum. I decided to measure polarization quantitatively where possible, using three measuring devices: the coding system, explained above, for pamphlets written by deputies; an examination of the margins of victory in those votes for which tallies were reported in the minutes; and a reconstruction of the alignment trajectories of those deputies for whom evidence exists of a shift to right or left between 1789 and 1791 (this evidence comes from measures of the decisions and actions of nobles and clergy in June, 1789, the swearing of the clerical oath, and membership in political clubs). These variables can be correlated with the scale of alignment to trace trajectories for some of the deputies.

Nobles and clergy are labeled "patriots" if they joined the National Assembly before the king ordered them to do so. The list for the clergy is made up of those who voted for a common verification of credentials on June 19; the nobles are those whose names appear on the roll call in the National Assembly on June 24, plus forty-two more nobles classified by James Murphy and Patrice Higonnet as liberals because of other indications that they supported the Third Estate.[19]

Finally, I tabulated membership lists for the Committee of Thirty that met in Paris in 1788 and 1789, for three moderate-to-right-wing clubs, and for Masonic lodges. All of these measures are used, singly or

19. For the clergy, the list is the *Procès verbal,* Vol. I, No. 4 (June 22, 1789), 11–16, referring to the June 19 vote. For the nobles, see *Archives parlementaires,* VIII (June 25, 1789), 154, and *Procès-verbal,* Vol. I, No. 7 (June 25, 1789), 9–12. The forty-two additional liberal nobles were so classified by Murphy and P. Higonnet, "Les Députés de la noblesse," 230–47.

in combination, to reconstruct alignment trajectories for those deputies on whom there is sufficient information.

Role Measures

The National Assembly presents many paradoxes. One of the most intriguing is that the deputies on the left did not form either a strong or a stable majority yet managed to secure a constitution more in accordance with their views than with those of the right-wing or center deputies. They managed to defeat proposals for an upper house, a permanent royal veto, a state religion, and a declaration of the duties of citizens. In order to analyze the nature of this influence, I designed various measures of roles that deputies could take within the National Assembly. As with alignment, I sought measures that would apply to all deputies from the least to the most active. To describe the structure of leadership in the National Assembly, I classified all deputies according to their roles in that body, and correlated this role scale with the political alignment scale.

Leaders and followers were defined according to seven different variables involving participation in debate, service on committees, and election as secretary or president of the Assembly. Information on these roles came from the *Archives parlementaires.* The scale for frequency of election as secretary or president ranges from "never" to "president two or more times"; these officers served for terms of two weeks or so and were elected by votes cast in the thirty separate bureaus to which all deputies were assigned.[20] Committees drew up legislative and constitutional proposals and reported out their drafts to the full Assembly. I recorded committee membership on a scale of one to nine committees—no deputy was a member of more than nine. I also selected two sets of committees to examine separately: the committees on the Constitution, whose work by definition addressed broad questions of legitimacy, and the two committees charged with managing communications between the National Assembly and the political nation outside of it.

There were three committees on the Constitution. The first consisted

20. On bureaus in the National Assembly, see Dawson, *Provincial Magistrates,* 230.

of thirty members elected July 6, 1789, with each of the bureaus of deputies choosing one member.[21] This was followed by a committee of eight elected on July 14 and itself replaced by another committee of eight chosen in September. The names of the members of each of these committees are recorded, with separate listing for those elected twice.

The two committees recorded separately were the Comité des Rapports and the Comité des Recherches. The Comité des Rapports was established to reduce the time in regular sessions devoted to receiving delegations; it was empowered to collect and answer written communications between the National Assembly and its constituents, particularly those in such corporate bodies as municipal governments or Jacobin Clubs that regularly sent petitions. The Comité des Recherches was established July 28, 1789, to investigate disturbances in the provinces. It was empowered to collect and look into information on conspiracies against the public safety. I chose these two committees because their members dealt with the tense issue of the National Assembly's authority over the rest of the nation and directly confronted the pressures that clubs, local governments, and popular violence could place upon the deputies.

In order to have a summary measure of leadership/follower roles, one that could be correlated with alignment and cross-tabulated with other biographical evidence, I constructed a five-point scale weighting the possible activities in which a deputy could engage in the National Assembly. Presumed least influential were the "listeners," deputies who never took part in debates and were not named to committees or elected as officers. "Participants" were not officers or committee members but did engage from one to five times in debate. "Active participants" served in one, but only one, of three categories: as officers, committee members, or frequent debaters. "Leaders" were those deputies who served in two of those same three categories, and "dominant leaders" served in all three.

The role scale thus ranks deputies from lowest to highest levels of involvement in the National Assembly, from listeners who took no active part to dominant leaders who were fully involved in the Assembly in all capacities. (I had initially included an intermediate category for "committee activists," men who did not hold other offices or debate often but served on two or more committees. Since I found only one deputy who met those

21. *Procès-verbal,* Vol. I, No. 17 (July 7, 1789), 6, 7.

criteria—he was on two committees but never engaged in debate and never served as an officer—I eliminated that category. Deputies did not tend to specialize as orators, committee participants, or officers. Either they remained inactive and silent or they emerged as recognized activists who participated vigorously in the Assembly's work.)[22]

Statistical Analysis

Most of the data in this book are presented in contingency tables that display relationships between two different measures; that is, they tell us that one measure, such as the alignment scale, is associated with another, such as deputies' estates. The tables report the percentages of frequencies for each combination of variables.

Results of the analysis of deputies' attitudes are presented mainly in chapters 3 and 4, where tables show associations between pairs of attitudes. Data on the behavioral measures of alignment and roles appear primarily in chapters 5 through 7. Some of the most interesting findings reveal associations between opinion variables and behavioral variables, such as a relationship between deputies' opinions on the king and their estates or pre-revolutionary experiences (see Table 8, page 57, for an example).

In many cases, in order to avoid presenting an enormous amount of detailed data, the full tables are not displayed. In chapters 3 and 4, I present "master" tables that simply list pairs of variables at two different levels of statistical significance, as well as those that are not significant. Table 5, page 53, is an example of such a combined table. Each listing is based on a computation of chi-square (to which I will return in a moment) performed for two related variables, but the complete tables are not displayed in the text. The combined lists show at a glance which relationships are strong and which are weak, while avoiding an endless parade of tabular data that would be tedious to read.

All of the attitudinal data and most of the information on deputies' careers after the close of the National Assembly in 1791 come from the

22. Dawson, *Provincial Magistrates,* 234, suggests that deputies did specialize, but my evidence shows that they did not.

regional sample of 247 deputies described earlier. For these data I report measures of statistical significance: chi-square values, degrees of freedom, and a probability estimate.

Statistical inference is a way of expressing the extent to which a characteristic of a sample is likely to be found in a whole population.[23] This likelihood is expressed in terms of statistical significance, which states the probability that a relationship between two variables in the sample could have occurred by chance alone. Social scientists generally accept as useful a probability of 5 percent or less (expressed as $p \leq .05$) that the relationship observed in the sample will *not* occur in the entire population.

Chi-square is a measure of statistical significance often used with nominal-level variables—classifications by categories that cannot be rank-ordered or averaged mathematically. Region is a good example of such a category: it would make no sense to average geographic regions, nor would it make sense to rank-order them by name only. Nominal measures cannot have a mean. Other variables used in this study are ordinal, such as the alignment scale or the role scale, on which the categories can be ordered from left to right or from least active to most active. Ordinal measures can be averaged. Although chi-square does not assume the computation of an average, it can be used for ordinal measures where means are generated. Chi-square expresses the difference between expected and observed values for two variables.

In order to interpret chi-square values, we also need a measure of degrees of freedom (abbreviated DF in the tables), which is computed by multiplying the total number of columns minus one by the total number of rows minus one. The greater the number of degrees of freedom, the higher the chi-square number must be to be significant.

Most of the behavioral data in this book apply to all the deputies and come from club membership lists, signatures on protest declarations, and information in parliamentary archives. For these measures, statistical inference is not appropriate, since the National Assembly is an entire population rather than a sample. In the interests of establishing standards for consistency and comparability, however, I have reported measures of statistical

23. These techniques are explained in detail in introductory statistics books. I have found most useful for political data the explanations in Louise G. White with Robert P. Clark, *Political Analysis: Technique and Practice,* (2d ed.; Pacific Grove, Cal., 1990), 350–58.

significance for some tables.[24] I have reported measures of statistical signifi-cance for findings presented in chapters 2, 3, and 6 that apply only to the sample of deputies and the pamphlets they wrote. For some of the tables in chapters 2 and 3, I have used significance levels to present evidence of relationships between pairs of variables that would otherwise take dozens of tables to provide. For example, Table 5 clusters pairs of relationships according to their significance levels, summarizing twenty-eight separate tables of cross-tabulated variables. I have made the assumption that the 370 pamphlets coded for this study approximate the range of opinions be-ing articulated in print throughout France between 1788 and 1791, and that adding more pamphlets to the analysis would not change the trends observed to any sizable degree.

One other measure is used here, an index of proportionality. The index is obtained by dividing the actual percentage of deputies in a specified category by the percentage to be expected from their numeric strength in the entire Assembly if they were distributed among all categories in pro-portion to their numbers. Perfect proportionality gives an index number of 1; a number higher than 1 indicates overrepresentation in that category, and a number lower than 1 indicates underrepresentation. This index is useful in demonstrating that members of one group—the nobility, for example—are more (or less) likely than their numbers would suggest to be classified in another group—deputies sitting on the right, for example.

The measures and methods explained in this chapter were selected to pro-duce a systematic tabulation of evidence that paints a group portrait of the deputies. By choosing not to focus on prominent, visible, and articulate leaders and activists, but to gather insofar as possible comparable informa-tion on every individual, I am making the same assumption of equality that the deputies themselves made when they created the National Assem-bly and began to vote by head. As the findings here will show, a system implementing majority rule was created by deputies whose representative base was redefined as the whole nation, but who failed to accept the concept of legitimate opposition that necessarily underlies majoritarian politics.

24. Sometimes measures of statistical significance are reported for entire populations in order to have what one author calls "a convenient method of establishing a threshold for analytic purposes." See Thomas R. Dye, "Taking, Spending, and Economic Growth in the American States," *Journal of Politics*, XLII (1980), 1085–1107.

Political Alignment in the
French National Assembly, 1789–1791

Alignment and Revolutionary Political Culture

National unity was valued by many eighteenth-century political theorists in the belief that special interests undermine any legitimate national political goal. French political thinkers insisted on one nation, indivisible, and unlike the Anglo-Americans, were not inclined to accept internal divisions as inevitable or to concern themselves with managing and controlling the effects of faction. The English, with a common-law tradition and parliamentary sovereignty, worked out a politics of consensus between government and opposition; the Americans forged a constitutional compromise with an ingenious mix of federalism, separation of powers, and checks and balances.

French political theorists and revolutionaries, sharing with the English and Americans the same Enlightenment natural-law convictions and the same unresolved tension between rights of the individual and needs of the community, achieved political consensus only episodically and ephemerally, but they laid down an enduring mystique of national unity that underlies the revolutionary tradition. As counterpoint to this faith in national unity, fundamental questions of political life were recurrently reopened. Ten years of revolution and three different constitutions produced no lasting agreement on the foundation of national sovereignty, the delegation and application of authority, the balance of executive and legislative powers, or the relation of individuals, groups, and classes to the state. Variant French political cultures produced extreme political fragmentation beneath an abstract unity that was declaimed in speeches and treatises, expressed symbolically in songs, flags, and uniforms, and dramatized in events both spontaneous and staged.

Students of the French Revolution, disagreeing on the origins of revolutionary conflicts, are returning their attention to the politics of revolution, looking anew at the institutions, symbols, and events that defined and determined the power struggles and established the patterns of two centuries of French political life. Beneath the incantation of national unity, what in fact were the lines of political cleavage that divided revolutionary participants? This study is concerned with locating the political bases of alignment among the first critically important leaders of the Revolution, the deputies to the Estates General/National Assembly, who were also the first to redefine national sovereignty in a written constitution for France.

Alignment in the National Assembly shaped the political environment for the deputies, who in turn set the precedents for modern French legislative politics. This first constituent assembly laid down procedures for passing constitutional decrees and other legislation, procedures that produced majorities and minorities in changing configurations and intensities on different issues. At certain moments, the most famous being August 4, 1789, the Assembly came close to unanimity; on other occasions, such as during the debate over declaring a state religion (April 12, 1790), the Assembly was evenly and bitterly divided. The deputies rhetorically perpetuated and extended the faith in national unity even as they developed a symbolic repertory of categories to isolate opponents and exclude them from the political nation and the sovereign people. Deputies across the spectrum from left to right did not hesitate to label their opponents enemies of the nation. They required oaths of one another, of the clergy, and of their presiding officers. These and other practices opened political rifts and rigidified resentments that persisted for decades and sometimes for centuries.

The concept of alignment also connects to more general and theoretical questions concerning interpretations of the French Revolution, beginning with the debate over continuity: whether the Revolution is best understood as a process that perpetuated even as it transformed a strong centralized French state, or whether the revolutionary years are most striking for political innovations and inventions. Furthermore, alignment in the National Assembly can illuminate the nature of divisions within the whole French political nation and can help us determine whether these national cleavages were formed mainly on the basis of divergent economic and material interests; differences of sensibility, style, habit, and custom; clashing ideological convictions; or competition between rival cliques for stakes in a new political game.[1] Finally, alignment can open a window on the nature of the strategies and tactics deputies within the National Assembly adopted, setting precedents that helped to establish the legislature as the continuing focal point of French political life.

Alignment divisions proved to be related to the roles deputies took within the Assembly as officers, committee members, frequent debaters, or silent attenders; and these roles set habits and styles of legislative politics for future assemblies. Most significant, alignment divisions were associated with differing and sometimes clashing convictions about political legitimacy and participation, convictions that connected deputies to the rest of the political nation, present and future. Neither deputies nor constituents ever developed concepts of loyal opposition and of majority rule and minority rights that could stabilize a liberal regime.

Historiographic Background

Historians of the French Revolution and political scientists working in the field of comparative politics in the last several decades have shared a concern to reinvestigate and redefine the meaning of politics. Beneath competing theories—Marxist or revisionist, behavioral or cultural, and structural-functional or statist—lies a fundamental question: do social constraints such as conflicts between classes, religions, and ideologies drive public

1. Alfred Cobban, *The Myth of the French Revolution* (London, 1955); Cobban, *The Social Interpretation of the French Revolution* (Cambridge, Eng., 1964); Jean Egret, *La Pré-Révolution française, 1787–1788* (Paris, 1962); Michael John Sydenham, *The Girondins* (London, 1961); Alison Patrick, *The Men of the First French Republic* (Baltimore, 1972); Michel Pertué, "Remarques sur les listes des Conventionnels," *Annales historiques de la Révolution française,* LIII (July–September, 1981), 366–78; Lemay, "La Composition de l'Assemblée nationale constituante," 341–63; Patrice Higonnet, *Class, Ideology, and the Rights of Nobles;* Guy Chaussinand-Nogaret, *La Noblesse au XVIIIᵉ siècle: De la Féodalité aux Lumières* (Paris, 1976); William Doyle, *Oxford History of the French Revolution* (New York, 1989); Norman Hampson, *Prelude to Terror: The Constituent Assembly and the Failure of Consensus, 1789–1791* (London, 1988).

policy and cause revolutions; or is "the state" an autonomous agent that ultimately grows stronger or weaker according to rulers' ability to employ and control coercive force and to manage or resolve conflicts, whether by bargaining, manipulation, or conquest? Debates over the social-constraint model versus the statist model have enlarged the concept of power beyond the pluralists' emphasis on competition for political influence and the Weberian emphasis on bureaucracy and administrative functions to encompass broader and deeper enforcement and coercion in most areas of social life, including spheres of economic exchange, communication of ideas, and moral convictions.[2]

This enlargement of the definition of politics and the accompanying debate over the nature of political change have of course affected interpretations of the French Revolution. Indeed, it can be argued that the expansion of the sphere of politics *began* at the time of the eighteenth-century French Revolution. The Marxist explanation, dominant among French historians of the Revolution for the first two-thirds of the twentieth century, makes politics narrow, part of a superstructure built upon a base of class relations of production, in which strains accompanying technological and social changes pitted a rising bourgeoisie against a declining aristocracy. Challenges to this Marxist paradigm are based upon alternative interpretations rooted in ideological conflicts, the creation and communication of a new language of politics, and the employment of that discourse in struggles involving the state (the king and the royal council) and other powerful institutions such as the church hierarchy, the parlements, the provincial estates, and the seigneurial courts.[3]

Recent interpretations of the causes and significance of the Revolution, particularly those set forth by Lynn Hunt, François Furet, and Keith Baker, reflect a shared aversion to linear, chronological, and hierarchical explanations. These scholars' formulations can be visualized as networks or mosa-

2. Charles S. Maier, Introduction to *Changing Boundaries of the Political: Essays on the Evolving Balance Between the State and Society, Public and Private in Europe,* ed. Maier (Cambridge, Eng., 1987), 21, 22.

3. Lengthy and complex arguments about the social and economic causes of the Revolution are interpreted by William Doyle in *Origins of the French Revolution* (New York, 1980). See also Georges Lefebvre's defense of the Revolution's radicalism in "Le Mythe de la Révolution française," *Annales historiques de la Révolution française,* CCLIX (January–March, 1985), 1–7.

ics, patterns of human relationships and fields of discourse that map po-litical culture. However, their rejection—based on quite solid empirical evidence—of the rising bourgeoisie as the cause of the Revolution has not yet been supplanted by an alternative list of equally empirical causes. Sym-bols and representations are offered and interpreted to supply descriptions of revolutionary political culture, but without specification of the rules for including and excluding evidence. One consequence of such writing is ab-straction; we learn much about iconographic representations of liberty, for example, but nothing about conflicts over freedom of association or quali-fications for voting.[4] A more serious consequence is that the Terror comes to dominate the understanding of the Revolution. As linear explanations of cause and effect have fallen from favor and have been replaced by a wider and deeper understanding of complex power struggle, determinism seems paradoxically to return. Anticipations of Terror are found, for example, in Enlightenment beliefs about progress and the possibility of transforming human nature, and all of the work of the National Assembly is seen as a "prelude to terror."[5]

The bicentennial commemorations of the French Revolution occasioned many clarifying summaries of the debates over Marxist and revisionist interpretations. There is no need to go over that ground again here, but it will be helpful to review the recent scholarship of several historians whose work provides a context for this study.

Writing the initial full-scale attack on the Marxist model in 1978, François Furet located the dynamic of the Revolution in the concept of equality and the conviction that political action could realize equality. The Revolution became a discourse about identity, about individuals finding

4. David P. Jordan, "Economics Versus Culture: Two Views of the French Revolu-tion," *Eighteenth Century,* XXVIII (1987), 83–90; Lynn Hunt, "Commentary on the Ori-gins of the French Revolution: A Debate," *French Historical Studies,* XVI (Fall, 1990), 761–63.

5. Hampson, *Prelude to Terror;* William H. Sewell, Jr., "Ideologies and Social Revo-lutions: Reflexions on the French Case," *Journal of Modern History,* LVII (1985), 57–85; Theda Skocpol, "Cultural Idioms and Political Ideologies in the Revolutionary Reconstruc-tion of State Power: A Rejoinder to Sewell," *Journal of Modern History,* LVII (1985), 86–96. See also three pieces in the special issue, entitled "François Furet's Interpretation of the French Revolution," of *French Historical Studies,* XVI (1990): David D. Bien, "François Furet, the Terror, and 1789," 777–83; Donald Sutherland, "An Assessment of the Writings of François Furet," 784–91; and François Furet, "A Commentary," 792–802.

who they were through the goals that drove their political acts. It was not inevitable and not a radical break with the past; the meaning of political acts simply was articulated and communicated in a new revolutionary language of public opinion, a language centering on equality and at least initially equating liberty with equality.[6] Once the Estates General was decided upon, elections focused attention on the notion that power was up for grabs. "The Revolution replaced the conflict of interests for power with a competition of discourses for the appropriation of legitimacy."[7] The language spoken by members of the political nation—that is, everyone who engaged in discourse about public life—set the standards of political legitimacy. People's identities no longer derived from their ascriptive status; a corporate society became a nation of individuals. The political legitimacy of the Old Regime's ruling institutions was no longer assumed, but tested against these new standards set by public discourse.

Picking up Furet's approach to revolutionary dynamics, Lynn Hunt moved from her first book's focus on the social history of elites in two towns to a study of the texts, rituals, and symbol systems that constituted revolutionary political culture. She attributed to Furet an enlargement of the meaning of politics, one that made it ultimately an instrument of coercion—Terror—to form and reshape society; but she faulted him for not suggesting how that new meaning came about. She focused less on causes and consequences of revolution and more on revolutionary processes as they unfolded from 1789 through 1799. She characterized the new political class as being not especially closely tied to Old Regime institutions, as being relatively inexperienced with democratic sociability, and as being much more likely to live in towns than the population as a whole. The new political class was indeed "bourgeois," but she noted that many antirepublicans were also bourgeois, so the Marxist paradigm was insufficiently discriminating to explain revolutionary dynamics. Hunt criticized revisionists as well, for failing to identify a new political class at all. Her revolutionary elites shared a set of Enlightenment values such as secularism, rationalism, and a belief in popular sovereignty, all originating in what she called "common cultural relationships." Hunt has been criticized for excluding a narrative of revolutionary events and accounts of the behavior of revolutionary

6. François Furet, *Interpreting the French Revolution*, trans. Elborg Forster (New York, 1981), 26–30.

7. *Ibid.*, 49.

activists, thereby producing an abstract and bloodless account of violent times, but her work illuminates revolutionary radicalization and the establishment of a tradition of democratic republicanism in France.[8]

In his recent work, both as editor and author, Keith Baker has investigated the dynamics of the French Revolution and reposed the old question of the ideological origins of revolutionary political culture. Like Furet, Baker views ideology not only as a tactic of revolutionary mobilization, but also as a dominant discourse that actually constitutes political power. What Baker calls the "court of public opinion" emerged after 1750 out of the expansion of print and oral communication, and especially after particular administrative crises and conflicts over religion produced a politics of contestation that made a great many writers and not a few administrators uneasy about instability. Therefore, once the court of public opinion was "clarified" by the decision to convoke the Estates General, the magistrates of this court—writers and editors—handed down nonconflictual, universal, and rational prescriptions for right behavior and consensus on values, transferring ultimate authority from "the public person of the sovereign to the sovereign person of the public."[9]

Public opinion—the flow of discourse within the political nation—functioned on the eve of the Revolution as a court of appeal, a legitimating standard, almost a sovereign entity that defined the national will. Public opinion in this sense was not an arena of partisan or factional conflict, but a tribunal that stood in judgment over reform attempts and public policy. Viewed in this light, the growing influence of public opinion, especially in 1788, did not create a style of politics that could produce majorities along with acceptance of opposing minorities. Instead, it fostered a myth of unity so powerful that those taking conflicting positions had to be forced to be free.[10]

8. Lynn Hunt, *Politics, Culture, and Class in the French Revolution* (Berkeley, 1984), chap. 5. The phrase quoted is on p. 179.

9. Keith M. Baker, "Politics and Public Opinion Under the Old Regime: Some Reflections," in *Press and Politics in Pre-Revolutionary France,* ed. Jack R. Censer and Jeremy D. Popkin (Berkeley, 1987), chap. 6; see p. 214. This essay was revised as "Public Opinion as Political Invention," in Baker, *Inventing the French Revolution: Essays on French Political Culture in the Eighteenth Century* (Cambridge, Eng., 1990), chap. 8; see p. 172; the phrase "court of public opinion" is on p. 199.

10. Baker, "Politics and Public Opinion Under the Old Regime," 241–44, and "Public Opinion as Political Invention," 194–97.

After the declaration of the National Assembly, constitution makers were driven by "the insoluble problem of instituting and maintaining a form of government in direct, immediate, and constant relationship to the general will."[11] In his volume *Inventing the French Revolution,* Baker consider public opinion not only as a tactic for acquiring, maintaining, and exerting power, but as the essence of power itself. To capture the discourse about sovereignty, legitimacy, representation, and revolution was to define and thereby acquire and use political power. In the revolutionists' claims to universal truth Baker finds assertions of the sovereign will of the nation, a will that was always prior to any constitution, always potentially revolutionary, and the point of origin for the Terror.[12]

Furet, Hunt, and Baker agree that the Revolution was driven by competition to control the new language of national will and popular sovereignty. I have set my study of political alignment in the context of that argument, using deputies' actions and language to analyze the shape and interpret the significance of their revolutionary roles and their concepts of legitimacy and participation. My understanding of discourse is, however, less all-encompassing than it seems to be for Furet, Hunt, and Baker. Capturing and controlling discourse was undeniably critical—as, for example, in the debates on June 16 and 17 in the Estates General over what name the Third Estate should adopt for the new body they were declaring themselves to be. But the deputies were also shaping and even inventing new forms, behaviors, and strategies for securing and using political influence. Decisions about the size, membership, and selection of bureaus and committees; the establishment of regulations for voting and tabulating votes; requirements to correspond regularly and publicly with electoral committees; and strategies to line up support from fellow deputies were all acts and styles of acting that determined not only outcomes within the Assembly, but also the institution's centrality in the whole arena of revolutionary politics.

Furthermore, these procedural decisions all fitted the principle of majority rule. Once the vote by head was assured, the rule of one man/one vote established equality among the deputies in place of deference to status and rank. Politics within the National Assembly became paradoxical; every

11. Keith M. Baker, "Fixing the French Constitution," in Baker, *Inventing the French Revolution,* 275.

12. *Ibid.,* 305.

vote divided the deputies into aye and nay voters, but they never accepted the principle that opposition could be loyal. In fact, their collective discourse pushed more and more toward the principle that the Assembly represented an indivisible and legitimately unopposable national will. That paradox informs the main lines of inquiry in this book.

The same democratic paradox, although expressed in different terms, is at the center of Alexis de Tocqueville's analysis of revolutionary politics. Furet, Hunt, and Baker have all made Tocqueville a point of departure for their own interpretations precisely because of his arguments for an inherently political continuity between the Old Regime and the Revolution. For Tocqueville, centralization was the bridge linking Old Regime, revolutionary governments, and subsequent political systems.[13] From his vantage point as a former legislator and minister forced into retirement by Louis Napoléon's coup d'état in 1851, Tocqueville first tried to explain the Revolution's legacy with reference to the politics and institutions of the First Empire. Upon reconsideration, he concluded that the possibility of establishing lasting democratic and free political institutions had been foreclosed earlier, even for the eighteenth-century revolutionaries, by the inimical effects of Bourbon centralization upon French social customs. Royal centralization created "class" hatreds by politically emasculating the aristocracy and by placing much of the professional Third Estate in the bureaucracy. (*Class*, for Tocqueville, did not imply any notion of shared identity or consciousness, or any idea of shared material interests. The word simply referred to divisions between the privileged and the nonprivileged.)[14] The kings also destroyed most of the traditional liberties in provincial and local government and thus eliminated one chance for meaningful political participation. Enlightenment and unsuccessful royal reform attempts inspired the revolutionaries to demand political liberty. Free institutions, established with constitutional monarchy, then failed in the First Republic because class rivalries and political inexperience made Frenchmen unable to cooperate. Fraternity existed ephemerally at moments of revolutionary

13. Richard Herr, *Tocqueville and the Old Regime* (Princeton, 1965); Alexis de Tocqueville, *L'Ancien Régime et la Révolution,* ed. J. P. Mayer and André Jardin, Vol. II of Tocqueville, *Oeuvres, papiers, et correspondances* (13 vols.; Paris, 1951–). Or see the English edition, *The Old Regime and the French Revolution,* trans. Stuart Gilbert (New York, 1955).

14. R. R. Palmer, *The Two Tocquevilles, Father and Son: Hervé and Alexis de Tocqueville on the Coming of the French Revolution* (Princeton, 1987), 25, 26.

epiphany, but fraternity as a political habit and style eluded the political nation. Liberal democracy, attempted again in the Second Republic in 1848, thus had too weak a base to incorporate the egalitarian demands of the radical urban classes.

Tocqueville's analysis of the evolution and transformation of political institutions and the behavior of people within them illuminates the operation of political power and accounts for the continuity of centralized bureaucratic rule in France from the seventeenth century forward, but as Furet reminds us, that analysis is less helpful in explaining successively radicalizing politics from 1789 to 1794, one consequence of deeply etched, intensely conflictual, and long-lasting political cleavages among elites.[15] Baker adds that Tocqueville downplayed mid-eighteenth-century conflicts among church, state, parlements, provincial estates, and ministers (conflicts that were expressed in terms of liberty against despotism) because his argument hinged on the supposed absence of any political liberty in prerevolutionary France.[16] Tocqueville's understanding of revolutionary dynamics was based in the growth of state power. He disregarded any impact of revolutionary ideologies, and he discounted revolutionaries' intentions. Hunt called him the first modernization theorist of the Revolution because of his insistence that state initiatives created revolutionaries who sought to control the exercise of state power themselves.[17]

Despite these criticisms and modifications, *The Old Regime and the French Revolution* is a very rich source of empirical statements about the causes and effects of the Revolution, statements that can be evaluated with the tools of modern research. One such contention is that the hatred of privilege so evident in the immediate prerevolutionary period was a consequence of the destruction of meaningful rights of nobles—rights earned by real social contributions—and the substitution of privileges not based in any social utility; another is that the bourgeoisie were split off from the

15. See the analysis of Tocqueville by Furet in *Interpeting the French Revolution,* chap. 2, 132–63. Like Keith Baker, Patrice Higonnet contends that Tocqueville underestimated ideology—"the increasingly contradictory world view"—and exaggerated institutional causes of the failure of the Revolution; Patrice Higonnet, *Sister Republics: The Origins of French and American Republicanism* (Cambridge, Mass., 1988), 9.

16. Keith M. Baker, "On the Problem of the Ideological Origins of the French Revolution," in Baker, *Inventing the French Revolution,* 20–23.

17. Hunt, *Politics, Culture, and Class,* 6–10.

common people by bourgeois preferences for living in town to escape paying and collecting the *taille* and by privilege-based distinctions among the Third Estate that, for example, divided artisans from presidial judges or notaries. Then there is Tocqueville's analysis leading us to expect that successful revolutionary elites would converge around a shared valuation of liberty and a common hatred of privilege—a convergence that would unite members of all three estates once the initial questions about the form and procedure of the Estates General were resolved.[18]

This converging-elites thesis was adopted by a group of contemporary historians who used it mainly to undermine the Marxist paradigm. William Doyle, Patrice Higonnet, Colin Lucas, Guy Chaussinand-Nogaret, and François Furet contended that the Revolution was mostly made by and for better-off property owners, both noble and bourgeois, who agreed on a program of careers open to talent, constitutionally defined and protected civil liberties, and laws to protect and encourage the ownership of property, and who disagreed only—and for no longer than a year or so after 1789—on the strictly political issue of the structure of voting in the Estates General. These authors amassed a considerable amount of evidence on comparative levels of wealth, demands in revolutionary cahiers, and ideological statements to show that the Revolution was not accomplished by a rising elite of class-conscious bourgeois protocapitalists. William Doyle made the case that nobility and Third Estate converged no later than mid-July, 1789, once the nobility had been denied their special prerogatives. In August deputies belonging to these two groups produced both "a statement of what had produced the Revolution"—the Declaration of the Rights of Man and of the Citizen—and "a statement of what the Revolution had produced"—the decree of August 11, 1789, abolishing feudalism.[19]

---

18. In Tocqueville's words, "No doubt it was still possible at the close of the eighteenth century to detect shades of difference in the behavior of the aristocracy and that of the bourgeoisie; for nothing takes longer to acquire than the surface polish which is called good manners. But basically all who ranked above the common herd were of a muchness; they had the same ideas, the same habits, the same tastes, the same kinds of amusement; read the same books and spoke in the same way. They differed only in their rights." Tocqueville, *Old Regime and the French Revolution*, 81.

19. Doyle, *Origins of the French Revolution*, 205. See also Chaussinand-Nogaret, *La Noblesse au XVIIIᵉ siècle*, 227–29.

Patrice Higonnet did further close analysis of the whole revolutionary period, arguing that the propertied elite did not come together before the end of the revolutionary decade. Convergence was sidetracked after 1789 by pressures from the demands of the urban poor and peasants, and then by foreign and civil war, producing a period of antinobilism, radical political egalitarianism (without, however, a redistribution of wealth), and Terror. Only with the Consulate and Empire did the components of the political elite reconverge to secure and codify, not a government facilitating the growth of entrepreneurial and industrial capitalism, but a government protecting property.[20]

Colin Lucas sought the root of the attack on privilege in 1788 and 1789, despite the permeability of the boundary of privilege through the purchase of ennobling offices and similar social practices characteristic of both nobles and non-nobles. He cited a narrowing of access to privileges as the source of non-noble resentment, but contended that the gulf that opened between nobles and the revolutionary bourgeoisie did so mainly because of mistaken perceptions of a unity of interests between the nobility and the monarchy. The Constitution of 1791 recemented former nobles and non-noble elites through a common base of wealth in landed property.[21]

The converging-elites thesis and the larger questions about centralization in which it is embedded form one dimension of my investigation. I look for the roots of revolutionary political alignment in deputies' backgrounds and experiences, and I find estate to be a much more powerful correlate of that alignment than the converging-elites theory would suggest. Another theme is the discourse about legitimacy and popular sovereignty, connected to the work of Furet, Hunt, and Baker and investigated through pamphlets authored by some of the deputies. I concur with Hunt that despite the flood of publications on revolutionary France produced to commemorate the bicentennial, there has been relatively little research, apart from narrative, on the unfolding *process* of revolution, the events fall-

20. Patrice Higonnet, *Class, Ideology, and the Rights of Nobles,* esp. chap. 5. This interpretation, incidentally, is not so different from that of the Marxist historian Georges Lefebvre, who argued that the vital revolutionary changes were economic freedom, equality before the law, and church-state conflicts. See Lefebvre, "Le Mythe de la Révolution française," 1−7.

21. Colin Lucas, "Nobles, Bourgeois, and the Origins of the French Revolution," *Past and Present,* LX (August, 1973), 84−126.

ing between the origins and outcomes that so compel the attention of historians.[22] This book is one effort to remedy that lack.

Historical Setting

The broad political question that ignited the French Revolution was about the locus and limits of sovereignty. Sovereignty was on the political agenda in 1788, as it in fact had been for three centuries of struggle between the sovereign courts and the king's council.[23] According to the *thèse royale*, the doctrine underpinning absolutism, the king had unlimited power to appoint his own advisers and issue his own decrees. Louis XVI articulated the thesis to the Paris Parlement in the *séance de la flagellation* during the d'Aiguillon affair in 1776: "To me alone belongs legislative power without dependence or division. . . . By my authority alone do the officers of my courts proceed, not to the formation of law, but to its registration, publication, and execution."[24]

Such an extreme claim to absolute power did not reflect reality. In fact, Tocqueville's thesis about the destructive political impact of centralization has to be modified when we take into account the effects of small increments of liberty produced by the attempted reforms in many administrative areas. A king who had once derived his legitimacy from a transcendental relationship with the church and who obligated obedience to his rule by divine right was becoming the executor of natural law, no longer the healer but the overseer.[25] Liberty was granted to some extent in the grain market,

22. Hunt, "Commentary," 761–63. See also Hunt's earlier essay, "French History in the Last Twenty Years: The Rise and Fall of the *Annales* Paradigm," *Journal of Contemporary History,* XXI (1986), 209–24.

23. Roland E. Mousnier, *The Organs of State and Society,* trans. Arthur Goldhammer (Chicago, 1984), 581–673, Vol. II of Mousnier, *The Institutions of France Under the Absolute Monarchy, 1598–1789,* 2 vols.

24. Jules Flammermont, *Remontrances du Parlement de Paris au dix-huitième siècle* (3 vols.; Paris, 1888–98), II, 557, 558.

25. This theme is traced through different dimensions of public policy in several recent studies. See, for example, Darline Gay Levy, *The Ideas and Careers of Simon Nicolas Henri Linguet* (Urbana, 1980); Steven L. Kaplan, *Bread, Politics, and Political Economy* (2 vols.; The Hague, 1976), esp. I, 154; and J. H. Shennan, *The Parlement of Paris* (Ithaca, 1968).

and sporadically censorship was curbed; but political liberty in the sense of a right of political opposition was never allowed. From the perspective of the king and his ministers, the nation was to be ruled by one will and one executive force, not by competing representatives of different interests.

An alternative thesis of royal legitimacy, the *thèse nobiliaire*, had been most concisely developed by Montesquieu. According to this thesis, repeatedly invoked by parlementary magistrates after their right to remonstrate was reinstated in 1715, the legitimate monarch had to exercise his sovereign will through intermediary institutions, the most important of which was the Parlement because its registration and judicial procedures guaranteed the rule of law. The Paris magistrates made their boldest claim to this checking and balancing power in remonstrances of May 3, 1788, wherein they listed the chief constitutional principles to which the king's authority was to be subordinated.[26]

Dale Van Kley's studies of the complicated relationships among the monarchy, the parlements, and the church have illuminated a series of conflicts, beginning about 1750, that disturbed the classical balance between church and state and worked to secularize and delegitimate the monarchy. Put simply, the *thèse nobiliaire* became complicated by the question of whether the church or Parlement should limit absolutism. Gallicans and Jansenists wanted the crown to be limited by Parlement's rights of registration and remonstrance; "devouts" wanted a king unlimited in his control over lay subjects but subject to an authoritarian church.[27]

These doctrines of sovereignty were debated, elaborated, and expanded until there was widespread belief that absolutism equaled despotism, especially during the struggles over royal reform attempts of the 1770s and 1780s that culminated in the decision to convene the Estates General. Conceptions of sovereignty were not fixed in rigid, traditional molds in the eighteenth century. Some were derived from Rousseau's idea of general will, others from absolutist theories of enlightened despotism, and still others from organic theories of complementary power, such as the *thèse nobiliaire*.

26. Speech by Jean Jacques du Val d'Eprémesnil, in Flammermont, *Remontrances*, III, 745, 746.

27. Dale Van Kley, *The Damiens Affairs and the Unraveling of the Ancien Régime, 1750–1770* (Princeton, 1984), chap. 4 and esp. p. 173. Also see Van Kley, "The Jansenist Constitutional Legacy in the French Pre-Revolution," *Historical Reflections/Réflexions historiques*, XIII (1986), 393–453.

But all of these theories of sovereignty had in common the myth of one France, of national unity that could not tolerate pluralistic politics.

Nonetheless, concepts defining the form and extent of influential political participation were shifting over these decades. The terms of political debate escalated as elites became more aware of the power of public opinion. In the political culture of the 1780s, the salons of the high Enlightenment, the coffeehouses and cafés of Grub Street, the reading rooms of provincial assemblies, the Masonic lodges—all were lively centers of debate for men and women with an increasing political consciousness, ready to reinterpret corporatism, constitutionalism, national sovereignty, and representative institutions. This broadening of political discourse enlarged and universalized concepts such as the rights of the nation, the historical understanding of the French constitution, and liberty within the context of debates on highly specific edicts and reform proposals.[28] Reforming ministers knew that they had to construct new supports for the monarchy, both fiscal and institutional, that would reflect expanding wealth (chiefly in agriculture and minerals) and that would recognize and accommodate the power aspirations of the owners of the property producing that wealth.[29] At the same time, parlementary magistrates, church leaders, leaders of privileged orders in provincial estates, and other notables recognized in those new institutional supports a threat to their own financial privileges and political prerogatives. They were determined that the ministers could not have it both ways, could not retain the traditional pillars of church, privileged orders, and sovereign courts while building new competing institutions that the crown thought it could control. Privileged notables were not happy with provincial assemblies that lacked distinction of orders, with a reformed treasury following regular procedures, and with appeals courts having no power to register laws.

All reforms stopped short of providing regularized political influence and a genuine pluralistic power base for new elites, and thus the reformers

28. Keith M. Baker, "On the Problem of the Ideological Origins of the French Revolution," in *Modern European Intellectual History: Reappraisals and New Perspectives,* ed. Dominick La Capra and Steven L. Kaplan (Ithaca, 1982), 197–219.

29. Mona Ozouf has underscored the manipulation of public opinion by spokesmen for the monarchy as well as by its opponents. Mona Ozouf, "L'Opinion publique," in *The Political Culture of the Old Regime,* ed. Keith M. Baker (New York, 1987), 419–34, Vol. I of *The French Revolution and the Creation of Modern Political Culture,* 3 vols.

failed to build a firm new support base for an enlightened monarch. For example, when the Jesuits were expelled in 1762, the crown replaced Jesuit schoolmasters and instructors in the *collèges* with teachers chosen deliberately to transmit secular values and patriotism, but the same change spread the teaching of Enlightenment values not necessarily supportive of monarchy.[30] Legal reforms also failed to create large numbers of new allies. Some of the law courts with status upgraded by the Maupeou reforms in 1771 did attract grateful provincial elites, but others had recruitment problems; in any case, the reforms were not in force long enough to convince men to trust the career opportunities they provided.[31] Likewise, the provincial assemblies created in 1781 and 1787 never seriously rivaled the prestige of the old provincial estates and were eclipsed by the popular radicalism of the reconstituted provincial estates of Dauphiné after 1787.[32] Closing recruitment to high officer rank in the army not only shut off advancement for *roturiers,* but also angered *simples gentilshommes* who felt they would be passed over in favor of court nobles.[33] Municipal reforms attempted in the 1760s produced only a small number of lawyers and judges glad to have the jurisdictions of their courts enlarged, whereas the changes were opposed by privileged defenders of the old municipal structures.[34] All these reforms, attempted and then usually rescinded, were changing customary routes to political influence and stirring up debates over who should be influential, in what ways, to what extent, and to whom accountable. Reforms raised these questions without settling them, and it was left to the deputies in the National Assembly to make careers open to talent one of the rights of man.

30. R. R. Palmer, *Catholics and Unbelievers in Eighteenth Century France* (Princeton, 1939), 9, 153; Palmer, *The Improvement of Humanity: Education and the French Revolution* (Princeton, 1985), 48–59. The government also weakened the moral force and retarded the modernization of the church by using ecclesiastical wealth to provide sinecures for nobles. See Guy Lemarchand, "L'Eglise, appareil idéologique d'état dans la France d'Ancien Régime (XVIe–XVIIIe siècles)," *Annales historiques de la Révolution française,* LI (April–June, 1979), 250–79.

31. Robert Villers, *L'Organisation du Parlement de Paris et des Conseils supérieurs d'après le Réforme de Maupeou, 1771–1774* (Paris, 1937).

32. Pierre Renouvin, *Les Assemblées provinciales de 1787* (Paris, 1921).

33. Egret, *La Pré-Révolution française,* 87–94.

34. Maurice Bordes, *La Réforme municipale du Contrôleur-Général Laverdy et son application, 1764–1771* (Toulouse, 1968), 256–70.

Once the decision was taken to convoke the Estates General, debate about political influence began to focus on the nature and limits of representation. Kenneth Margerison has used pamphlets written in 1787 to show that writers drew upon an ancient tradition of assemblies of the Estates General on the Champ de Mars to justify their claims that the nation's representatives had once exercised legislative functions, the three estates working together in a single, powerful authority. The invocation of these historical arguments stopped with the declaration of the National Assembly, when the nature of political representation could no longer be defined by precedent.[35] From that point on, privilege could no longer serve as a medium of exchange, a "good" that the crown could dispense for services (or money) rendered and that holders of privilege could use to curb a despotic state. According to Michael Fitzsimmons, arguments in the cahiers separated the interests of the privileged from the national interest. The unanimity among deputies the night of August 4, 1789, gave them a new identity as representatives of the nation, no longer delegates representing social categories.[36] Beneath that new identity were fissures so deeply etched that the deputies could never lay the foundation of trust that is necessary for the effective operation of majority rule.

Formulations of sovereignty, legitimacy, and authority were the main issues over which the deputies clashed, and which divided them into left, center, and right in the National Assembly. An examination of the ideological and behavioral differences that characterized deputies in different alignments can help to clarify both the continuities between Old Regime and revolutionary political culture and the radicalizing tendencies that established a revolutionary tradition in French politics. These alignments formed early in the revolutionary period and became embryonic political parties, whose members engaged in campaigns for office, formulated issues for debate, lobbied for votes on the floor of the legislature, published journals, and organized all kinds of political communication. Such competition and conflict were not carried on beneath consensus about legitimacy and participation; in fact, the very nature of participation and legitimacy was contested in partisan struggle.

35. Margerison, "History, Representative Institutions, and Political Rights in the French Pre-Revolution," 68–98.
36. Michael P. Fitzsimmons, "Privilege and the Polity in France, 1786–1791," *American Historical Review,* XCII (1987), 269–95.

By the time the Constitution of 1791 was completed, the National Assembly, debating the formulation of rights and powers, had replaced an absolute sovereign monarch with a sovereign nation. Title III of the Constitution unified the nation by decree: "Sovereignty is one, indivisible, inalienable, and imprescriptible. It appertains to the nation; no section of the people nor any individual may assume the exercise thereof."[37] The king was declared to be one of the nation's representatives and the recipient of executive power delegated to him by the nation. This study focuses on the opinions and behavior of the more than thirteen hundred deputies who transformed a sovereign absolute monarch, legitimate by birth and divine right, into a constitutional king legitimate only if he served the will of the sovereign nation.

37. The Constitution of 1791, translated and printed in John Hall Stewart, *A Documentary Survey of the French Revolution* (New York, 1951), 234.

Chapter 1

Elections to the Estates General

When the crown's increasingly desperate search for ways to augment the tax returns culminated in the decision of July, 1788, to convoke the Estates General, electoral regulations became the focal point of political conflicts throughout France. In some places political passions escalated to the point of violence, and lives were lost. In quieter areas, struggles for position generated what amounted to genuine election campaigns. In the final reckoning, the election rules reinstated the political importance of the socially obsolete three estates, ensured that well-placed institutional elites would win election as deputies, and produced an Estates General with disproportionately more sword than robe nobles, more lawyers than judges, more parish priests than bishops, more bureaucrats than farmers, and fewer rural and village dwellers than urbanites.

The Paris Parlement decreed on September 23, 1788, that the forthcoming Estates General should be constituted with three equal estates, as it had been in 1614, each of which would vote separately. This declaration marked the rupture between the magistrates, heretofore acclaimed for their resistance to despotism, and "patriot" leaders demanding that the Estates be a body of equal deputies representing not orders, but the nation. Complex political questions throughout France were thus reduced to the extent and meaning of privilege. Two issues had to be settled: the number of deputies for each order, and the method of voting to be used in the Estates. Would the deputies vote "by head"—that is, as individuals—or as members of their order, so that two orders could together overrule a third?

In December and January, the finance minister Jacques Necker led the royal council to two decisions that seemed to favor the Third Estate but that left enough technical details unsettled to create different interpretations of royal intentions and to increase the rancor between patriots and aristocrats. The December 27 declaration doubled the number of Third Estate deputies. In the report accompanying the Order in Council, Necker stated that the Estates would normally vote by order, but might decide to vote by head on fiscal issues. The *règlement* of January 24, 1789, maintained separate procedures for the three orders but equalized the requirements for voters within one order.[1] These aspirations to electoral uniformity were condemned by provincial officials and individual correspondents asking the ministers for allowances and exceptions for areas with special claims to historic privileges—ducal apanages, privileged cities, and *pays d'états*. In many cases, notably for Paris, Necker and his fellow minister François de Barentin upheld these claims, with the result that national regulations were modified by local applications reflecting local politics. Nor was the impact of this localization neutralized by crown leadership; the king and ministers did not campaign for any program of reforms or for a slate of candidates.[2] Freedom of the press was guaranteed in the *règlement,* and polemicists for both the privileged orders and the Third Estate escalated debate over the nature of political representation.

Central Provinces

The *règlement* of January 24, outlining electoral procedures for 80 percent of France, classified voters by estate. All Catholic ecclesiastics could vote for deputies for the First Estate, the clergy. Monastic houses assembled and chose representatives to the general assembly of the clergy; all other clergymen, priests as well as bishops, who held benefices with cure of souls could

1. "Résultat du conseil d'état du roi, tenu à Versailles le 27 décembre 1788," in Armand Brette, *Recueil de documents relatif à la convocation des Etats généraux de 1789* (4 vols.; Paris, 1894–1911), I, 37–38. The "Réglement général du 24 janvier" is *ibid.,* 64–103.

2. Augustine Cochin, *Les Sociétés de pensée et la Révolution en Bretagne, 1788–1789* (2 vols.; Paris, 1925), I, 428, 429.

attend personally and vote in the general assembly. Second Estate representatives were to be chosen in a general assembly of all nobles possessing fiefs and by all others over twenty-five years of age who could prove acquired and/or transmissible nobility. For the Third Estate, voters were to be all male citizens over twenty-five who were regular residents of their locality and were inscribed on the tax rolls. This suffrage was broader than that designed by the Constitution of 1791, but its democratic effects were modified by indirect elections and voting in stages. The geographic units for the elections were judicial territories, either bailliages or sénéchaussées. Men of the Third Estate were convoked in two-, three-, or four-stage assemblies, depending on population density.

Electoral strategy in the three estates was shaped in part by these official rules. Within the clergy, the curés had a vote equal to that of bishops and canons, and in some localities particular circumstances combined with this rule gave the curés significant voting strength. In Berry, for example, the diocese of Bourges had lacked an archbishop since September, 1787; this vacancy allowed the curés to enlarge their influence by writing to curés in other dioceses to oppose the upper clergy and to complain about ecclesiastical abuses. They campaigned actively and quite successfully for seats in the Estates General: of the twenty-five deputies the clergy of Berry sent to Versailles, thirteen were curés.[3] In the bailliage of Blois in Orléanais, the bishop failed to be elected because of the hostility of his curés. One of the churches in his diocese possessed relics that were displayed in the streets during an annual festival, occasioning much travel to the town and income for the curé, as well as for the shops, inns, and families who provided lodging. In 1788 the bishop angered the lower clergy and the townspeople by ordering that the relics be no longer venerated because their authenticity was doubtful. The bishop also lost favor because he had opposed the doubling of the Third Estate when he sat in the second Assembly of Notables in the fall of 1788. In the electoral assembly in March, 1789, the clergy passed over him and elected a curé, Michel Chabault.[4] In the bailliage of Auxerre, the bishop Jean Baptiste Marie Champion de Cicé was

3. Marcel Bruneau, *Les Débuts de la Révolution dans les départements du Cher et de l'Indre, 1787–1791* (Paris, 1902), 12–15.

4. Adrien Thibault, "L'Abbé Michel Chabault, député aux Etats-Généraux de 1789," *Mémoires de la Société des sciences et lettres de Loir-et-Cher*, XIV (1900), 37–44.

elected by only a small majority after he had sent Necker a protest against the *règlement* of January 24 and had spoken to the three orders of his electoral assembly against the vote by head. The curés who opposed him were able to elect their choice to be secretary of the Assembly and to revise Cicé's proposed cahier draft, but they could not defeat him as a candidate for deputy.[5]

For the nobles, the electoral rules were intended to equalize the old nobility and the more recently ennobled judicial or bureaucratic nobility. But there was built-in discrimination. Nobles possessing fiefs were convoked by name and allowed to send representatives with proxy votes to their electoral assemblies; women possessing fiefs also had this privilege. Nobles without fiefs were convoked collectively. They had to have hereditary nobility, to reside in the bailliage where they attended the electoral assembly, and to attend in person.[6] These distinctions could cause confusion and conflicts, such as the struggle between bailliage officeholders of Saint-Pierre-le-Moutier in Bourbonnais and the seigneurial officials of the duc de Nevers. The bailliage officials wanted to strengthen their influence by denying proxy votes to fiefed nobles, but the denial was ultimately not permitted by the royal council.[7]

For the Third Estate, the electoral rules ensured that the electors and the deputies themselves would be middle- and upper-middle-class officials, professionals, and businessmen. Not only was there a tax qualification for voters, but the multistage electoral process meant that peasants in parish assemblies and urban artisans in town assemblies chose not deputies to the Estates General, but delegates to the next higher assembly.[8] Procedures for the Third Estate assigned the chief civil judge (the *lieutenant-général* of the

---

5. Charles Porée, "Mémoire du chanoine Frappier sur le clergé d'Auxerre, pendant la Révolution de 1789 à l'an IV," *Bulletin de la Société des sciences historiques et naturelles de l'Yonne,* LXXVII (1923), 101–42; Jean-Baptiste Marie Champion de Cicé, *Discours prononcé . . . le 23 mars 1789, dans l'assemblée des trois ordres réunis du bailliage d'Auxerre et imprimés sur leur demande* (N.p., 1789).

6. Georges Lefebvre, *Etudes orléanaises* (Paris, 1962), 109.

7. Brette, *Recueil,* III, 531, 536.

8. There were some spokesmen for the interests of cultivators and artisans; some were nobles looking for allies among the "Fourth Estate," and some were minor officials who wrote Necker and Barentin on behalf of the poor. See Patrick Kessel, *La Nuit du 4 août 1789* (Paris, 1969), 22.

bailliage) and the king's counsel (the royal *procureur*) to positions of leadership within the electoral assemblies. Both officials were usually candidates for election and thus had an advantage; they often competed for the right to make the opening speech or influence the order of procedure, or to draft the general cahier in the assemblies.[9]

For all three estates, the votes taken to choose deputies were by secret written ballot, so a candidate had to be known and respected by his fellow delegates. It was considered indecent to electioneer on one's own behalf. Electoral strategy involved such maneuvers as getting elected secretary of the assembly, making a speech containing suggestions for the general cahier, circulating one's pamphlets, and trying to be placed on the cahier-drafting committee. The assemblies of the bailliage of Bourges in Berry offer examples of both successful and unsuccessful campaigns. Jérôme Le Grand, Etienne François Xavier Sallé de Chou, and Guillaume Barthélemy Boëry were the three electors from the Third Estate sent as representatives to the nobles' assembly to propose a common cahier. They might well have been elected because they had held posts in the royal judiciary or a royal tribunal; some of the nobles may have known them, and would in any case have respected them for their professional connections. Negotiations with the nobles ultimately failed, but the three representatives were all chosen as deputies, and Le Grand became the primary author of the Third Estate's cahier. In the nobles' assembly, the comte de Guibert was a likely candidate for deputy and undoubtedly sought election. He had been a member of the *conseil de la guerre* and had sponsored reforms in promotion and rank in the military. Neither this experience nor his patriot sympathies supporting the Third Estate made him popular with his fellow nobles, and when he tried to make a speech at an assembly of the three orders at Bourges on March 18, he was literally shouted down by noble opponents. Members of the Third Estate who approved of his views asked that he be allowed to speak, but the nobles refused. Ultimately, Guibert was able to make his opinions known only by having the president of the assembly of the nobles, the comte de Lachastre, read a printed *mémoire*. Guibert made no attempt to attend any more sessions and did not cast a vote for his order's deputies. Lachastre himself asserted his authority to insist that the *mémoire* be read,

9. Brette, *Recueil*, III, 26.

but he did nothing else on behalf of Guibert and did not endanger his own ultimately successful election as a deputy.[10]

Paris

Different sets of electoral rules, in response to demands from law courts and provincial estates, were set up for Paris, Brittany, and Dauphiné in this sample, and in total for the 20 percent of France not included in the general *réglement*. The controller-general, Charles Alexandre de Calonne, had convoked the Assembly of Notables at Paris—not Versailles—in 1787 to publicize and win support for his reforms and to restore the government's credit.[11] But the belief was growing among young liberal magistrates in the Paris Parlement and others that reform should come through the Estates General, as the only proper body to represent the nation. These men, all of them future deputies, became the leaders of what in 1788 was called the "National party"—men like Adrien Jean François Du Port, a magistrate in the Paris Parlement who wanted nothing less than a new written constitution; Jean Jacques du Val d'Eprémesnil, a councillor in the Chambre des Enquêtes and a staunch supporter of the aristocratic magistrates' tradition of opposing royal despotism; Emmanuel Marie Michel Philippe Fréteau de Saint-Just and Pierre Samuel Du Pont de Nemours, who were inspired by American revolutionary issues; and Louis Philippe Joseph, duc d'Orléans, prince of the blood, who was personally hostile to the king and queen and had an agent in Parlement urging magistrates to oppose royal decrees. These leaders influenced the younger councillors of the separate chambers of the Parlement (Enquêtes and Requêtes), who were also urged on by several thousand enthusiastic *avocats, procureurs, clercs,* and *secrétaires* sitting in the galleries of the Palais de Justice. The National party's views

10. Thomas Lemas, *Etudes sur le Cher pendant la Révolution* (Paris, 1887), 1–35; Egret, *La Pré-Révolution française,* 80–94; Louis Hector Chaudru de Raynal, *Histoire du Berry depuis les temps les plus anciens jusqu'en* 1789 (4 vols.; Bourges, 1844–47), IV, 499–506.

11. William Doyle, "The Parlements of France and the Breakdown of the Old Regime," *French Historical Studies,* VI (1970), 450, 451; Vivian R. Gruder, "A Mutation in Elite Political Culture: The French Notables and the Defense of Property and Participation, 1787," *Journal of Modern History,* LVI (1984), 598–634.

were reflected in Parlement's remonstrances of July 26, 1787, refusing to register a new tax and demanding that the Estates General have the right of consent to any new taxes. The remonstrances were printed and sold.[12] On August 6, the tax edicts were forcibly registered; when the magistrates' protests were supported by enthusiastic demonstrations in the streets, Parlement was exiled to Troyes. Even when the magistrates yielded on taxes and returned to Paris, they continued to insist that the Estates General alone could vote taxes.

The coup by Etienne Charles Loménie de Brienne, then minister of finance, against the parlements on May 8, 1788, caused the first split in the National party when the younger liberals like Du Port predicted that the royal Edicts would be so strongly opposed that the king would be forced to resort to the Estates General. When that prediction came true on July 5, the Parlement divided into "patriots," who wanted liberal reforms from the Estates, and "aristocrats," who supported traditional prerogatives. The latter, led by du Val d'Eprémesnil, won the first round when Parlement declared on September 23 that the Estates should be constituted as they had been in 1614, that is, by equal orders. The Parlement now moved away from the patriot cause. This shift drove a wedge between many magistrates and their erstwhile supporters in the lower levels of the judiciary, foreshadowing the split between the nobility and the Third Estate that characterized the early sessions of the Estates General nine months later. The publicity of political views through pamphlets became an even more important tactic for liberals once they lost the Parlement as a forum. The patriot nobles also lost a base of operations in the Parlement, and the Parlementary magistrates fell into popular disfavor.

The Patriot party was led by a group of liberal nobles, clergy, and wealthy members of the Third Estate who together constituted the Society of Thirty, which began to meet regularly at the home of Adrien Du Port in November, 1788.[13] They sought to influence elections in order to get liberals into the Estates General and control its agenda so as to produce a written constitution. They shared a conception of the nation as a society of

12. Doyle, "Parlements of France," 456–58.

13. Egret, *La Pré-Révolution française*, 326–31; Elizabeth L. Eisenstein, "Who Intervened in 1788? A Commentary on *The Coming of the French Revolution*," *American Historical Review*, LXXI (1965), 77–103; Daniel L. Wick, *A Conspiracy of Well-Intentioned Men: The Society of Thirty and the French Revolution* (New York, 1987).

property-owning equal citizens; they advocated the abolition of privilege and the establishment of a regular legislature that would represent the national will. Initially they concentrated on persuading the ministers to double the Third Estate's representation, a decision with which Necker concurred.

The doubling of the Third Estate did not preclude further electoral controversies in Paris, centering on rival claims of the Châtelet and the Hôtel de Ville to historic rights to choose deputies and draw up the cahiers for the Estates General. The struggle for influence pitted the centralizing and regularizing monarchical administrators not only against the remaining representatives of the old corporate society, such as the *prévôt des marchands,* but also against ambitious and wealthy bourgeois. Spokesmen for the Châtelet argued that as the administrative body for the prévôté and vicomté of Paris, analogous to a bailliage court, it alone could convoke the three orders. Although the royal rules of January 24, with no decision on the Paris election, expressly prohibited municipalities from sending deputies directly to Versailles, the Hôtel de Ville argued that the *prévôt des marchands* had always had the right to convoke the Commune of Paris.[14]

On March 28 and April 13 a widely unpopular compromise settled the matter. The Châtelet was empowered to convene the clergy and nobles in the city of Paris, and all three orders in Paris outside the walls. The *prévôt des marchands* would convene the Third Estate in Paris in sixty different districts. As François Furet has suggested, the decision produced a strange amalgam of a traditional convocation of corporate bodies and a modern representative electoral system.[15] The *prévôt de Paris,* through the Châtelet, would preside over the drawing up of cahiers and the election of deputies for all three orders, but the *prévôt des marchands,* through the Hôtel de Ville, would preside over the convocation of the Third Estate. Preliminary elections would select 150 electors for the clergy, 150 for the nobles, and 300 for the Third Estate; these men would meet to elect deputies and draft cahiers, either separately or together. The forty deputies of the Third Estate

14. Between January and March, numerous pamphlets supporting both sides, as well as official decrees from both institutions, were printed and sent to the royal council.

15. François Furet, "La Monarchie et le règlement électoral de 1789," in *Political Culture of the Old Regime,* ed. Baker, 383.

for the Estates General would then meet with the *corps municipal* at the Hôtel de Ville to draw up a separate cahier of municipal demands.[16]

Before the March 28 decision, patriot and aristocratic opinion did not align neatly behind the rival institutions competing to control the elections. Some patriot pamphlets objected to an urban oligarchy under the *prévôt des marchands* and recommended that the Third Estate choose its deputies by guilds, corporations, Paris quartiers, and communities. They were arguing for somewhat less elitist and more democratic procedures. At least one pamphlet demanded nearly universal manhood suffrage by removal of tax qualifications for voters. Others argued that because the *prévôt des marchands* and the Hôtel de Ville could convene electors without regard to orders, they would best serve the interests of the Third Estate. Still others maintained that Paris nobles would lose their rights as citizens if they were not convened by the Hôtel de Ville.[17]

The generally unpopular electoral forms effectively disfranchised about one-fourth of the citizens of Paris because the tax qualifications for voting were higher there than elsewhere in France.[18] The multistage election reduced the influence of artisans, craftsmen, tradesmen, and domestics. All 497 electors ultimately chosen were middle-class professionals in law, commerce, public service, or the army.

The multistage election also transformed the old process for the nobility. No longer were all Paris nobles called directly to a bailliage assembly, as they were in the *pays d'élections;* like the Third Estate, they now gathered initially in primary assemblies to select delegates to the whole electoral assembly. Only the clergy were convoked according to traditional corporate practices. These procedural differences go far toward explaining why the Paris noble deputies were among the most liberal of all nobles in the Estates General, whereas the clergy's deputies were among the leaders of the conservatives.

16. Charles L. Chassin, *Les Elections et les cahiers de Paris en 1789* (4 vols.; Paris, 1888–89), I, 333–36, 399–405. See also Robert Barrie Rose, *The Making of the Sans-Culottes* (Manchester, Eng., 1983), 23–41.

17. See Chassin, *Les Elections et les cahiers de Paris,* I, 158–61, 166–75, 453–74 for examples.

18. J. M. Thompson, *The French Revolution* (Oxford, Eng., 1964), 9; Jacques Godechot, *La Prise de la Bastille* (Paris, 1965), 169–73; Rose, *Making of the Sans-Culottes,* 36–39.

Primary assemblies for the Third Estate often rejected the presiding officers named by the municipality, and they chose 407 electors instead of the 300 to which they were entitled. The electors in turn agreed to choose as a deputy no member of the clergy or nobility who was not already a Third Estate elector, and indeed, for the first nineteen of their deputies, they alternated between selecting a man from the professions, finance, or commerce on one round of voting and a lawyer on the next. The abbé Emmanuel Joseph Sieyès was proposed as the twentieth and last deputy, since he had been excluded by the clergy of both Orléans and Paris.* Sieyès was elected only after a lively evening of debate over whether to break the rule excluding the clergy in order to bring into the Estates General the most famous exponent of the rights of the Third Estate. Eight electors who were not selected as deputies inserted a formal protest in the procès-verbal.

On April 23 the electors of the three orders met together, 344 for the clergy, 223 for the nobles, and 407 for the Third Estate. Although willing to exchange information on their cahiers with the nobles, the Third's electors refused to unite with the other two orders because they would then have been in the minority.[19] Once they had finished their assigned task, the electors of the Third Estate decided not to disband until the end of the Estates General, and to remain as a correspondence committee with the Paris deputies in Versailles. In July they invited the noble and clerical electors to join them, and seventeen nobles and twenty-five clergy did so. These 449 members of the Assemblée générale des électeurs de Paris became the municipal government of Paris during and after the attack on the Bastille.

The deputies for the Paris clergy, the only ones elected according to ancient corporate practices, were predominantly conservative, led by the archbishop Antoine Eléonor Léon Leclerc de Juigné, who was so unpopular that he was attacked in his carriage by a stone-throwing street mob in Versailles in June. The clerical delegation did include a liberal member of

---

*With Sieyès' name, I have adopted the almost universal modern usage of the lone *accent grave* (the accentuation *Siéyès* often appeared formerly). Otherwise, for consistency in spelling and accentuation of deputies' names, I have followed the style used by Brette, *Recueil*, II, 35–333, although this sometimes differs from preferred modern spellings. I have not hyphenated forenames. Where secondary sources on the deputies are cited, I have followed whatever style the author used.

19. Chassin, *Les Elections et les cahiers de Paris,* chap. 1.

the Society of Thirty, Charles François Perrotin de Barmond, and the rector of the University of Paris and future Jacobin, Jean Baptiste Dumouchel. The noble delegation from Paris produced leaders of the forty or so liberal nobles in the Estates General, especially the parlementary magistrates Adrien Du Port, Achille Pierre Dionis du Séjour, and Louis Michel Lepeletier de Saint-Fargeau. The Third Estate deputies included prominent patriots, two of whom were members of the Society of Thirty: Du Pont de Nemours and the abbé Sieyès. The avocat Camus had resigned as avocat of the clergy of France before the Parlement because he ardently opposed Maupeou's reforms.[20] Others had become known for their writing. Sieyès' pamphlet *Qu'est-ce que le Tiers-état?* had sold over 30,000 copies in a few days after its January, 1789, publication.[21] Dr. Joseph Ignace Guillotin, popular for challenging the Parlement on collective petitions, had written a pamphlet, *Pétition des citoyens domiciliés à Paris,* which he had given to the six corps of the marchands de la ville for deliberation and signatures. On December 19, 1788, Parlement had confiscated the document and required Guillotin to appear for a hearing; when he emerged from the Palais de Justice, he was greeted by an enthusiastic crowd.[22] Another pamphlet, a *mémoire* of December 18, 1788, requesting that citizens, rather than the Hôtel de Ville, elect deputies, seemed to be almost a campaign manifesto. The pamphlet had 108 patriot signatures, including those of three nobles later chosen as deputies, Hugues Thibault Henri Jacques Luzignem and Charles Philippe Simon de Beaufort-Canillac Montboissier from Paris and Antoine Louis Claude de Stutt de Tracy, elected from Moulins. Six future Third Estate deputies also signed, three from Paris (Jean Silvain Bailly, Jean Nicolas Démeunier, and Jean Baptiste Pierre Bevière) and three others (Pierre Joseph Grangier, from Bourges; Jean Marie Garnier, from Brittany, and Jean Bazin, from Orléans).[23] Many future Paris deputies for the Third Estate had become fa-

---

20. Michel Prévost *et al.,* eds., *Dictionnaire de biographie française* (Paris, 1933–), VI (1956), 1010.

21. Barthélemy Pocquet, *Les Derniers Etats de Bretagne* (Paris, 1885), 55, Vol. II of Pocquet, *Les Origines de la Révolution en Bretagne,* 2 vols.

22. Joseph Ignace Guillotin, *Pétition des citoyens domiciliés à Paris, 8 décembre 1788* (Paris, 1788); E. Pariset, "Guillotin, à propos d'une récente thèse allemande," *La Révolution française,* XXV (1893), 437–62; Chassin, *Les Elections et les cahiers de Paris,* I, 35–46, 56–71.

23. Chassin, *Les Elections et les cahiers de Paris,* I, 79–83.

mous for success in other areas, like Bailly for the studies of astronomy that had won him membership in the Royal Academy, and Démeunier for political geographies of North America.

The delegation from the three estates in Paris arrived late in Versailles, after the opening of the Estates General, but many of its members promptly became very active deputies and placed themselves across the alignment spectrum from the far left to the far right. Many of the Paris clergy became prominent conservatives, and many of the nobles were leaders of the small group of liberal nobles whose votes were critical for the success of the constitutional reformers.

Brittany

The deputies from Brittany, selected in the most tumultuous election of all France, were extraordinarily politically involved; most of them were frequent writers of pamphlets who had served in the rebellious provincial estates of 1788–1789. The prerevolution in Brittany had featured conflicts both between the crown and the province and between the Third Estate and the Breton aristocrats.

These conflicts originated in the provincial estates and parlement at Rennes, two powerful institutions that had maintained more autonomy for Brittany, since its incorporation with the French crown in 1532, than any other region enjoyed. The estates had the right to set amounts and allocations for all royal taxes, which also had to be registered in the Breton parlement.[24] These arrangements, although legal, had led to periods of conflict between the province and royal agents since the seventeenth century, culminating in the "affaire de Bretagne," a seventeen-year struggle between the chief judge in the parlement and the royal comman-

---

24. The parlement, founded in 1554, actually had greater leverage than the estates because by remonstrating and declining to register edicts it could prevent crown agents from collecting a tax. It could publish its decrees and remonstrances and oversee town finances and administration. See Armand Rébillon, *Les Etats de Bretagne de 1661 à 1789* (Rennes, 1932), 197–212.

dant in Brittany, resolved finally only by Maupeou's attempt to replace all parlements.[25]

Brittany's assertion of limits to royal jurisdiction within its boundaries not only unified its parlement and estates, but also defined the relationship between royal authority and the whole nation. Breton leaders of the Third Estate, mainly wealthy Nantes merchants and the judicial bourgeoisie in Rennes, did not fully support provincial privileges above all else. Throughout the reign of Louis XV, merchants from the larger commercial ports such as Nantes, Redon, Lorient, and Saint-Brieuc were well aware that their fortunes were tied to national trade and international politics, and they often deemphasized provincial claims and supported the intendant. In the 1770s leaders of the Third Estate expressed resentment of tax inequalities inherent in the *capitation* (head tax) and the *octrois* (city tax). Jean Denis Lanjuinais, a professor in the law school at Rennes and a future deputy, had proposed changes in the Breton constitution in 1782 to improve the fiscal and political situation of the Third Estate.[26]

At first it seemed possible that the May Edicts of 1788 would reunify Brittany in defense of provincial privileges and against this latest centralizing effort of the crown.[27] Breton nobles, who held the most power in the provincial estates, had little difficulty in winning the support of their colleagues in the clergy (all upper clergy) and the mayors of the forty-two privileged cities. In addition, the protests of the Rennes parlement against the Edicts were supported by the procureurs, avocats, law students, and townspeople of Rennes whose income derived from the parlement, and there were riots until the end of July. The nobles tried to mobilize additional support within the Third Estate throughout Brittany, but because the new courts included in the May Edicts would profit the cities where they would be located, these efforts were not successful in

25. Henri Fréville, *L'Intendance de Bretagne, 1689–1790* (3 vols.; Rennes, 1953), II; Barthélemy Pocquet, *Le Pouvoir absolu et l'esprit provincial: Le Duc d'Aiguillon et La Chalotais* (3 vols.; Paris, 1900–1901); Marcel Marion, *La Bretagne et le duc d'Aiguillon, 1753–1770* (Paris, 1898).

26. Fréville, *L'Intendance de Bretagne*, I, 41–303; II, 118–20; Rébillon, *Les Etats de Bretagne*, 738; Jean Egret, "Les Origines de la Révolution en Bretagne, 1788–1789," in *New Perspectives on the Revolution in France*, ed. Jeffry Kaplow (New York, 1965), 136–52.

27. Egret, "Les Origines," 137–40.

Nantes and in other towns, especially those in the dioceses of Quimper and Tréguier.

The decision to call the Estates General had a particular impact on the Breton Third Estate, who feared their interests would be underrepresented if Brittany's deputies were chosen in the provincial estates.[28] The notables at Nantes, led by the *anobli* Jacques Edme Cottin, made the revolutionary demands for doubling of the Third Estate and for the vote by head. On November 6 a new and irregular assembly at Nantes sent twelve delegates to the king to request the right to elect its own deputies. The twelve included five who later were chosen to go to the Estates General: Cottin, Etienne Chaillon, Jean François Girard, François Joseph Jary, and François Pierre Blin.[29] In the next weeks at least seventeen cities out of the forty-two privileged ones ordered their deputies to the coming session of the provincial estates to demand the vote by head.[30]

The more liberal nobles in the provincial estates from Rennes and Nantes were unable to win concessions from their rural colleagues on the demands of the Third Estate. From December, 1788, to March, 1789, the sequence of events polarized opinion in Brittany, aligning the Third Estate and curés with the royal government and against the nobles and upper clergy. On October 25 a group of nobles had published a declaration at Rennes supporting vote by order and insisting on the firmness of provincial privileges; this was answered by Lanjuinais' *Réflexions patriotiques,* a bitter denunciation of the nobles' "enslavement" of two million Bretons.[31] From then on, many pamphlets representing both sides circulated through the province. Playing an active part in this mobilization were the deputies from Nantes at Versailles and Paris, now joined by Augustin Bernard François Le Goazre de Kervelegan and François Jérôme Le Déan from Quimper, Julien François Palasne de Champeaux from Saint-Brieuc, Jean Pierre Boullé

28. Participation in the provincial estates of Brittany was restricted to privileged persons. All nonrobe nobles had the right to sit. The clergy were represented by nine bishops, forty abbots, and the representatives of the nine Breton cathedrals, but no lower clergy. Third Estate deputies were all mayors or procureurs-syndics of forty-two privileged towns, most of whom had purchased their offices. See Rébillon, *Les Etats de Bretagne,* 109–27.

29. Cochin, *Les Sociétés de pensée et la Révolution en Bretagne,* II, 30.

30. Egret, "Les Origines," 143.

31. Jean Denis Lanjuinais, *Réflexions patriotiques, sur l'arrêté de quelques nobles de Bretagne, du 25 octobre 1788* (N.p., 1788).

from Pontivy—all future deputies—and many others. These men wrote regular bulletins home that were read publicly. In Paris they met representatives from Dauphiné and the leaders of the patriot movement.[32]

On December 27, representatives of the Third to the provincial estates met at Rennes and decided to demand double representation for their order and the vote by head. When the provincial estates opened on December 29, the "Résultat" of December 27 had reached Rennes with the news that Necker had decreed the doubling of the Third for the Estates General. Heralding tactics they would recommend at Versailles in May, the Third refused to conduct any business in the estates at Rennes until their demands were granted, and they met each evening to coordinate their tactics. The nobles were equally adamant, and the estates were deadlocked until the king suspended the session on January 3.

The break between the Third and the aristocracy was sealed absolutely by an armed clash in Rennes from January 26 to 28, involving law students supporting the patriots against servants supporting the nobles. On January 20, the king had authorized the privileged cities to double their deputies and to have them elected by the inhabitants. The nobility and the urban bourgeoisie both tried to mobilize opinion; these activities may have contributed to the outbreak of violence in Rennes.

The whole matter was not finally settled until March 16, when a royal order declared that deputies to the Estates General would be elected in three different ways: the nobles and clergy by an assembly at Saint-Brieuc (plus diocesan assemblies to complete the clerical election), and the Third in assemblies by judicial districts. The privileged orders met from April 16 to 20 and refused to name deputies, on the grounds that the only legal representation could come from an election held in the provincial estates.[33]

Thus it happened that Brittany, with the strongest nobility outside the royal court in all of France, sent only deputies from the Third Estate and the lower clergy to Versailles. These men had learned well the principles they were to practice and describe: that the king was basically in favor of liberty; that aristocrats were permanent and intransigent enemies who

32. Charles Kuhlmann, "Influence of the Breton Deputation and the Breton Club in the Revolution, April–October, 1789," *University Studies* (University of Nebraska), II (1902), 223, 224.

33. Pocquet, *Les Origines de la Révolution en Bretagne,* II, 169, 170. See also Jean Meyer, *La Noblesse bretonne au dix-huitième siècle* (2 vols.; Paris, 1966).

could be defeated only by uncompromising firmness; that deputies should meet together outside the Estates to coordinate their actions; and that the common people were easily manipulated and could be persuaded to support their aristocratic patrons. When the Breton deputies got to Versailles, it was only six weeks until a majority of the Third Estate accepted much of their program.

Dauphiné

As in Brittany, Dauphiné's union with the French monarchy had brought guaranteed special privileges. But Dauphiné's provincial estates had ceased to meet in 1628, leaving only the parlement at Grenoble to combat the royal will. Before the mid–eighteenth century, this parlement was docile enough in its relations with the intendant and the crown, but after 1756 it joined other parlements in resisting tax reforms. Politics in the prerevolutionary period in Dauphiné were marked by a struggle to fuse the defense of provincial privileges with a defense of the nation's rights. There was considerable coordination among the leaders of all three estates, in direct contrast to the extreme hostility between patriots and aristocrats in Brittany.

Relations between the privileged and the nonprivileged in Dauphiné contained the potential for developing hostility as bitter as that in Brittany. By the middle of the century only eleven members of the Grenoble parlement were *anoblis* or of *roturier* origin. A 1762 decision required that new recruits for the Grenoble parlement who did not have ancestors from the magistracy had to prove four generations of nobility on their father's side. Even under the supposedly open recruitment for the Maupeou court, only two avocats were admitted as judicial officers and then only after some conflict; one of these was the future deputy Alexis François Pison du Galland.[34] After the parlement was restored, avocats were not deferential to the magistrates; in 1780 and 1781 the bar and the parlement fought over the avocats' right to hold meetings; the matter was settled only after the avocats went on strike.[35]

34. Jean Egret, *Le Parlement de Dauphiné et les affaires publiques dans la deuxième moitié du XVIIIᵉ siècle* (2 vols.; Grenoble, 1942), I, 17–36, 293–95.
35. *Ibid.*, II, 85–89.

These conflicts were prevented from enlarging by conciliatory leadership from the Third Estate and the willingness of a group of nobles and upper clergy to cooperate to ensure the reestablishment of their provincial estates. As early as 1783, Jean Joseph Mounier and Antoine Pierre Joseph Marie Barnave had requested these estates and demanded a new written constitution for Dauphiné. The magistrates in parlement, too, welcomed the idea of an institutional ally, and had begun to request the estates after 1750 and more frequently after 1778. In 1779 Dauphiné was granted a provincial assembly similar to that in Berry. It was to levy taxes and participate in administrative tasks, although, like Berry's assembly, it had no right of consent to taxes and could not prevent their collection. Although this was much less autonomy than Dauphiné's ancient estates had enjoyed, parlementary magistrates were willing to accept limits because they wished to retain exclusive power to register tax decrees.[36] The opening of the provincial assembly was delayed by rivalries among cities that wished to host it and among bishops who wished to preside. Necker's dismissal came in 1781, and the assembly was never operative.

After 1775 the Grenoble parlement did not act in concert with other parlements but concentrated instead on defending provincial privileges. In 1787 this emphasis dovetailed with national politics. In remonstrances favoring the maintenance of the *corvée* in March, the parlement asked again for the provincial estates; but after the Assembly of Notables in Paris recommended provincial assemblies, the magistrates feared the new institution would provide another device to increase taxes. In June the magistrates issued an edict describing the nature of the estates they desired, including a doubled Third Estate and the vote by head, but retaining the registration of tax laws by parlement. This request was denied. In July Dauphiné was given a provincial assembly like those in the central provinces, quite subservient to the intendant and the royal council. The assembly was constituted and met in October, whereupon it was promptly declared illegal by the parlement. Although the magistrates were looking to preserve their own interests, some future radicals, chiefly Barnave, agreed with their condemnation of the assembly's lack of autonomy.[37] Throughout the winter of 1787–1788 a struggle between the Grenoble parlement and the central gov-

36. This is Egret's contention. *Ibid.*, II, 134, 135.
37. *Ibid.*, II, 190, 191.

ernment remained unsettled until the May Edicts curtailed the parlement's political role and severely limited its juridical functions. The Grenoble magistrates were sent on vacation, but they met on May 20 and drafted their bitter objections. On June 6, lettres de cachet arrived exiling them as punishment.

The Day of Tiles at Grenoble, June 7, saw the most famous of the violent incidents that followed the May Edicts and the magistrate's resistance to them. Law students and clerks led a protest that began in the markets and ended in a violent clash between the crowd and two regiments of royal soldiers. When news of it spread nationally, the event was described as an uprising of the entire province in resistance to despotism. Jean Egret's analysis of the episode emphasizes both its limited nature (it did not go beyond Grenoble) and its failure (the exiled magistrates left the city as soon as they could).[38] Crown officials did permit the first major move in Dauphiné's revolution, the meeting of Mounier and a group of notables at Grenoble on June 14. The declaration drafted at this meeting gave provincial privileges a national scope; the return of the Grenoble parlement and the provincial estates with a freely elected doubled Third were demanded, but the call for the Estates General was stressed equally.[39]

During the summer of 1788, Mounier and Barnave led an extraordinary campaign to mobilize their province and publicize their revolutionary program throughout France. The June 14 declaration was sent to many communities throughout Dauphiné, and personal letters were mailed to lawyers outside Grenoble. Mounier and Barnave wrote dozens of pamphlets, many anonymous, paid for most probably by magistrates and liberal nobles. Intendants and subdelegates countered with pamphlets suggesting that the government was the true defender of ordinary people against the selfish presumptions of magistrates.[40] Mounier and Barnave stressed their ultimate concern for the Estates General and not just the province's right to have a sovereign court.

In July the government tried to fragment the opposition to the May

38. Egret, *La Révolution des Notables: Mounier et les monarchiens, 1789* (Paris, 1950), 7–9.

39. Jean Joseph Mounier, *Délibération de la ville de Grenoble, 14 juin 1788* (N.p., 1788).

40. Blanchard, "Une Campagne de brochures dans l'agitation dauphinoise de l'été 1788," 225–41. See also Egret, *Le Parlement de Dauphiné*, II, 246–59.

Edicts by promising that Dauphiné could convoke its provincial estates. On July 21, Mounier led five hundred men at Vizille in an assembly that tightened the unity of all three orders by securing agreement on demands for the recall of the Grenoble parlement, the reconstitution of the provincial estates with a doubled Third, and the immediate convocation of the Estates General. The government countered with a decree convoking a legal assembly at Romans in August to prepare the provincial estates; in effect, the ministers wanted to trade support for the May Edicts for concessions on the provincial estates. This tactic posed a dilemma for the leaders of the movement; the nobles especially had a tendency to divide on the issue of support for the parlementary magistrates. In the end, 51 percent of the communities of Dauphiné (including 95 percent of those in the *élection* of Grenoble) chose deputies not for the legal convocation, but for an illegal one at Grenoble.[41] On the first of September these men met at Grenoble and agreed to go to Romans later if they could insist on their right to discuss what they chose.

In the September assembly at Romans, the plans drawn up for the provincial estates undercut the parlement's role in relations with the king and in the registration of laws. When they returned to Grenoble, the magistrates did not agree with Paris Parlement's declarations that the Estates General should be constituted as it had been in the seventeenth century; thus the magistrates appeared to support the provincial estates. But from then on the political initiative remained with the estates, and those magistrates were quite ineffectual who opposed Dauphiné's new constitution as well as the election of deputies to the Estates General in the estates.

The estates of Dauphiné met from December, 1788, to January, 1789, elected deputies to Versailles, gave them a mandate, and chose an interim commission to carry on its administrative work when it was not in session. All but two of the deputies were members of the provincial estates (all three orders were represented), and most had participated in the assemblies and the pamphlet campaign of the summer of 1788. Some were known throughout the province as leading spokesmen for their orders in that campaign: the comte de Virieu for the nobility, the archbishop of Vienne, Jean Georges Le Franc de Pompignan, for the clergy, and Barnave for the Third Estate. Mounier had become nationally famous for his activities and his writings.

41. Egret, *Le Parlement de Dauphiné*, 315.

Dauphiné's new constitution resolved the tension between provincial privileges and national issues: the estates declared that only the Estates General could levy taxes, but the local body reserved to itself all internal administrative matters and relations with the crown. The deputies to Versailles were mandated to refuse to deliberate as separate orders and not to vote until the forms of the Estates General were decided.

The political experience of the Dauphinois deputies was in many ways opposite to that of the Bretons. The Dauphinois learned that conciliation worked among the three orders; that the king was well intentioned and could be persuaded to yield to the imperatives of liberty over the heads of his more despotic ministers; and that the individual leadership of one man, Mounier, had been decisive. Whereas in Rennes in January the lowest classes, depending on robe nobles for their employment and livelihood, supported aristocrats against young students, in Dauphiné the *menu peuple* played only a small role in Grenoble during the Day of Tiles. Dauphiné's constitution specifically kept from a political role the stipended clergy, who were the poorest and closest to the masses, and the rural *fermiers*. The Bretons had seen the lower classes manipulated for political ends, but the Dauphinois had ignored or excluded their role. With Barnave's pamphlets as a conspicuous exception, the writings of the Dauphinois later in 1789 expressed revulsion against violence; the Bretons were more inclined to recognize its usefulness.

Church politics in Dauphiné were likewise very different than in Brittany. For several decades the curés of Dauphiné had been contesting with church officials over their economic situation and their parish responsibilities. At Romans the curés unsuccessfully protested their under-representation. The upper clergy were able to maneuver to keep them out; not one curé was elected to the Estates General.[42] In Brittany, curés were able to ensure that they dominated the choice of clerical deputies for Versailles.

Mounier expected to lead the Third Estate at Versailles as he had at Grenoble, but some of his independent overtures won him only the resentment of his fellow deputies. More important, he had foreseen neither the intransigence of the upper orders nor the ambiguity of the king's attitude to-

---

42. Timothy Tackett, *Priest and Parish in Eighteenth Century France* (Princeton, 1977), 225–54.

ward the Estates. He was finally to achieve the presidency of the Assembly only a few days before he left it in bitter disillusionment.

A Collective Portrait of the Men of the Estates General

The complexity of the national electoral rules produced an Estates General very close to the proportions of estates specified by the decision to increase the number of Third Estate deputies. Among the 1,318 who eventually sat in the Estates General/National Assembly there were 332 clergy (25 percent), 311 nobles (24 percent), 645 Third Estate (49 percent), and 30 deputies (2 percent) taking seats after June, 1789, who were not elected according to estate.

Many studies of the Estates General have remarked upon the skewing of the First Estate delegation toward the lower clergy. Only 15 percent of the clerical deputies were bishops and archbishops, 20 percent were middle clergy, and 65 percent were curés and priests. The top of the power structure of the church, one of the most politically potent institutions in the Old Regime, could easily be outvoted in the sessions of the clergy in May and June, 1789. The numerical strength of the lower clergy pulled the order to the left and was a factor in the close votes on clerical issues later, in the National Assembly.

For the Second Estate, the impact of deputies' institutional backgrounds is not so clear. More than two-thirds of the noble deputies were nobles of the sword, representing those connected to the court or the army to a much greater extent than those in parlements. This underrepresentation of robe nobles should not be assumed to account for the conservatism of much of the Second Estate. Only a few of the younger magistrates in the Paris Parlement were members of the Patriot party in 1788 and 1789, whereas many magistrates from the Grenoble parlement supported the revolt in Dauphiné. Ninety or so noble deputies took liberal positions in the Estates General and the National Assembly; as we shall see, they became a most significant group of actors in determining internal legislative politics, as well as legislation, between 1789 and 1791.

Historians have made many classifications of occupations for the 675 deputies who represented the Third Estate or were replacements not elected by estate. Beginning in the spring of 1789, publicists noted that these deputies were hardly representative of the "Fourth Estate" of peasants and urban artisans; there was not a poor man among them. The single largest group of Third Estate deputies were avocats, but there is disagreement about how to differentiate among positions and offices. Alfred Cobban's classification, initially presented in 1954 and published in 1955, supported his argument that the bourgeois revolution was a process of upward occupational mobility by which former minor officials sitting as deputies created new high-level judicial and administrative posts that they themselves filled from 1791 through the Napoleonic era. The category he called "officers in state services" is larger than it should be, since he included both those who were proprietors of venal offices and those, like *subdélégués* under intendants, who did not own their own offices. His category "avocats du roi" should be included with officers of bailliages and sénéchausées, since all three groups were royal officials. Edna Lemay, in an article published in 1977, used similar categories, also combining venal and nonvenal offices, but came up with slightly more *officiers* and *négociants* and somewhat fewer avocats and others than Cobban.[43]

The occupational categories presented in Table 1 separate judicial and administrative officeholders, and distinguish royal officeholders from provincial administrators, mayors, and seigneurial officeholders. For most deputies, the occupation given is the first one listed in Armand Brette's biographical sketch of deputies. Using that information, supplemented by additional biographies, I tried to determine what a deputy spent most of his working time doing and/or how he earned his living.[44] The first cate-

43. Cobban, *Myth of the French Revolution;* Lemay, "La Composition de l'Assemblée nationale constituante," 341–63. Other recent occupational categorizations were not relevant for this study, either because they apply to lower social strata than are appropriate for deputies or because they are too broad. See, for example, A. Daumard and François Furet, *Structures et relations sociales à Paris au milieu du XVIIIᵉ siècle* (Paris, 1961); Donald Greer, *The Incidence of the Terror During the French Revolution* (Cambridge, Mass., 1935), and *The Incidence of the Emigration During the French Revolution* (Cambridge, Mass., 1951); and Jean Sentou, *Fortunes et groupes sociaux à Toulouse sous la Révolution (1789–1799): Essai d'histoire statistique* (Toulouse, 1969).

44. Brette, *Recueil,* II, 35–333; Prévost *et al., Dictionnaire de biographie française;* Adolphe Robert, Edgar Bourlotin, and Gaston Cougny, *Dictionnaire des parlementaires français* (5 vols.; Paris, 1891–95).

gory, officeholder in the royal judiciary, includes all those who were members of the corporate group of judges and lawyers in a parlement, a bailliage, a *châtellenie,* or another royal court. *Avocats du roi* and *procureurs du roi* are included here, but judges in seigneurial jurisdictions are not, because the latter position took up at most one or two days a week of a man's professional time. *Avocats, procureurs,* and *notaires* were all lawyers. Avocats were generally trained in French law, could represent plaintiffs and defendants in litigation, submitted written briefs and often made oral arguments, but could not participate in the taking of evidence. Most frequently they worked in parlementary cities, although in theory they could practice anywhere within the territory of that parlement whose judges had supervised their admission to the bar. They did not own their own offices. Procureurs did own their offices; they organized lawsuits and drew up written briefs presenting the facts of a case rather than its legal precedents. Their profession was organized by corporations that maintained their monopoly and set requirements for training as apprentice clerks. Notaires were similarly organized and trained. They purchased their offices, but they did not plead cases. Their main function was to draw up official documents for marriages, commercial dealings, and contracts, and to witness signatures. Such documents were not necessarily part of briefs for lawsuits, and notaires, unlike avocats and procureurs, were not primarily involved in litigation.

Royal administrators were judges and lawyers who practiced before royal administrative courts, such as *greniers à sel* (administration of salt tariffs), *traites* (administration of trade), *élections* (administrative subdivisions that assessed the direct tax, the *taille,* owed by parishes), *foraines* (customs), and *maîtrise des eaux et forêts* (water and forest administration).

The next seven categories include other professionals. Men with high-level commercial and financial occupations or judges in commercial tribunals included *négociants, marchands en gros, juges consul,* and *banquiers. Médecins* were doctors and professors of medicine. Bourgeois and *propriétaires* lived off of invested income, usually in real estate, and had no other occupation listed by Brette or in other biographical dictionaries. Farmers were usually quite well off; they either owned or managed lands themselves. *Armateurs* were entrepreneurs in shipping, important in Brittany and especially in Nantes. *Maîtres de forges* either operated mines or produced iron. Occupations listed as other or multiple are indicated in the notes to the table. The category of mayor includes law enforcement officers. Officers in

Table 1

Occupational Profile of Third Estate Deputies

Occupation	Frequency	% of Total	% of Third Estate
Royal judiciary	169	12.8	25.0
Avocat	188	14.3	27.9
Procureur	3	.2	.4
Notaire	12	.9	1.8
Royal administrator	39	3.0	5.9
Merchant	75	5.7	11.1
Doctor	20	1.5	3.0
Bourgeois	22	1.7	3.2
Farmer	35	2.7	5.2
Armateur	3	.2	.4
Forge master	4	.3	.6
Army	11	.8	1.6
Other[a]	9	.7	1.3
Unspecified	5	.4	.7
Mayor	37	2.8	5.5
Seigneurial judge	8	.6	1.2
Two or more occupations listed[b]	12	.9	1.8
Officer, provincial administration	7	.5	1.0
Noble, clergy: deputy for Third	16	1.2	2.4
First, Second Estate	643	48.8	—
Total	1,318	100.0	100.0

[a]Deputies with occupations coded "Other":

1. Anson, Pierre Hubert, professor on the law faculty at Grenoble, then receveur-général des finances of Grenoble.

2. Bailly, Jean Silvain, in 1754 garde-général des tableaux du roi, member of French Academy; astronomer.

3. Cocherel, Nicolas de, lieutenant des maréchaux de France.

4. Cottin, Jacques Edme, sécrétaire du roi, chancellery court attached to the parlement of Brittany.

5. Démeunier, Jean Nicolas, royal censor, secretary of comte de Provence.

6. Gillet de la Jaqueminière, Louis Charles, procureur-syndic in 1787; had been director of postes.

7. Laboreys de Châteaufavier, Pierre Augustin, subdélégué to intendant, inspector of royal manufacturing.

8. Perisse du Luc, Jean André, imprimeur-libraire at Lyon.

9. Rabaut de Saint-Etienne, Jean Paul, protestant minister.

Table 1 (*continued*)

---

[b]Deputies with two or more occupations given:

    1. Alquier, Charles Jean Marie, procureur du roi at the bureau of finances, premier avocat du roi en la sénéchaussée, and mayor of La Rochelle.

    2. Chambon de la Tour, Jean Michel, had been a lieutenant-principal du sénéchal at Uzès in 1786; in 1789 was an avocat and mayor of Uzès.

    3. Dubois, Jean Claude, royal procureur in the sénéchaussée de Châtellerault and mayor after 1785.

    4. George, Robert François, elected December 12, 1789, and admitted January 14 to replace Dupré de Ballay; George was conseiller garde-scel for the bailliage of Varennes, mayor of Varennes.

    5. Gontier de Biron, Guillaume, lieutenant-général de la sénéchaussée and mayor of Bergerac.

    6. Latour, Jean Pierre, doctor and mayor of Aspet.

    7. Laurence, Jacques, sheriff and merchant at Poitiers.

    8. Laziroule, Georges Bergasse de, former artillery officer, avocat and mayor of Saurat en Foix.

    9. Leroux, Charles Florimond, former merchant, former mayor of Amiens, administrator of Hôpital Saint-Charles.

    10. Mougins de Roquefort, Jean Joseph, mayor, first consul, avocat en parlement, lieutenant-général de police et chef de viguerie, député électeur de la sénéchaussée de Grasse.

    11. Scheppers, Louis Joseph Leclercq, merchant, judge in the chambre consulaire of Lille.

    12. Viefville des Essars, Jean Louis de, avocat and subdélégué of the intendant of Soissons.

Source: Brette, *Recueil,* II, 35–333.

provincial administration were independent of the royal government and connected with an autonomous province such as Brittany.

The occupational frequencies presented in Table 1 indicate just how many Third Estate deputies were tied by their occupations to the judicial and administrative structures of the Old Regime. The single largest plurality, 28 percent, were avocats who did not own their offices. Another 25 percent were royal judges, and 6 percent were royal administrators; most of these men owned their offices. Some 20 percent of the deputies were independent professionals: merchants, doctors, farmers, armateurs, and forge masters. Only 8 percent were judges or administrators not connected to royal government. As we shall see, occupational categories correlated to some degree with alignment, although not particularly strongly; there was a slight tendency for royal administrators and judges to be more to the right and center than avocats and independent professionals.

Estate was interconnected with political opportunity. A minority of deputies had had experience in political and administrative institutions before their elections to the Estates General; 16 percent of the total membership had sat in provincial estates or assemblies, and 29 percent were expe-

Table 2

Index of Proportionality for Experience in Prerevolutionary Assemblies,
by Deputies' Estate

	Clergy (N = 332)	Nobility (N = 311)	Third Estate (N = 645)	Not in Estate (N = 30)
Assembly of Notables and provincial estates	1.9	1.2	.4	—
Assembly of Notables only	1.2	2.6	.1	—
Provincial estates	.8	.5	1.4	—
Provincial assembly	.7	1.6	.9	—
Estates of Dauphiné	.5	1.5	1.1	—
Departmental or municipal assembly	.6	1.3	1.1	—
Not in assembly	1.0	.9	1.0	1.2

rienced in courts of law or administrative posts. Nobles had had more opportunities than clergy or members of the Third Estate to acquire influence in prerevolutionary assemblies, and they profited from Necker's and Calonne's expansion of these opportunities. When the royal council drew electoral circumscriptions along judicial boundaries (bailliages) instead of empowering provincial estates to elect deputies in *pays d'états,* it reduced the influence of entrenched privilege, particularly noble, in those estates; however, those same provincial elites were known in their bailliages and had an advantage in the competition for election.[45] In addition, they were disproportionately more likely than clergy or Third Estate deputies to have served in a provincial assembly: 10 percent of them had done so, compared with 4 percent of the clergy and 6 percent of the Third Estate.[46] In fact, noble deputies were overrepresented in the Assembly of Notables, provincial assemblies, the Dauphiné estates, and assemblies at the regional, town, and village levels (Table 2). In Brittany and Dauphiné, provincial politics created influential roles for the Third Estate in provincial estates, and many

45. Donald M. G. Sutherland, *France, 1789–1815: Revolution and Counter-revolution* (New York, 1986), 33–43.

46. These findings contradict William Doyle's statement that the nobles who were elected to the Estates General were politically inexperienced. See Doyle, *Origins of the French Revolution,* 153.

Table 3
Index of Proportionality for Experience in Law Courts and Administrative Posts,
by Deputies' Estate

	Clergy (N = 332)	Nobility (N = 311)	Third Estate (N = 645)	Not in Estate (N = 30)
Court	—	2.0	1.1	—
Parlement	—	1.6	1.3	—
Intendancy	—	—	2.0	—
Bailliage court	—	.2	1.8	3.1
Administrative court	—	—	2.0	—
Royal law court	—	.5	1.7	3.2
Provincial administration	.8	—	1.5	—
Municipal administration	—	.3	1.8	1.3
Not in institution	1.4	1.2	.7	.7

future deputies sharpened their political skills and made names for themselves in their provinces.

Nobles were also overrepresented among those who had had experience at the royal court or in a parlement; they were unlikely to have served in a lower-level law court or an administrative post (Table 3). Third Estate deputies were overrepresented among those with experience in lower courts and administrative tribunals or offices; half of them had experience in administrative judicial posts, contrasted with only 14 percent of the nobles and 1 percent of the clergy. One hundred fifty Third Estate deputies—nearly a fourth—had practiced before a bailliage court, and about another fourth were connected to other governing institutions.

One final variable that differentiated the men elected to the Estates General was Masonic affiliation. Beginning with Augustin Cochin's pioneering work, twentieth-century historians have considered the rapid spread of Freemasonry in the second half of the eighteenth century to have been instrumental in the delegitimation of monarchy and the growth of new forms of democratic sociability, especially those based on equality and individual autonomy.[47] One direct route to political influence for Freemasons would

47. See Cochin, *Les Sociétés de pensée et la révolution en Bretagne,* I, 34–39, 263, 264; Augustin Cochin, *Les Sociétés de pensée et la démocratie* (Paris, 1921), 159, 160; Ran Halévi,

have been through election as deputies. As many as 244 of the 1,318 deputies (19 percent) may have been Freemasons: 204 were listed on the membership rolls of the Grand Orient, an additional 13 each put a Masonic symbol with their signatures on the Tennis Court Oath, and 27 others were probable Freemasons (some of the names on Masonic lists have the same patronymic as known deputies, but there is insufficient information to make the linkage certain).[48] Of the possible Freemason deputies, 135 (55 percent) were Third Estate, 75 (31 percent) were nobles, and 28 (8 percent) were clergy. If we reverse the data, we find that 24 percent of the nobles, 21 percent of the Third Estate, and 8 percent of the clergy were Masons. Freemasons were more likely than other deputies to have sat in provincial estates or assemblies or the Assembly of Notables; 21 percent of the Masons had such experience, compared with 13 percent of the non-Masons. Freemasons were also disproportionately represented among those who had experience at the court at Versailles or before a parlement or in a municipal or seigneurial jurisdiction. Data in this book will show that some of these Masonic deputies did in fact join other influential revolutionary groups but were by no means universally men of the left.

Portrait of Deputies in the Regional Sample

Because the sample used to locate pamphlet authors was drawn to reflect the most and least centralized regions, it might not be as representative of the total membership of the National Assembly as a sample selected randomly. Local phenomena skew the data somewhat. For example, Brittany elected no noble deputies and 32 percent curés, whereas Dauphiné elected no curés but 11 percent upper clergy and 4 percent vicars or canons. Thus the distribution of representatives of the three estates is different in the sample than for the whole Assembly, with the sample containing slightly

---

Les Loges maçonniques dans la France d'Ancien Régime aux origines de la sociabilité démocratique (Paris, 1984); and Roger Chartier, *The Cultural Origins of the French Revolution,* trans. Lydia G. Cochrane (Durham, N.C., 1991), 162–68.

48. Pierre Lamarque, *Les Francs-Maçons aux Etats généraux de 1789 et à l'Assemblée nationale* (Paris, 1981). The explanation for the categories is on pp. 5–13.

Table 4

Authors and Nonauthors: Index of Proportionality for Prerevolutionary
Political Experience (Deputies in Sample)

Old Regime Affiliation	Authors N = 114	Nonauthors N = 133
Court	1.6	0
Parlement	2.7	.8
Intendancy	1.3	3.3
Bailliage court	.8	1.0
Administrative tribunal	0	1.5
Royal judiciary	1.7	1.4
Provincial administrative post	0	0
Municipal administration	.8	1.6
Not in institution	1.0	1.0
Affiliation with Political Assemblies		
Assembly of Notables and provincial estates	0	1.0
Assembly of Notables only	1.5	.5
Provincial estates	3.9	2.3
Provincial assembly	1.6	.8
Estates of Dauphiné	4.4	6.0
Departmental or municipal assembly	2.5	.6
Not in assembly	.7	.9

more clergy and Third Estate deputies and appreciably fewer noble deputies. Of the 247 deputies in the sample, 28 percent were clergy, compared with 25 percent of the entire membership, 19 percent were nobles, compared with 24 percent, and 53 percent were Third Estate, compared with 49 percent (plus 2 percent not chosen by estate).

In addition, the authors in the sample differed from the nonauthors (Table 4). For purposes of the analysis of attitudes, these differences need to be underlined. The authors were much more likely to be experienced in political and administrative institutions before their election as deputies. Clearly, the motivation to write and publish a political pamphlet, to form a political opinion and want to publicize it as widely as possible, was connected to experience in a parlement or to sitting in provincial estates or assemblies. Interestingly too, 28 percent of the sampled authors were Freemasons, compared with 14 percent of their nonauthor colleagues from the same regions.

The political alignment of the first revolutionary deputies grew out of their origins as strategically placed elites in the Old Regime, elites schooled in the laws and institutions that got them started in public life. The deputies arrived at Versailles in the spring and early summer of 1789 already experienced in particular provincial permutations of a national politics emerging from three decades of attempted reforms and reactions to those reforms, capped by an electoral period of intense agitation and conflict. These men came with strong opinions, and many had the rhetorical skills to defend their views. It is striking how consistent their initial alignment remained throughout two years and a summer of writing the Constitution and making a revolution.

Chapter 2

Deputy Opinion, May, 1788, to June, 1789

Compromise was not a characteristic political practice in the National Assembly. The deputies had their dramatic displays of unity and their bitterly contested debates, but they treated very few issues that they were able to resolve through workable compromise. Of the major constitutional questions, only the king's suspensive veto represented a negotiated agreement, having been worked out between supporters of an absolute veto and those who preferred none at all. In most other areas, the majority (most of the time on the left, occasionally on the right) had its way without having to make many concessions. Sometimes victory came through parliamentary tactics such as calling the previous question or moving to adjourn or postpone debate, and sometimes it came after long and impassioned argument.

The polarization of legislative politics pulled deputies toward opposite positions with a wide gulf between them, rather than pressuring them to avoid extremist positions and search for compromise. Ironically, probably the most straightforward argument against the vote by order in the Estates General had been based on the fear of polarization: the vote by order would allow the first two orders to combine against the Third Estate. The vote by head was thought to be a mechanism to weaken, if not eliminate, the political influence of the defenders of privilege vested in the upper clergy and conservative leaders of the Second Estate. The vote by head was the legislative tactic of fraternity: individual votes would undercut the structural effect of elections designed to represent all three orders, and would create a majority of Third Estate, lower clergy, and liberal nobility, who would unite against privilege and win converts by the just nature of their demands on behalf of the whole nation. The political struggles of the first six weeks of the Estates General gave the lie to this vision of national unity. Once the National Assembly was in place, polarization produced, by August at the latest, a visually apparent left-right division rooted in the estates and career routes from which deputies came.

The development of public opinion as the ultimate court of appeal, with universal authority, produced a model of what Keith Baker has labeled "rational consensus" between the threatening extremes of unbridled liberty and intolerable despotism. In Baker's words, "public opinion was consistently depoliticized," that is, disconnected from political conflict. This passion for consensus grew out of several centuries of monarchical centralization, as well as from enlightened growth in public opinion, the ultimate arbiter of political legitimacy. Furthermore, many French observers saw English politics negatively, as being tumultuous and subject to unbridled and passionate conflict that could not lead to sound law or an ordered society. Political conflict had characterized reactionary aristocratic and absolutist politics; better to create a new political universe on a foundation of consensus. Baker argues that the legitimacy and authority commanded by this concept of public opinion facilitated calls for the reclamation of rights.[1]

Baker is certainly right that public opinion had broadened the political agenda by 1788, but from the deputies' perspective, it did not facilitate agreement. Within days of their arrival at Versailles, some deputies realized that no rational consensus existed among their colleagues, nor was one likely to be produced in the Estates General. As early as the first debates over the forms of representation and the methods of voting that would be applied to the Estates General, some pamphlet writers grasped that national sovereignty was the real issue, and that national sovereignty could only be realized in some form of majority rule. More troublesome was the political space to be occupied and the political leverage to be exerted by those outside of that majority. Very little in either the deputies' personal political experience or their knowledge of royal French politics under the Bourbons over several centuries gave them any reason to believe that opposition could be tolerated, much less structured into political institutions, without eroding leadership and national strength. From 1788 on, partisan

1. Baker, "Public Opinion as Political Invention," 196–99.

battles raged under the banner of unity inherited, paradoxically, from both the monarchical tradition and Enlightenment doctrine, and within a concept of nationalism that undermined the possibility of limited and legitimate opposition and consensus politics.

To determine the distances between future deputies' positions on specific substantive issues before they gathered at Versailles, I analyzed pamphlets printed in the twelve months preceding the opening of the Estates General. Ninety pamphlets were written between May, 1788, and June 17, 1789, by men who were elected deputies from the regions I chose to sample: Paris, Brittany, Dauphiné, Auxerre, and the central provinces. These pamphlets indicate a sharp, extensive, and consistent polarization, mainly along lines of estate, of elite opinion on issues of participation in politics and legitimacy of political institutions.

The ninety pamphlets were written by forty-two different authors, who were disproportionately likely to represent the Third Estate, to be lawyers, and to have served in prerevolutionary political assemblies. Sixty of the ninety were written by Third Estate deputies. Fifty, or 56 percent, were written by men experienced in assemblies—a sizable overrepresentation, since only 16 percent of the total of 1,318 deputies had sat in previous assemblies. Lawyers wrote twenty-four of the ninety (27 percent); judicial officers wrote fourteen (16 percent). Those who found it possible and useful to publish pamphlets were, in short, men experienced in political communication and public life. Also, they were likely to have come from regions where prerevolutionary political conflicts had been intense; seventy-three of the ninety pamphlets were written by men from Paris, Brittany, and Dauphiné. Of the pamphlets discussing the function of the Estates General and the method of voting in it, the majority followed the opinion of the Patriot party in Paris. Forty pamphlets addressed the issue of function, and twenty-five of them stated that the Estates General should receive legislative power under a new constitution or act as the repository of national sovereignty. The pamphlet authors also wanted the vote by head in the Estates; of thirty-one pamphlets on the subject, only eight favored a compromise or the retention of the vote by order.

Generally speaking, the pamphlets supported the more radical and abstract conceptions of legitimacy over the traditional interpretations and were less, rather than more, apprehensive about disorder and violence. The authors inclined toward change rather than continuity and tradition, but only a handful expressed complete acceptance of a constitution based on national sovereignty. There was a fairly large minority of traditional or centrist views.

When two variables were compared, this division of attitudes was found to be consistent and coherent. A statistically significant relationship between legitimacy and popular participation was found for twenty-eight pairs of variables (Table 5). These data evince a connection between support for strengthening the traditional monarchy and apprehension about change and violence: a patterned conservative viewpoint. On the other hand, men who in spring, 1789, were already committed to making France a constitutional monarchy were less apprehensive about broadening popular roles in politics, although only one pamphlet went so far as to concede that violence, while regrettable, could sometimes be a necessary political tactic. Because only ninety pamphlets make up the data base, the number expressing opinions on any given pair of variables was sometimes quite small, but the consistency is noteworthy.

Several attitudinal measures merit special attention because of their implications for developments in the relations between Louis XVI and the National Assembly after the move to Paris in October, 1789. The first measure associates views on the sources of legitimacy with attitudes toward popular participation. Those pamphlets exhibiting the view that the nation's legitimacy derived from the general will or a sovereign assembly were likely to support mobilizing the people for political activity. Those that based legitimacy on tradition argued that people should be calmed or restrained. The same measure of the source of legitimacy, when correlated with opinions about the king, indicates that traditionalist views were associated with traditional faith in the king as the center of authority, whereas Enlightenment views on the sources of legitimacy were coupled with criticism of the king as weak or untrustworthy (Table 6). Similarly, correlation of views on the function of the Estates General with opinions on the king shows that authors committed to a constituent assembly were more likely to distrust the king than those who favored limiting the Estates to traditional functions of advice and representation of the three orders (Table 7).

Opinions coded from the ninety pamphlets cluster around two poles defined by the issues of legitimacy and participation. A majority liberal view favoring a constitutional monarchy and enthusiastic for a further mobilization of supporters, and not apprehensive about violence or instability,

Table 5

Relationships Between Attitudes on Legitimacy and Participation in Ninety
Pamphlets Printed Before June 17, 1789

Pairs of variables with the strongest significant relationship ($p < .001$).
Sources of legitimacy with:
        attitudes toward the masses
        definitions of revolution
        attitudes toward the king
Meaning of "nation" with:
        definitions of revolution
        perceptions of causes of revolution
Interpretation of constitution with:
        attitudes toward the king
        definitions of revolution
        causes of revolution
Purpose of Estates General with:
        general attitudes toward authority
        opinions on faction
        definitions of revolution
        perceptions of causes of revolution
        attitudes toward the king
Attitudes toward fellow deputies with:
        perceived political divisions

Pairs of variables with strong significant relationships ($.001 < p < .05$).
Sources of legitimacy with:
        opinions on faction
        causes of revolution
        general attitudes toward authority
Meaning of "nation" with:
        attitudes toward popular violence
        opinions on faction
        attitudes toward the King
        general attitudes toward authority
Interpretation of constitution with:
        attitudes toward the masses
        attitudes toward popular violence
        opinions on faction
        attitudes toward the National Assembly
        general attitudes toward authority
Attitudes toward fellow deputies with:
        attitudes toward the masses
        general attitudes toward authority

Table 6

Attitudes Toward the Masses and the King by Opinions on Sources of Legitimacy, Pamphlets Printed Before June 17, 1789

	Sources of Legitimacy					
	Fundamental Laws (N = 10) %	King + Estates General (N = 13) %	Natural Law (N = 7) %	General Will (N = 11) %	Sovereign Assembly (N = 10) %	Legitimacy not Mentioned (N = 39) %
Attitudes Toward the Masses:[a]						
Mobilize	10	61	29	37	40	5
Educate	10	8	—	27	30	13
Calm	40	—	14	18	—	13
Restrain	20	—	—	—	—	2
Not mentioned	20	31	57	18	30	67
Totals	100	100	100	100	100	100
Attitudes Toward the King:[b]						
Traditional ruler	30	—	—	—	—	10
Supporter of liberty	—	46	43	55	30	33
Center of authority	60	16	29	9	—	—
Weak, misled	10	23	—	18	—	13
Untrustworthy	—	—	14	—	30	—
Not mentioned	—	15	14	18	40	44
Totals	100	100	100	100	100	100

[a]Chi-square = 70.75; DF = 20; $p < .001$
[b]Chi-square = 83.24; DF = 25; $p < .001$

Table 7

Attitudes Toward the King by Opinions on Purpose of Estates General, Pamphlets Printed Before June 17, 1789

		Purpose of Estates General			
	Oversight $(N = 7)$ %	Share Legislative Powers $(N = 8)$ %	Separation of Powers $(N = 15)$ %	Popular Sovereignty $(N = 10)$ %	Purpose of Estates not Mentioned $(N = 50)$ %
Attitudes Toward the King:[a]					
Traditional ruler	15	—	—	—	12
Supporter of liberty	14	13	53	30	36
Center of authority	57	63	13	—	—
Weak, misled	14	12	14	—	14
Untrustworthy	—	—	7	30	—
Not mentioned	—	12	13	40	38
Totals	100	100	100	100	100

[a]Chi-square $= 68.16$; DF $= 20$; $p < .001$

contrasts with a minority conservative view respectful of monarchical authority, content to regularize and codify a traditional constitution granting representatives of the three orders an advising role in public policy, and fearful of popular protest and crowd violence.

The Antecedents of Opinion: Deputies' Political Backgrounds

Attitudinal polarizations do not automatically create political factions. Men holding similar views must be brought together to articulate them and to act on them. The first step in this process for the deputies may well have been commonality of background and, for some of them, shared experiences. As was displayed in the collective portrait of deputies in chapter 1, those who published pamphlets were disproportionately likely to have been affiliated with a political institution in the Old Regime and to have served in a political assembly.

The distribution of authors' opinions on any given issue was related to differences in their estates, occupations, and prerevolutionary political experience. Tables 8 through 11 summarize twenty contingency tables, relating the distributions of five different opinions to four variables concerning deputies' backgrounds: province of origin, estate, occupation (for Third Estate deputies), and service in a political assembly before the Estates General was convoked at Versailles. Relationships between attitudes and province (Table 8), although not statistically significant, reflect the regional differences in prerevolutionary politics. A large majority of the pamphlets written by deputies from Brittany and Orléanais defined the key political conflict of 1789 as between those who were privileged and those who were not. In contrast, the eighteen pamphlets whose authors were from Dauphiné were evenly divided; half mentioned the privileged-nonprivileged division and half cited a conflict between despotic government and the nation. The Breton and Orléanaise pamphlets were the most favorable toward extending the revolutionary participation of the masses; those from other regions were more concerned with calming and restraining people. The Breton deputies, reflecting their successful struggle to defeat the first two orders and control their provincial estates, approved of the political tactic of organizing factions to further political influence; in April they had themselves begun to meet together at Versailles to coordinate their efforts in the Estates General.

The authors from Dauphiné, fresh from a two-year struggle with the court over the reconstitution of their provincial estates, were the most likely to see the king as a weak ruler misled by his advisers and to fear excessive centralized authority. Their distrust of authority was coupled with ambivalence over factions, concerning which the eighteen Dauphinois pamphlets were split evenly. Since these men had not been divided along lines of estate in their province, they had considerably more faith than the Bretons in conciliation and compromise.

The pamphlets written by Parisians show opinions distributed more randomly across these issues, reflecting the presence in the delegation of radicals and conservatives, as noted in the earlier categorization of authors. Patriot-aristocrat divisions are obvious on issues of legitimacy and participation.

Among the Third Estate as categorized by occupation (Table 9), law-

Table 8

Distribution of Attitudes on Five Issues by Deputies' Political Background,
Pre–June 17, 1789

	Province				
	Brittany (N = 26) %	Paris (N = 29) %	Dauphiné (N = 18) %	Orléanais (N = 11) %	Other (N = 6) %
Political Cleavages					
Political conflicts:					
are between privileged, nonprivileged	92	72	50	91	67
are between despotic gov't., nation	0	14	50	9	33
Attitudes Toward the Masses					
Deputies should					
mobilize	11	21	33	36	33
educate	31	10	6	9	0
calm	11	14	11	9	33
restrain	4	3	6	0	0
Attitudes Toward Factions					
Pamphlet:					
approves of organized factions	65	41	33	36	16
disapproves of organized factions	4	17	33	45	0
Attitudes Toward Monarchy					
King is:					
traditional ruler	4	10	11	9	0
supporter of liberty	50	31	22	27	33
center of authority	4	14	11	18	33
weak and misled	4	0	39	27	0
untrustworthy	0	7	6	9	0
Attitudes Toward Authority					
Author:					
stresses liberty, fears excessive authority	15	28	39	18	33
fears disorder	4	24	17	27	0
believes strong government needed for order	0	7	11	0	16

Note: Not all percentages sum to 100 percent because "not mentioned" categories have been omitted.

Table 9

Distribution of Attitudes on Five Issues by Deputies' Occupation (Third Estate only), Pre–June 17, 1789

	Occupation		
	Judge (N = 16) %	*Lawyer* (N = 27) %	*Other* (N = 17) %
Political Cleavages Political conflicts:			
are between privileged, nonprivileged	69	78	82
are between despotic gov't., nation	25	15	18
Attitudes Toward the Masses Deputies should:			
mobilize	19	26	29
educate	6	26	29
calm	19	11	0
restrain	6	0	0
Attitudes Toward Factions Pamphlet:			
approves of organized factions	46	59	65
disapproves of organized factions	25	4	6
Attitudes Toward Monarchy King is:			
traditional ruler	13	0	0
supporter of liberty	31	33	53
center of authority	13	7	0
weak and misled	19	26	0
untrustworthy	0	4	12
Attitudes Toward Authority Author:			
stresses liberty; fears excessive authority	13	33	47
fears disorder	19	7	0
believes strong government needed for order	13	0	6

Note: Not all percentages sum to 100 percent because "not mentioned" categories have been omitted.

yers were not uniformly the most radical; their pamphlets expressed less enthusiasm about mobilization and less concern about excessive governmental authority than pamphlets written by men in other occupations. However, lawyers were the most likely to approve of factions and criticize the king as weak or untrustworthy. Judges' pamphlets were least supportive of mobilization, most disapproving of factions, most respectful of royal authority, and most conscious of the need for stability and order.

Opinions varied along lines of authors' estate (Table 10) more consistently than for any other dimension of deputies' previous experiences. For the clergy, the pattern is clear. Authors from the First Estate were most fearful of mobilization, most disapproving of factions, and most likely to mention the king as a traditional ruler or the center of authority. The clerical pamphlets express respect for existing institutions and traditional legitimacy. Divisions between the upper and lower clergy that became obvious when the National Assembly was declared on June 17 do not emerge from the pamphlet data, most likely because the more liberal curés wrote fewer pamphlets than the more conservative bishops, vicars, and canons.

Noble deputies were the most likely to cite the key political conflict as being between the privileged and the nonprivileged. They were also the most confident that the king was a supporter of liberty, although they were not as likely to mention his authority as were the clergy. Nobles were even more concerned about the danger of disorder and the need for strong government than were the clergy.

Members of the Third Estate were consistently the most likely to hold Enlightenment views on legitimacy and participation. Noteworthy are their strong support for factions as a political tactic, their stress on liberty rather than governmental authority, and their enthusiasm for educating the masses politically.

Finally, deputy opinion varied according to whether authors had sat in political assemblies before the opening of the Estates General (Table 11). Those who had been in the Assembly of Notables—by and large, members of the clergy and the nobility—were the most conservative in their views: opposed to mobilization and factions, supportive of the traditional monarchy, and fearful of disorder. Those who had sat in provincial assemblies in the Ile-de-France and the central provinces were less uniform in their views and more likely to distribute across the range of opinions.

Men from the estates of Dauphiné are kept separate here because of their

Table 10

Distribution of Attitudes on Five Issues by Deputies' Estate,
Pre–June 17, 1789

	Estate		
	First (N = 15) %	Second (N = 15) %	Third (N = 60) %
Political Cleavages			
Political conflicts:			
are between privileged, nonprivileged	60	87	77
are between despotic gov't., nation	20	13	18
Attitudes Toward the Masses			
Deputies should:			
mobilize	7	33	25
educate	0	0	22
calm	33	7	10
restrain	13	0	2
Attitudes Toward Factions			
Pamphlet:			
approves of organized factions	13	27	57
disapproves of organized factions	53	20	10
Attitudes Toward Monarchy			
King is:			
traditional ruler	33	0	3
supporter of liberty	13	40	38
center of authority	33	13	7
weak and misled	7	0	17
untrustworthy	0	7	5
Attitudes Toward Authority			
Author:			
stresses liberty; fears excessive authority	13	13	32
fears disorder	27	33	8
believes strong government needed for order	7	7	5

Note: Not all percentages sum to 100 percent because "not mentioned" categories have been omitted.

Table 11

Distribution of Attitudes on Five Issues by Deputies' Experience
in Political Assemblies, Pre–June 17, 1789

	Pre-1789 Political Assembly				
	Notables (N = 5) %	Prov. Estates (N = 18) %	Prov. Assembly (N = 9) %	Dauphiné (N = 18) %	Not in (N = 40) %
Political Cleavages					
Political conflicts:					
are between privileged,					
nonprivileged	60	89	67	50	85
are between despotic					
gov't., nation	0	6	33	50	8
Attitudes Toward the Masses					
Deputies should:					
mobilize	0	17	33	33	23
educate	0	33	11	6	12
calm	40	11	22	11	10
restrain	20	6	0	6	0
Attitudes Toward Factions					
Pamphlet:					
approves of organized					
factions	0	67	56	33	42
disapproves of					
organized factions	40	6	11	33	18
Attitudes Toward Monarchy					
King is:					
traditional ruler	20	0	0	11	10
supporter of liberty	0	50	22	22	40
center of authority	40	6	22	11	10
weak and misled	0	6	0	39	8
untrustworthy	0	0	22	6	3
Attitudes Toward Authority					
Author:					
stresses liberty; fears					
excessive authority	0	28	33	39	20
fears disorder	40	6	11	17	18
believes strong					
government needed					
for order	20	0	22	11	0

Note: Not all percentages sum to 100 percent because "not mentioned" categories have been omitted.

unique experience in winning their struggle with the crown to gain a reconstituted and revolutionized provincial estates and a provincial constitution. Because the eighteen pamphlets written by Dauphinois before June 17, 1789, were all by men who had sat in the provincial estates, the frequencies of their opinions as veterans of political assemblies in Table 11 are exactly the same as those given in Table 8 for the province of Dauphiné, reflecting distrust of royal authority and ambivalence toward factions.

The most radical opinions were held by the eighteen Bretons deputized to the provincial estates from Brittany in its last sessions. In direct contrast to the Dauphinois, these men were the most likely to see the king as a supporter of liberty, to advocate mobilizing and educating the masses, to approve of factions, and to encourage liberty and fear strong government.

In the broad sense, these regional, occupational, and estate variations corroborate standard interpretations of the stalemate during the first six weeks of the Estates General. Deputies of the Third Estate, often lawyers, led by the Bretons, cajoled, persuaded, threatened, stonewalled, maneuvered, and finally frightened a majority of Third Estate deputies and a few curés into confronting the two upper orders with a *fait accompli* on June 17, a National Assembly that they had either to join or to disown and abandon. However, what is dramatically revealed here is the width of the gulf between patriot reformers and conservative deputies. The predominance of conservative views among deputies of the First and Second estates makes it clear that there was little basis for a negotiated compromise with the radicals in the Third.

The most powerful predictor of authors' attitudes was the estate they represented. The relationship between estate and opinions was statistically significant at the 1-percent level for issues concerning mobilization and the king; it was significant at the 5-percent level for attitudes about factions. Despite the incongruence between the medieval structure of a corporate society of orders and the late-eighteenth-century French society with new sources of wealth and status, estate returned to the political center stage because it was used to organize the convocation of the Estates General. The ensuing struggle over numerical representation and the form of voting brought debates about privilege to the forefront of political life. Other, broader issues also divided the deputies according to estate: the clergy were most supportive of traditional legitimacy, the nobility most trustful of royal support for liberty and most fearful of crowds, and the Third Estate most enthusiastic about liberty and broader participation. The association between deputies' estate, their attitudes, and their behavior did not disappear after the establishment of the National Assembly, but it became more complex as divisions within estates began to deepen and sharpen.

Chapter 3

Alignment and Opinion
in the National Assembly

At the opening convocation of the Estates General, on May 5, 1789, deputies representing each estate were placed in traditional locations in relation to the king's throne: the First Estate to his right, the nobles to his left, and the Third Estate at the rear of the hall.[1] Three months later, observers were commenting on the spatial placement of factions, with those who shared liberal, "patriot" views on the left and conservatives on the right. As deputies were transformed from royal consultants into representatives of the nation, their physical placement no longer symbolized an organic society of orders but a constitutional nation of individuals. Gaining experience with legislative politics, deputies sat near their allies and distanced themselves from their adversaries, making it easier to organize tactics, to play to the galleries, and eventually to coordinate their activities with political journalists and clubs outside the Assembly.

In the first six weeks of the Estates General politics centered on issues of political participation and legitimacy. Disagreeing over the voting method, awaiting the delayed arrival of the Parisian deputation, and challenging the credentials of some of their colleagues, deputies recognized that such seemingly minor and insignificant questions as what constituted proper clothing for the Third Estate or whether to permit applause after speeches were in fact fraught with implications for the significance and even

---

1. Lawrence M. Bryant, "Royal Ceremony and the Revolutionary Strategies of the Third Estate," *Eighteenth-Century Studies,* XXII (1989), 421–26.

the survival of the Estates General.[2] All three orders initially avoided any decisive action, not even electing a presiding officer before credentials were verified, so as not to limit their tactics in the power struggle within the Estates.

The deputies were not inexperienced. All shared at least rudimentary exposure to political maneuvering within their electoral assemblies. More than half of them had come from careers in a court, a provincial assembly, a provincial estates, or an administrative institution. They had had opportunities to develop tactical skills, and many of them had formed definitive judgments about who or what was the most significant threat to their particular vision of national regeneration. Many deputies had instructions to communicate regularly with the electoral committee for their bailliage.[3] They did not select regular recording secretaries to draw up official minutes, fearing that such actions would be interpreted as constituting separate orders. Gabriel Honoré de Riquetti, comte de Mirabeau, was much criticized for publishing and circulating his *Courrier de Provence*.[4]

The "patriots" did not have a solid majority within the Third Estate on the fifth of May, but by refusing to compromise on the issues of common sessions and the vote by head, the patriot leaders eventually created the National Assembly and compelled the king to acquiesce. The struggle was lengthy and complex. From May 5 to late June, the number of nobles and clergy who supported common sessions and the vote by head did not change very significantly. In the Third Estate, the shift was more dramatic. On May 18, a majority of 360 votes favored compromise, supporting Jean Paul Rabaut de Saint-Etienne's motion to send commissioners to conciliatory conferences with the nobles and clergy. By June 17, the Third Estate pro-

---

2. Jacques Antoine Creuzé-Latouche, *Journal des Etats-Généraux et du début de l'Assemblée nationale, 18 mai–29 juillet 1789,* ed. Jean Marchand (Paris, 1946), 11; Olga Ilovaïsky, ed., *Les Séances de la Noblesse, 6 mai–16 juillet 1789* (2 vols.; Paris, 1974), I, 208–24, Tome 2 of *Recueil de documents relatifs aux séances des Etats généraux,* 2 vols. in each of 2 tomes (Tome 1 [2 vols.; Paris, 1953] was edited by Georges Lefebvre and Anne Terroine). The hyphenated version of Creuzé de Latouche's name is as it appears on the title page of his *Journal*.

3. In Brittany there were official correspondence bureaus at Rennes, Nantes, Saint-Brieuc, Guérande, and Lorient. See Kuhlmann, "Influence of the Breton Deputation," 212.

4. Gustave Rouanet, "Les Premiers Leaders parlementaires en France," *Annales révolutionnaires,* VIII (1916), 616.

duced a majority of 491 votes to end efforts at cooperation and to take the radical step of declaring the National Assembly.[5]

Meeting separately on May 6, the day following the opening convocation, each of the three orders took a different stand. The Third Estate did nothing, many of the deputies hoping for a royal decision ordering them to meet in common session and vote by head. The nobles made the first decisive move when they voted overwhelmingly in favor of verifying noble deputies' credentials within their own order. The clergy, more evenly divided on the issues of common sessions and the vote by head, proposed that each order name commissioners to meet together and effect a compromise.

Conservative nobles outnumbered their patriot peers by a four-to-one ratio. When the nobles met on May 6, they voted on a motion to verify their powers within their own order. The results of the roll call were 188 votes to verify within the order, 46 to verify in common with the other two orders, and 3 abstentions.[6] Noble deputies from Dauphiné defended the interests of the Third Estate in the initial debates over verification of powers, but they were never able to gain more than a handful of adherents to their side. During the second session, on May 11, between twenty and twenty-five clergy and nobles from Dauphiné were admitted to the chambers of the nobility to protest the provincial constitution that the estates of Dauphiné had voted, to declare the elections of deputies from Dauphiné to have been illegal, and to demand new elections. Their protest was ultimately dismissed, but the deputies from Dauphiné did not deliberate that day and did not vote on a motion determining that the nobles had verified enough credentials of deputies to declare themselves constituted.[7]

Conservatives within the nobility tried very hard to uphold tradition in every possible way and to mute evidence of dissent over the legitimate structure and procedures of the Estates General. In the May 11 session, the comte d'Antraigues gave an address recommending that the Estates conduct sessions according to traditional forms, at least until new ones could be agreed upon. His speech was applauded. Another member promptly

5. For the May 18 vote on Rabaut Saint-Etienne's motion, see Jean François Gaultier de Biauzat, *Correspondance,* in *Gaultier de Biauzat,* ed. Francisque Mège (2 vols.; Paris, 1890), II, 65–70. For the June 17 vote, see Jean Pierre Boullé, Letter of June 17, 1789, in "Documents inédits," *Revue de la Révolution,* XIII (1888), 14.

6. Ilovaïsky, ed., *Les Séances de la Noblesse,* I, 226.

7. *Ibid.,* 222, 354–60, 377–79.

stood up and demanded that all speeches be greeted with silence; applause and expressions of disapproval should both be disallowed. His recommendation, too, was greeted with applause.[8] Sessions of the nobles were full of disruptions and delays caused by stormy debates over what should be communicated to the other two orders. The number of patriot nobles was somewhat augmented when the Paris delegation arrived on May 25, but still only forty-eight nobles took the definitive step in June of joining the National Assembly before the king ordered all deputies to do so.

Within the First Estate, division between the upper clergy and the curés was marked at the opening ceremonies by the placement of clerical deputies according to rank. Politically they were very evenly divided, deciding on May 6 by 133 votes to 114 to verify credentials within their own order.[9] The next day a delegation from the Third Estate proposed common verification, and immediately following their departure the clergy voted "à la pluralité des voix" to name commissioners to work with those from the other orders to determine the manner of voting. Although most of those in favor of common verification were curés, both the patriots and conservatives were led by members of the upper clergy. The archbishops of Vienne and Bordeaux were the leaders of the popular party of curés; the archbishops of Arles and Aix led the conservatives.[10] When the Parisian delegation arrived and de Juigné, the archbishop of Paris, entered the meeting room of the clergy, he was greeted by "mocking murmurs" from the seats of the curés.[11]

Following two sets of unsuccessful conferences from May 23 to 25 and May 30 to June 9, the Third Estate declared itself the National Assembly on June 17; two days later the clergy voted on whether to order all their deputies to join the Third Estate.[12] According to one participant, Canon Sigisbert Etienne Coster, the clergy's initial vote produced 136 votes to

8. *Ibid.*, 332.

9. *Archives parlementaires,* VIII, 27.

10. Albert Houtin, ed., *Les Séances des députés du Clergé aux Etats généraux de 1789: Journaux du curé Thibault et du chanoine Coster* (Paris, 1916), 4; Rouanet, "Les Premiers Leaders parlementaires en France," *Annales révolutionnaires,* IX (1917), 20. See also *Archives parlementaires,* VIII, 27.

11. Paul Christophe, *Les choix du Clergé dans les révolutions de 1789, 1830, et 1848* (2 vols.; Lille, 1975–76), I, 21.

12. Creuzé-Latouche, *Journal des Etats-Généraux,* 102, 106, 107, 119, 120.

support the king's plan for conciliation, 127 votes for common verification (in effect supporting the Third Estate's invitation to join the National Assembly), and 10 votes for common verification provided that the Third Estate recognize the independence and distinctiveness of the three orders. Supporters of common verification threatened those 10 deputies with recriminations from a crowd of two thousand outside the meeting hall unless they eliminated their qualification. Such pressure changed their votes on a second roll call, for a new total of 137 votes for common verification and 136 for conciliation. Different sources give different totals for the final June 19 vote, ranging between 149 and 137 in favor and between 115 and 136 against. A minority report, signed by Cardinal de La Rochefoucauld as president and the abbé Charles François Perrotin de Barmond as secretary, even claimed that there were in fact three roll calls and a different outcome, with the most votes for maintaining the clergy as a separate order.[13] This report was wishful thinking, because those who wanted to join the National Assembly prevailed, but the winning margin was narrow, somewhere between 1 and 34 votes. Whatever the exact outcome, the results were not far different from the May 6 vote as an indication of the patriot-conservative split.

These votes indicate that in the aggregate there was very little change in the numbers of men on both sides within the two upper orders. Most nobles remained adamantly opposed to any deviation from the vote by order because it would nullify their order's veto and weaken and even destroy their influence on decisions taken in the Estates General. The four dozen patriots in their midst, most of whom were from Dauphiné and Paris, were unsuccessful in persuading others to their point of view. The clergy re-

---

13. The tallies are as follows: *Ibid.*, xxi (tally: 149 to 135); Houtin, ed., *Les Séances des députés du Clergé*, 134 (tally: 137 to 136); [Jacques Rangeard], *Procès-verbal historique des actes du Clergé par un député à l'Assemblée des Etats généraux des années 1789 et 1790* (Paris, 1791), 138 (tally: 149 to 132); [the attribution to Rangeard is by Célestin Port, *Dictionnaire historique, géographique, et biographique de Maine-et-Loire* (3 vols.; Paris, 1878), III, 225]; Pierre Pinsseau, *Un Curé constitutionnel: L'Abbé Vallet, député à l'Assemblée nationale constituante* (Clermont-Ferrand, 1941), 66 (tally: 149 to 115); J. J. Brethé, ed., *Journal inédit de Jallet, curé de Chérigné, député du Clergé du Poitou* (Fontenay-le-Comte, 1871), 93 (tally: 148 to 136); Emmanuel Barbotin, *Lettres de l'abbé Barbotin, député à l'Assemblée constituante* (Paris, 1910), 15 (tally: 144 to 135). The minority report was printed as a sequel to the *Journal* of Thibault and is published in Houtin, ed., *Les Séances des députés du Clergé: Appendice au journal de Thibault*, 59 (tally: 130 to 137).

mained closely divided, but there was a very significant shift of about two dozen votes in favor of the patriots, which gave them a majority of the clergy and enabled them to outmaneuver the minority of opposing nobles. There were 114 patriot clergy on May 6, judging on the basis of opposition to a motion to verify credentials within the First Estate. On June 19, there were at least 137 patriots voting to join the National Assembly.

In the Third Estate, the political drama climaxing with the formation of the National Assembly was played out between three groups: traditionalists who wanted the three separate estates of the realm to retain and strengthen their influence upon a monarchy they intended to reform, moderates who hoped to persuade the first and second orders to meet as one body and vote by head, and radicals who accepted Sieyès' contention that the Third Estate was everything and therefore could not accept the veto power of the other two orders. Initially the Third Estate refused to conduct any business until sitting in common with the other two orders. This was a compromise to buy time for the Paris deputies to arrive, to allow supporters in the clergy to persuade their fellow deputies, to rein in the radical Bretons, and to permit Jean Joseph Mounier's liberal noble colleagues from Dauphiné to try to influence their order. Most Third Estate deputies were convinced that a further compromise with the other two orders on the voting issue was illogical and practically impossible. Either deputies would vote as individuals or orders would vote as orders. The deputies, the king, and the royal council would eventually have to come down on one side or the other, unless the Estates were simply disbanded and the deputies sent home, leaving the king with no constitution (which he would have preferred), no taxes (which he could not afford), and an aroused citizenry (whom he did not dare to leave dissatisfied). The six weeks of immobility played into the hands of the radicals. The Third Estate's meeting rooms admitted spectators, and many hundreds attended; there was room for more than three thousand. Most spectators, well-dressed bourgeois or aristocratic friends of deputies, were patriot sympathizers whose shouted interjections from the galleries put significant pressure on the moderate and conservative deputies.[14]

Reformers in the Third Estate agreed that the legitimacy of the French

---

14. Gustave Rouanet, "Les Débuts du parlementarisme française," *Annales révolutionnaires,* VIII (1916), 188–91; Creuzé-Latouche, *Journal des Etats-Généraux,* 29.

monarchy needed to be buttressed by a written constitution and a re-established permanent Estates General. When it came to strategies, they divided into moderates and radicals. Mounier, foremost of the moderates, was one of the few Third Estate members with a national reputation, earned by leading the successful struggle to regain the provincial estates of Dauphiné; he was, according to Gustave Rouanet, the "second most popular man in France." [15] Having worked closely with bishops and nobles in his own province, Mounier was convinced that the nation's representatives had to belong to all three orders, not just the Third Estate, and that at Versailles the three would soon recognize their common interest in regularizing taxes, reshaping the traditional constitution into a written document, and restraining arbitrary rule. After he resigned from the Assembly in the fall of 1789, Mounier published an explanation of his conduct, depicting himself as a very cautious compromiser during the first six weeks. Actually, he was just as committed as the Bretons to common sessions and the vote by head, but he differed radically with them over tactics. Because the Dauphinois delegation had been elected by a united provincial estates without regard to orders, they discussed whether they should work together as a body at Versailles. When his colleagues rejected that strategy and decided to sit in their three separate orders, Mounier aspired to become a leader of the entire Third Estate and work with the patriots in the first two estates toward uniting all the orders. [16] His chief rival within the Third Estate was the abbé Sieyès, with whom he had major ideological differences.

The theoretician of the Third Estate, Emmanuel Joseph Sieyès was a member of the Society of Thirty in Paris, a political associate of the duc d'Orléans, and author of the most famous pamphlet of all, "What Is the Third Estate?" The last elected of the delayed Paris deputation, Sieyès did not arrive in Versailles until after the selection of commissioners to meet with those from the other two orders. He presented himself to the king on May 24 and took his first important action on May 27, when he drafted a proposal that the clergy meet with the Third Estate to coordinate efforts. [17]

15. Rouanet, "Les Premiers Leaders parlementaires," 492.

16. Egret, *La Révolution des Notables,* 52.

17. Murray Forsyth, *Reason and Revolution: The Political Thought of the Abbé Sieyès* (New York, 1987); Paul Bastid, *Sieyès et sa pensée* (Paris, 1939), 59.

The evening of May 29, the Third Estate voted to send delegates to a second set of conferences with men from the other two orders, in the presence of royal commissioners. When these conferences ended in impasse, Sieyès determined it was time to act. On June 10, he recommended that the Commons call the nobles and clergy to a joint session to verify powers. After an hour, the roll of electoral circumscriptions would be called and any absent deputies declared in default. The tactic marked a definite breach with Mounier's policy of compromise, and it split the Third Estate nearly in two after an intense debate: the vote on the motion was 247 for calling for the joint session, 246 preferring a formal reclamation against the principles contained in statements from the conferences on conciliation, and 41 recommending sending the issue to the bureaus for additional discussion.[18]

Mounier opposed Sieyès' motion. He believed that the term *National Assembly* excluded nobles and clergy from the right to represent any part of the nation. So as not to destroy all possibilities of compromise, Mounier proposed that the Third Estate designate themselves "the Assembly formed by representatives of the greatest part of the Nation."[19] But the majority of the Third Estate were not in a mood to cooperate after the failure of conferences, the nobles' refusal to sign minutes referring to the Third Estate as "the Commons," the fear of royal dissolution of the Estates, and mounting demands for action from the clamorous galleries.

Sieyès' motion was sent to the clergy and nobles on June 12, and the roll call began that evening to verify the powers of the deputies attending. When verification was completed on June 14, debate began on the next step; since only nineteen curés, out of all the nobles and clergy, had come over to join the Commons, some dramatic act appeared necessary to forestall royal intervention. Sieyès proposed that the Commons declare itself the assembly of representatives, known and verified, of the French nation. On June 15 and 16 the Third Estate argued intensely over this and other proposed titles. Tension escalated and the first use of the phrase "national assembly" in debate, by the deputy Jérôme Le Grand, passed almost un-

18. Creuzé-Latouche, *Journal des Etats-Généraux*, 94.
19. Egret, *La Révolution des Notables*, citing AN C 27, pp. 188–192. Creuzé-Latouche, *Journal des Etats-Généraux*, 110, gives Mounier's words as "representatives of 25 million citizens forming the majority of the Nation."

noted until Sieyès spoke again and used that title. By June 16, moderates and patriots agreed that the Third Estate had to take a definite step, but they disagreed on whether the Third alone could dare to define its members as the only true representatives of the nation. The patriots used threats of retribution from the people to create a majority of votes for Sieyès' motion that the Third Estate declare itself the National Assembly; the motion passed by 491 votes to 90 on June 17.[20] The Third Estate shifted from the conciliatory position of Mounier to the assertive position of Sieyès because of the unyielding posture of most deputies of the first two orders, the fear that the ministers would have the Estates dissolved by force if necessary, the pressure from gallery spectators and radical publicists and spokesmen, and finally, the concerted efforts of the deputies from Brittany.

Most of the Breton deputies were experienced in organized political action. Ten of them had represented Brittany's interests in Paris six months earlier and had met regularly among themselves and with leaders of the patriots in Paris.[21] When the Bretons got to Versailles at the end of April, they held regular meetings and were soon labeled the Breton Club. Within a week of the opening convocation, at least some of them were prepared to urge the Third Estate to declare themselves the whole nation's representatives if compromise failed. On May 12, Jean François Pierre Poulain de Corbion wrote his constituents at Saint-Brieuc that if overtures to the nobles and clergy produced no results, the Third Estate would make such a declaration; Poulain was certain that the king would not object.[22] The Bretons unanimously supported Issac René Guy Le Chapelier's unsuccessful motion of May 14 to invite the first two orders to a common session to

20. *Procès-verbal de l'Assemblée nationale* (77 vols.; Paris, 1789–91), Vol. I, No. 1 (June 17, 1789), 1–4.

21. The ten were Cottin, Blin, Jary, Duplessix, and Chaillon from Nantes; Le Chapelier, Lanjuinais, Varin, and Glezen from Rennes; and Boullé from Pontivy. See Kuhlmann, "Influence of the Breton Deputation," 222–25. Palasne de Champeaux, Coupard, Kervelegan, Le Déan, Le Roulx, and La Chapelle (*sic;* Chapelières?) sometimes attended.

22. Julien François Palasne de Champeaux, Letter of May 1, 1789, in *Mémoires de la Société d'émulation des Côtes-du-Nord,* XXVI (1888), 218; Laurent François Le Gendre and Ildut Moyot, Letter of May 1, 1789, in *La Révolution française,* XXXIX (1900), 518; Jean François Pierre Poulain de Corbion, Letter of May 12, 1789, in *Mémoires de la Société d'émulation des Côtes-du-Nord,* XXVI (1888), 221, 222.

verify credentials.[23] On the evenings of June 8 and 9, the Breton Club discussed a motion similar to the one presented by Sieyès on June 10.

Sensitive to public opinion, the Bretons were eager to enlist the support of spectators, their electors, and the people of Paris in the early months of the Revolution. Two Breton deputies, Laurent François Le Gendre and Ildut Moyot, criticized Mirabeau for his incendiary style and counseled moderation so that the Third Estate would retain public favor. Just before the first set of conferences among the three orders, another Breton, Jean Pierre Boullé, remarked that the Third Estate should take care that "public opinion" did not blame them for the impasse between the three orders.[24] Throughout the week preceding the proclamation of the National Assembly, the Bretons rallied the spectators and cajoled or threatened their colleagues. During the sessions of June 16, the radicals tried to get a quick vote on the declaration of the National Assembly, while conservatives lengthened debate and tried delaying tactics. The presiding officer, Jean Silvain Bailly, wrote that three hundred to four hundred deputies in front of him were urging a prompt vote, while a hundred or so noisy opponents behind him wanted to disrupt the session and prevent a vote.[25] Jacques Antoine Creuzé de Latouche, who supported the Bretons and Sieyès' motion, feared that delay could occasion a royal decree dissolving the Estates General; he mentioned "a party" of about eighty or so "bad citizens" whose tactics included a motion that every deputy should speak on the National Assembly proposal before a vote was taken.[26]

Many deputies grasped the profound significance of pressure from public opinion on the question of declaring the National Assembly. Creuzé de Latouche astutely recognized the potency of the conservative claim that deputies' votes could not be free if spectators intervened in debate. On the other hand, delaying the vote overnight could give the advantage "to *courtisans* and to our enemies." The Breton Boullé was less apprehensive, be-

---

23. Kuhlmann, "Influence of the Breton Deputation," 247–50.

24. Le Gendre and Moyot, Letters of May 8, 13, 1789, in *Mémoires de la Société d'émulation des Côtes-du-Nord,* XXVI (1888), 521, 522; Jean Pierre Boullé, Letter of May 15, 1789, in *Revue de la Révolution,* XIII (1888), 12, 13.

25. Jean Silvain Bailly, *Mémoires de Bailly avec une notice de sa vie* (3 vols.; Paris, 1821–22), I, 153–56. See also Rouanet, "Les Débuts du parlementarisme française," 180.

26. Creuzé-Latouche, *Journal des Etats-généraux,* 121.

lieving that the king's reasons for calling the Estates in the first place would suffice for him not to disband them. He wrote his constituents that the opponents of Sieyès' motion were never a threat.[27] His colleague Palasne de Champeaux was angrier: "Discussions are very long, and as we have among us some scoundrels delivered over to the aristocracy who create a thousand difficulties, you see, Sirs, how much time we lose; however, the majority of well-intentioned men is considerable, and I hope we will carry the day over the cabal." Carry the day they did. Pierre Victor Malouet reported that the evening of June 16 there were two hundred opponents of the motion, but that under the pressure of shouts from the galleries their numbers shrank to ninety by the time the vote was taken the next morning. He himself was seized by the collar by an angry spectator.[28] The names of all ninety opponents of the National Assembly cannot be reliably documented. Significantly, key members of this opposition were from Dauphiné (Mounier, Pison du Galland) and Paris (François Denis Tronchet, Du Pont de Nemours, Guy Jean Baptiste Target), where they knew liberal nobles and clergy who supported the patriot cause. Despite the label "traitors" that radical spokesmen attached to them, they certainly did not oppose common verification, the vote by head, and a written constitution.

In the next days, nearly half the clergy and many of the patriot nobles joined the new National Assembly, the legitimacy of which was now the central political question. The king, deciding that the time had come to regain some initiative, convoked a royal session for June 23. On the twentieth, the men who had formed the National Assembly, finding themselves locked out of their meeting hall, convened in an indoor tennis court at Versailles and swore their famous oath not to disband until they had given France a constitution. Louis XVI attempted a *coup d'authorité* in the *séance royale* on June 23. He surrounded the meeting hall with troops, nullified

27. *Ibid.*, 123; Boullé, Letter of June 16, 1789, in *Revue de la Révolution*, XIII (1888), 12, 13.

28. Palasne de Champeaux, Letter of June 16, 1789, in *Mémoires de la Société d'émulation des Côtes du Nord*, XXVI (1888), 234. For the vote on Sieyès' motion, see Boullé, Letter of June 16, 1789, pp. 12–13. Malouet's observation about spectator influence is from Pierre Victor Malouet, "Lettre à ses commettans," as quoted in Kessel, *La Nuit du 4 août 1789*, 101; the collar-grabbing incident is in Pierre Victor Malouet, *Mémoires de Malouet*, ed. le baron Malouet (2 vols.; Paris, 1874), II, 10, 68, 69.

the declarations of June 10 and June 17, urged the orders to sit together and vote by head on most matters, reserved a veto for two-thirds of any order, and announced that the deputies had no authority to deny his wishes or to enforce their own. When the king and ministers left, most of the bishops and nobles followed; the supporters of the National Assembly remained in session against royal command and decreed the personal inviolability of every deputy. Between the evening of the twenty-third and the twenty-sixth, more clergy and nobles joined the National Assembly. Finally, on June 27, the king yielded and ordered the remaining nobles and clergy to join the National Assembly. The decree gave the stamp of legitimacy to the new institution. Furthermore, when the king stated that some deputies would have to ask their electors for new mandates, he implicitly recognized that the representative base of the defunct Estates General had been radically transformed.

Alignment: Attitudinal Measures from Sampled Regions

As the twenty-seven months of the National Assembly passed, many deputies continued to write pamphlets and have their speeches printed, often to explain an act of the Assembly to their constituents or to justify their personal conduct. The 280 pamphlets written during the period of the National Assembly, from June 17, 1789, to September 30, 1792, cover dozens of specific topics on general questions of legitimacy and participation. Since many pamphlets do not address any particular issue, the percentages for any one category may appear to be small, but they do reveal a consistent division into left, center, and right clusters of opinions. Fundamental ideological differences in attitudes can be identified among these clusters. The distributions of opinions on seven issues concerning legitimacy and participation exhibit left-wing attitudes in from 8 to 56 percent of the pamphlets, depending on the issue. From 10 to 24 percent state centrist views, and from 8 to 26 percent contain rightist opinions. The only measure for which any faction's views represent a consensus majority is attitudes toward the

National Assembly, with 56 percent of the pamphlets enthusiastically supportive (Table 12).[29]

Left-wing opinion was the closest in outline to the Constitution of 1791. It defined the nation as the sovereign people, emphasized liberty rather than the need for order, and understood legitimacy as originating in the acts of a sovereign legislative assembly. Left-wing pamphlets enthusiastically supported the work of the Assembly and criticized the king for either his weakness or his untrustworthiness. The authors of these pamphlets might regret violence but argue that it was sometimes necessary to carry forward the revolution, and they tended to advocate the view that the people should be mobilized or educated for extended political activity.

Right-wing pamphlets described opposite views on these issues. The nation's essence was the king and the traditional constituted bodies. Legitimacy was traditional, and a strong government was needed to keep order. The king was supported in his traditional place as the embodiment of the nation and center of authority. Of the 280 pamphlets, 15 percent expressed shock over revolutionary violence.

Centrist views reflected an Enlightenment theory of regulated monarchy. Centrists rejected popular sovereignty. The National Assembly was sovereign, and the nation's representatives acted in the name of the legitimate general will. These authors neither feared nor favored strong authority, but emphasized stability and were concerned that violence was destabilizing. Less apprehensive than the right about mass behavior, they recommended calming the people. They were mildly supportive of the Assembly and praised the king as a supporter of liberty.

These clusters of opinions consistently varied together. When two issues, the source of legitimacy and the definition of the nation, were cross-tabulated with ten other measures of legitimacy and participation, nineteen of twenty tables were significant at the .1-percent level (Table 13).

This documentary evidence portrays the deputies as caught between the king and the people. Right-wing pamphleteers inclined toward making the Constitution a bulwark of support for the king; left-wing authors were

29. Because so many of these issues are not discussed in any given pamphlet, these attitudinal frequencies cannot be used to estimate proportionate size of factions in the National Assembly. Grouping deputies according to their actions, not their attitudes, is a much more valid measure of alignment.

Table 12

Distribution of Left, Center, and Right Opinions on Seven Variables (Pamphlets Written from June 18, 1789, to September 30, 1791; N = 280)

Left-wing Opinions	%	Centrist Opinions	%	Right-wing Opinions	%
Mobilize, educate the masses	25	Calm the masses	20	Do not mobilize	15
Violence is necessary	8	Violence is destabilizing	24	Violence is frightful	15
King is weak, untrustworthy	17	King supports liberty	10	King is needed for traditional authority	15
Enthusiastic support is given Assembly	56	Mild support is given Assembly	13	Assembly is criticized	21
Liberty is stressed	8	Stability is stressed	24	Need for order is stressed	26
Legitimacy = sovereign constituent assembly	24	Legitimacy = general will	10	Legitimacy = tradition	14
Nation = sovereign people	12	Nation = representatives in Assembly	15	Nation = king plus his supporters	8

Table 13

Relationships Between Opinions on Legitimacy and Participation (Pamphlets Written from June 18, 1789, to September 30, 1791; $N = 280$)

Pairs of variables with the strongest significant relationships ($p < .001$)

    Sources of legitimacy with:

        perceptions of political cleavages

        attitudes toward the masses

        attitudes toward popular violence

        definitions of *revolution*

        opinions on causes of revolution

        date author wishes Revolution to end

        attitudes toward the king

        attitudes toward the National Assembly

        general attitudes toward authority

    Meaning of *nation* with:

        perceived political divisions

        attitudes toward the masses

        attitudes toward popular violence

        opinions on factions

        definitions of *revolution*

        opinions on causes of revolution

        date author wishes Revolution to end

        attitudes toward the king

        attitudes toward the National Assembly

        general attitudes toward authority

Pair of variables with strong statistical relationship ($.001 < p < .05$)

    Sources of legitimacy with:

        opinions on factions

---

more concerned that the king might enforce his authority and squelch the revolution they were making. The pamphlets show that the attitudinal polarization was not so complete as to eliminate the ideological center. An average of 17 percent of the pamphlets exhibited centrist views, 17 percent rightist, and 21 percent leftist. It is striking that the center was the same size as the right, and that it had some ideological coherence. There is additional fragmentary evidence that centrist views on legitimacy were weak-

Figure 1

Changes in Distribution of Left-Wing Views in Pamphlets

———————— Violence is necessary.

– – – – – King is weak and untrustworthy.

·—·—·—·—·— Enthusiastic support is given Assembly.

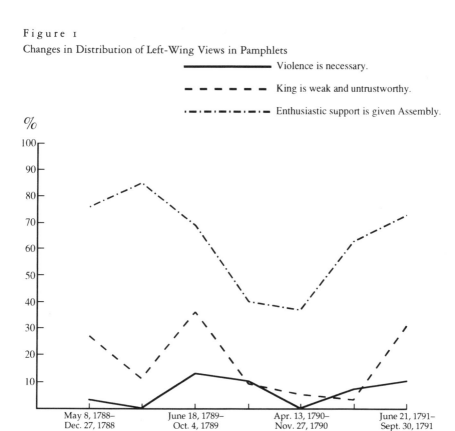

ened by divisions on issues that were essentially uncompromisable, especially the political role of the king. Seventeen pamphlets that defined the nation in terms of its representatives were also codable according to opinions on the king; they distributed nearly evenly across the range of views, suggesting an absence of centrist cohesion on this issue. Six said the king supported liberty, six called him the center of power, and five stated he was untrustworthy. Sixteen pamphlets defining legitimacy as natural law or the general will similarly disagreed on the king, with three calling him a sup-

Figure 2

Changes in Distribution of Centrist Views in Pamphlets

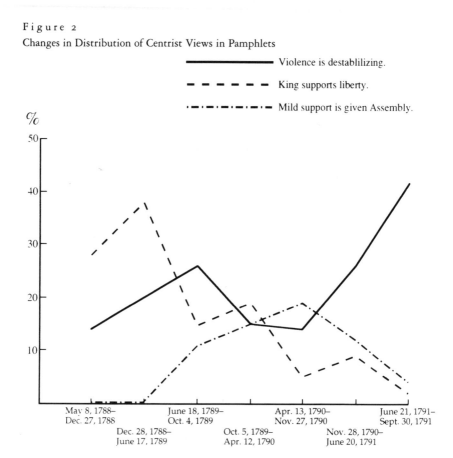

porter of liberty, six the center of authority, and seven untrustworthy. Right-wing pamphlets more uniformly agreed that the king was a traditional ruler or the center of authority; likewise, left-wing pamphlets either said the king supported liberty or called him untrustworthy. Only a few pamphlets can be paired on these variables, but the fragmentation of centrist opinions on the king also appears when centrists are defined according to their actions and not their attitudes (see pp. 87–93).

Figures 1, 2, and 3, representing different degrees of coherence among leftist, centrist, and rightist opinions, indicate increasing polarization

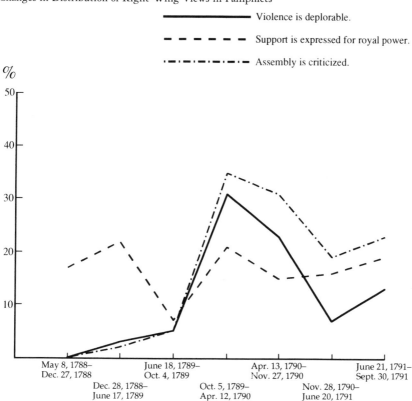

Figure 3
Changes in Distribution of Right-Wing Views in Pamphlets

————————— Violence is deplorable.

— — — — — — Support is expressed for royal power.

·—·—·—·—·—· Assembly is criticized.

and the decline of the center after the king's flight to Varennes. Although the left-wing attitude toward the Assembly—enthusiastic support—was always more frequently mentioned, the three left-wing opinions on the king, the Assembly, and violence tended to vary together. The frequencies for right-wing views did the same, and the frequencies were even closer. The frequencies for the centrist views show a different pattern, and indicate how the dilemma over the king polarized the Assembly and weakened the center. Opinion that the king supported liberty declined steeply after June, 1789, and again after October 5. The view that violence is destabilizing increased after the October Days and again, considerably, during the final year of the Assembly, suggesting that the king's flight simply left the centrist deputies without an anchor for their beliefs about authority.

These differences of opinion were formed and shaped by deputies' early political experiences. Attitudinal configurations of left, center, and right proved to be associated with differences in the prerevolutionary roles and the estates of pamphlet authors. In the pre–June 17, 1789, pamphlets, the distribution of opinions on political cleavages, the masses, factions, monarchy, and authority was associated with authors' province, occupation, estate, and membership in a prerevolutionary political assembly. Evidence developed in chapter 2 indicates that estate was the most significant determinant of these attitudes, with service in a prerevolutionary assembly the second most significant. For the pamphlets distributed after June 17, I have dropped the cross-tabulation with political cleavages, since that issue had been settled by the formation of the National Assembly. Attitudes toward the masses in politics did not vary significantly with any of the four background variables. The results for the remaining three issues are replicated, with the addition of attitudes toward violence and toward the National Assembly, in Table 14. Just as in the earlier period, estate turned out to be the most important predictor of opinion, with statistically significant relationships on all five issues. Occupation of Third Estate deputies was the second most powerful determinant, significant at less than the 5-percent level for attitudes toward the king and toward factions, and not significant for attitudes about violence. Deputies' province of origin was closely related to the distribution of opinion on the Assembly; less strongly related to views on the king, authority, and faction; and not significantly related to views on violence. Attendance at a prerevolutionary political assembly, which was an important determinant of attitudes before June 17, was thereafter significantly related only to views on the Assembly. It is possible that the common denominator of experience in the National Assembly lessened the effect upon attitudes of previous association with an assembly.

In the strong association of province with opinions on the National Assembly, Bretons were far and away the most likely to support the Assembly enthusiastically, whereas opinions from the other provinces were more evenly divided between support and criticism. Pamphlets by Dauphinois authors were more likely to range across the categories of each issue than those by authors from other provinces, reflecting the split between the Monarchiens, led by Mounier, and a left-wing group led by Barnave.

Contemporaries who commented upon the occupations of deputies elected to the Estates General often noted the large number of lawyers, whom they sometimes blamed or praised for the rapidity of political change in 1789. When I investigated lawyers' opinions expressed before June 17, I found them not to be uniformly the most radical, nor were they so later on—in fact, for the duration of the National Assembly. However, on two significant variables, lawyers do stand out: they were the strongest supporters of the National Assembly and the severest critics of the king.

The continuing strong relationship between deputies' estate and their attitudes as revealed in the pamphlets written after June 17 follows unsurprising patterns. The clergy's pamphlets accepted the traditional role of the king and were most critical of the Assembly. Nobles' pamphlets most frequently expressed concern for strong government and disapproved of factions. Third Estate pamphlets reveal the largest number of opinions consistently on the left: recognition of the utility of violence, criticism of the king, strong support for the Assembly, and emphasis on liberty. However, taking all pamphlets together and disregarding their authors' estate, I found that majority opinion was not very radical. The largest plurality of pamphlets did not accept violence, stressed strong government over liberty, and disapproved of factions.

Although the association between prerevolutionary assembly and opinions was not as strong as that between estate and opinions, the frequencies do reveal historically important patterns. All 10 pamphlets written by members of the Assembly of Notables were conservative; so, in general, were the 153 pamphlets whose authors had not served in any assembly. The most liberal pamphlets were the 43 by men who had served in provincial estates.

In sum, estate once again proved to be significantly related statistically to deputies' opinions on various dimensions of participation and legitimacy. In fact, estate was the only variable concerning deputies' backgrounds that was correlated at a highly significant level with opinions on violence. All the background variables, on the other hand, were associated significantly with views on the National Assembly.

These data underline once again the political centrality of estate as the

Table 14

Distribution of Opinions on Four Issues After June, 1789, by Authors' Political Background

	Province						Occupation (Third Estate)			Estate			Pre-1789 Political Assembly					
	Brittany N = 87	Paris N = 106	Dauphiné N = 28	Bourges N = 12	Bourb./Moulins N = 14	Orléanais N = 33	Judge N = 43	Lawyer N = 75	Other N = 46	First N = 41	Second N = 76	Third N = 163	Notables N = 10	Prov. Estates N = 43	Prov. Assembly N = 39	Dauphiné N = 28	Departmental/Municipal N = 7	Not in assembly N = 153
	p = .232 (n.s.)*						*p* = .16 (n.s.)			*p* = .005			*p* = .355 (n.s.)					
Opinions on violence																		
Approves: necessary	12	5	11	0	7	9	9	11	13	2	4	11	0	16	8	11	14	5
Disapproves: destabilizing	38	21	11	8	21	18	35	31	22	20	18	28	10	35	26	11	14	25
Disapproves: intolerable	6	22	21	0	7	24	16	5	2	20	28	9	30	5	18	21	14	16

Opinions on king			_p = .025_				_p = .023_			_p < .001_			_p = .158 (n.s.)_					
Traditional ruler	0	4	0	8	7	6	0	0	0	17	1	0	10	0	0	0	0	5
Supporter of liberty	13	11	4	0	14	6	9	12	7	10	11	10	10	16	10	7	29	9
Center of authority	1	22	29	8	7	3	19	1	7	12	24	7	20	0	13	29	0	13
Weak, misled	6	4	0	0	0	6	2	5	2	2	5	4	0	9	3	0	0	4
Untrustworthy	18	7	25	0	7	18	7	28	15	0	8	19	0	9	10	25	14	14
Opinions on Assembly			_p < .001_				_p < .001_			_p < .001_			_p < .001_					
Enthusiastic support	86	43	50	33	50	36	63	76	74	24	38	72	10	91	33	50	57	56
Support	6	16	21	25	0	15	9	12	7	17	17	10	50	5	18	22	14	10
Criticism	3	29	18	33	43	30	23	3	19	44	37	8	20	5	41	18	14	22
Opinions on authority			_p = .002_				_p < .001_			_p < .001_			_p = .075 (n.s.)_					
Stresses liberty	8	6	21	0	0	12	7	17	15	0	0	14	0	12	5	21	7	7
Fears disorder	38	13	18	17	50	21	42	27	11	34	15	26	40	35	21	18	57	21
Strong government	15	39	25	25	21	15	19	17	13	22	37	22	30	12	23	25	14	31
Opinions on factions			_p = .02_				_p = .03_			_p = .004_			_p = .054 (n.s.)_					
Approves	17	16	11	0	14	27	12	20	24	7	16	22	0	23	13	11	43	16
Disapproves	41	33	39	8	43	30	56	31	19	29	41	24	20	47	36	39	33	32

*n.s. = not statistically significant.

Old Regime came to its end. The largest difference in pamphlet opinions expressed during the National Assembly was just as closely associated with the authors' estate as had been the case with prerevolutionary pamphlets. Political outlooks shaped by different occupational and public service opportunities did not disappear once the deputies moved together into a constituent assembly.

Alignment: Behavioral Measures

According to the alignment scale devised for all the deputies, 47 percent of the total membership of the National Assembly were right-wing, 18 percent were in the center, and 35 percent were on the left (see the Introduction for a complete explanation of this scale). Table 15 presents a more

Table 15
Frequencies of Alignment, All Deputies

	Frequency	%
Consistent right	108	8
Moderate right	315	24
Center right	147	11
Resigning right	51	4
Right center	13	1
Contradictory	44	3
Unclassifiable	173	13
Ministerial left	184	14
Shifting left	176	14
Consistent left	107	8
Total	1,318	100
Right	621	47
Center	230	18
Left	467	35
Total	1,318	100

Table 16

Relationships Between Behavioral Alignment and Attitudes

Relationships showing strongest statistical relationship (p < .001)
    Behavioral alignment with:
        perceptions of political cleavages
        attitudes toward popular violence
        opinions on factions
        definitions of *revolution*
        date author wishes Revolution to end
        attitudes toward the king
        attitudes toward the National Assembly
Relationships showing a strong statistical relationship (.001 < p < .05)
    Behavioral alignment with:
        attitudes toward the masses
        general attitudes toward authority

---

detailed breakdown of the frequencies and percentages for all ten alignment categories.

Since the measures for the alignment scale are based on deputies' behavior and not their opinions, the scale can be correlated with scales of opinions coded from the pamphlets. A summary of these correlations (Table 16) shows that the alignment scale is catching historical reality; there is a consistent statistically significant relationship between alignment and nine of the sixteen attitudinal scales.

When all 280 pamphlets written during the National Assembly are matched with their authors' behavioral alignment, it is clear that men of the left, center, and right differed significantly on the issue of royal legitimacy (Table 17). The 92 pamphlets written by right-wing deputies were three times more likely than their number would suggest to respect the king as traditional ruler. Centrists, despite their relatively infrequent mentions of the topic, were disproportionately likely to approve of the king as a supporter of liberty; the left-wing deputies were disproportionately likely to consider him untrustworthy. Royal legitimacy was thus a central issue dividing the deputies into factions.

Observers of the pageantry surrounding the mass and opening session of the Estates General often remarked upon the distinctive appearance of

Table 17
Index of Proportionality for Attitudes Toward the King by Behavioral Alignment

	Left N = 159	Center N = 29	Right N = 92
Attitude toward the king:			
Traditional ruler	0	0	3.0
Supporter of liberty	1.2	1.4	.5
Center of authority	.3	.8	2.2
Weak and misled	1.0	0	1.5
Untrustworthy	1.4	.8	.5
Not mentioned	1.1	1.1	.8

men of the three orders: curés in clerical collars, upper clergy in robes of office; nobles in the cordon bleu, symbols of privilege, military insignia, or judicial robes; and Third Estate deputies in plain black suits. Such visible distinctions among the orders paralleled less obvious but more significant distinctions among the left, center, and right. Province of origin, estate, occupation, and prerevolutionary careers all proved to be associated with factional differences.

Most striking is the relationship between alignment and estate (Table 18). Noble deputies predominated among the extreme right and were a strong presence in all right-wing categories. Clerical deputies were somewhat more likely to appear across the alignment spectrum, but they too were disproportionately represented in all the right-wing categories. (Seven of the thirteen members of the right center were clergy, assigned there because I could find no other evidence of their alignment besides the attribution by a supporter of the left wing.) Members of the clergy were more likely than nobles to be in the center and on the extreme left. In contrast to both groups, the Third Estate, with half the total membership, overwhelmingly dominated the left-wing alignments, especially the shifting left and the center left. The only exception to this pattern was their presence among the resigners, and even there they were slightly less than proportionate to their numbers.

Experience in a political assembly before the Estates General does not differentiate as strongly as estate among the alignment categories, although the 16 percent of the deputies who had such experience were somewhat

Table 18
1789 Profile of All Deputies in Each Alignment Category

	Prerevolutionary Assembly (%)	Estate[a]				Prerevolutionary Institution (%)	Freemasons (%)
		1st	2d	3d	(Not)[b]		
			(%)				
Consistent right	18	44	48	8		15	12
Moderate right	17	42	38	19	(1)	15	14
Center right	23	33	40	27		19	17
Resigning right	10	26	29	43	(2)	25	20
Right center	0	54	8	38		31	15
Contradictory	9	27	16	55	(2)	32	23
Unclassifiable	12	14	8	73	(5)	40	16
Ministerial left	17	10	14	73	(3)	48	23
Shifting left	20	9	9	80	(2)	36	29
Consistent left	6	14	5	77	(4)	38	17

[a] Percentages on estate sum to 100 percent by row.
[b] Elected after abolition of estates.

overrepresented among the center right and the shifting left, and under-represented among the consistent left. A clearer pattern appears with a third variable, experience in a prerevolutionary institution: 29 percent of the deputies had connections with a prerevolutionary institution, but the percentages were considerably higher for left-wing deputies. The fourth variable, Freemasonry, is the least distinct predictor of alignment. The 244 likely Freemasons, 19 percent of the total membership, are found in all alignment categories, being appreciably overrepresented only among the shifting left (the index of proportionality for that category is 1.6). Masonic deputies were somewhat more likely to be on the left than on the right, but their distribution across the alignment spectrum undermines the thesis that Freemasons plotted a revolution or at least supported revolutionary ideals.[30]

To summarize, estate was not a simple determinant of alignment. At

30. The list of Freemasons is from Pierre Lamarque, *Les Francs-Maçons aux Etats généraux de 1789 et à l'Assemblée nationale* (Paris, 1981).

the most general level, it was quite an accurate predictor: right-wing deputies were more likely to be clergy or nobility, center deputies to be clergy or Third Estate; left-wing deputies were predominantly Third Estate. These quantitative descriptions do not deviate from the patterns long described by observers and historians of the National Assembly, but they do point up certain anomalies that should be pursued. The 15 percent of the clergy and 12 percent of the nobles who sat on the left contributed key votes on certain issues; we need to understand what determined their behavior and made them different from the other members of the first two estates. The center deputies (17 percent of the total membership) are so categorized because they did not sign protests or join clubs or bring themselves to the attention of observers. We should investigate whether they were merely inactive, perhaps not wanting to adhere to a particular set of opinions, or whether they articulated a centrist position that was internally consistent and coherent.

Alignment also varied according to occupational differences within the Third Estate, and prerevolutionary experience or the lack of it in assemblies and institutions (Table 19). Occupation had a greater impact on alignment than career experience for left and center deputies. Lawyers, men in agriculture, and those in the anomalous category of "other" occupations (a law professor, an astronomer, a printer, etc.) contributed more disproportionately to the left than judges, royal administrators, other professionals, town officials, and clergy or nobles representing the Third Estate. Attendance at a prerevolutionary assembly did not tend discernibly to make one left-wing, at least not independently of one's estate.

The center was composed disproportionately of bureaucrats and professional men, who were roughly twice as likely to sit there as their numbers would indicate. Centrists were also drawn from among those with experience in an administrative office or a court. The center was not a hotbed of prolific pamphleteers: of the 280 pamphlets printed after June, 1789, only 29 were written by centrist deputies. Those that could be coded on four issues concerning participation and legitimacy took what I have defined elsewhere as centrist positions. The authors wanted to calm crowds, considered violence destabilizing, and stressed stability rather than liberty or authority. A greater percentage of these pamphlets, compared with those by leftist or rightist authors, expressed belief in the king's support of liberty, although an even greater plurality were unsure of the king. In short, the

Table 19
Index of Proportionality for Alignment by Deputies' Background Characteristics

	Left (N = 467)	Center (N = 230)	Right (N = 621)
Estate (Expanded)			
Clergy			
Upper	.2	.2	1.9
Middle	.4	.7	1.5
Lower	.5	.9	1.4
Nobility			
Sword	.5	.4	1.6
Robe	.8	.2	1.4
Other	.3	.5	1.7
Third	1.6	1.4	.4
Occupation			
Judge	1.5	1.3	.5
Lawyer	1.6	1.2	.4
Royal administrator	1.2	2.0	.5
Professional	1.4	1.9	.4
Agriculturist	1.9	1.4	.2
Other	1.7	.9	.5
Town official	1.4	1.2	.6
Clergy/noble: Third	1.5	.8	.7
Noble/clergy	.4	.6	1.6
Prerevolutionary Assembly			
Notables + prov. estates	.5	.5	1.4
Notables only	.4	.2	1.7
Provincial estates	1.4	1.0	.8
Provincial assembly	1.1	.5	1.1
Dauphiné	.7	.9	1.3
Dept./municipal assembly	1.2	1.2	.8
Not in assembly	1.0	1.1	1.0
Prerevolutionary Institution			
Court	1.6	.6	.7
Parlement	1.5	.8	.7
Intendancy	.9	1.9	.7
Bailliage court	1.4	1.3	.6
Royal Adm. court	1.1	2.4	.4
Royal jurisdiction	1.5	1.4	.5
Provincial administration	1.1	1.6	.6
Municipal administration	1.4	1.4	.6
Not in institution	.8	.9	1.2

Table 20
Alignment by Region

	Paris	Normandy	East	West	Aquitaine Basin	Nord
Alignment (%)						
Left	33	35	42	49	32	34
Center	22	18	16	13	14	27
Right	45	47	42	38	54	39
	100	100	100	100	100	100
	Massif Central	Rhone Delta	Jura Alps	Midi / Corsica	Colonies	
Left	25	40	35	35	32	
Center	13	13	13	11	42	
Right	62	47	52	54	26	
	100	100	100	100	100	

Whole Assembly: Left = 35%, Center = 18%, Right = 47%

centrists tended to be supporters of a constitutional monarchy who did not very frequently express trust in their monarch.

Right-wing deputies were disproportionately drawn from the upper clergy and from those who had attended the Assembly of Notables and/or served in provincial estates (excluding the estates of Dauphiné). These were traditional Old Regime elites from whose numbers the reactionary forces within the National Assembly were drawn.

Widely divergent prerevolutionary politics influenced deputy alignment. The estates of Dauphiné and Brittany, for example, became unique institutions in 1788 and 1789, and attending them had to have been a dramatic and formative experience. Similarly, the patriot party had come together in Paris and most of the nobles and Third Estate deputies in the Paris delegation adhered to its ideology.

The regional variation represented in Table 20 reflects the incompleteness of developing national politics and institutional unity in France at the end of the Old Regime. Provincial estates, assemblies, and parlements differed considerably from place to place, and each had a different impact on the deputies elected to the Estates General. As we have seen, estate varied more closely with alignment than did any other variable, including region. However, a regional pattern can be discerned: deputies on the left were disproportionately likely to have come from the eastern or western regions and the Rhône delta, center deputies from the northern provinces and the colonies, and right-wing deputies from the Aquitaine Basin, the Massif Central, the Jura Alps, and the Midi and Corsica.

Estate determined deputy alignment to a greater degree than any other variable, but it was neither a simple cause nor a direct effect. It would be quite accurate to say that the Third Estate created the National Assembly and dominated it throughout its two-and-a-half-year existence, but such a conclusion would mask the complexity of internal politics and distort the roles played by such important subgroups as Jacobin members, liberal nobles, and left-wing curés. Where the evidence permits, a look at deputies' alignment trajectories that accompanied increasingly radical actions by the Assembly can help to clarify the dynamics of the early years of the Revolution.

Chapter 4

Alignment Trajectories

In his report to the royal council on December 27, 1788, Jacques Necker spelled out the alignment he perceived forming over the issue of the size of the Third Estate's representation in the Estates General. The majority of the Notables, the majority of the clergy and nobility (the Breton nobility especially), the parlementary magistrates, and most of the princes of the blood wanted to restrict the Third Estate to one-third of the total deputies. Those in favor of doubling the Third Estate constituted a minority of Notables, albeit the most distinguished; delegates from the estates of Dauphiné, Languedoc, Provence, and Hainaut; provincial commissioners; and many correspondents from cities and communities throughout the nation.[1] Necker saw very clearly that the Estates General would be a forum for a power struggle dividing the first two orders from the third. Only "patriot" nobles and curés would stand significantly outside this basic pattern of alignment by estates. This political configuration did in fact appear in the National Assembly and was remarkably enduring throughout the complex interplay of events and internal politics between May, 1789, and September, 1791.

Revisionist historians writing since the 1970s explain the swiftly advancing radicalism characteristic of the French Revolution as a consequence of political power struggle, rather than class war. They claim that after August 4, 1789, liberal patriot deputies lost control of the political agenda

---

1. Jacques Necker, "Rapport fait au roi dans son conseil, par le ministre de ses finances, le 27 décembre 1788," *Archives parlementaires,* I, 490, 491.

as they maneuvered between an obstructionist monarch and the insatiably demanding popular classes, whose leaders and orators made sure to remind the deputies in the National Assembly that popular violence had saved them from being sent packing by a royal coup. The evidence available to trace alignment trajectories does not support the idea that August 4 or indeed any other specific event represented a turning point that dramatically altered alignment within the Assembly.

The August 4 decrees eliminating the seigneurial system, albeit with compensation, were passed during a high-pitched, almost orgiastic night of renunciation, paradoxically the last moments of near-unanimity that the Assembly would ever know. Orchestrated in advance at the Breton Club, motions to abolish "feudal" rights were the product of an effort to come to terms with a summer of sporadic violence in the countryside and an even more extensive wildfire of rumor and fear, coupled with continuing concern that the king would use force to rein in the constitutional ambitions of the National Assembly.[2] August 4 brought the deputies together around a concept of national unity built upon fraternal bonds between individual citizens, bonds that could be weakened or snapped by exclusive privileges.[3]

This moment of unity itself produced conflictual issues. The decrees of August 4 and the enabling legislation that followed defined the nature of the right to property that the new Constitution was designed in part to protect. The Assembly did not accept the arguments of some of the clerical deputies that church tithes were not identical to secular feudal rights and should not be abolished, since they were a form of property. This dispute was followed by deeper schism in late 1789 and 1790 over the nationalization of church property to undergird a new currency and fiscal and monetary reform. Debate began in August on the Declaration of the Rights of Man and of the Citizen and on the constitutional construction of executive authority and legislative structures and powers, and the direction it took angered right-wing supporters of a strong monarchy and advocates of an upper aristocratic house in the legislature.

The abstraction of a political left and right originated with the concrete

2. Fabio Freddi, "La Presse parisienne et la nuit du 4 août," *Annales historiques de la Révolution française,* LVII (1985), 46–59; Sutherland, *France, 1789–1815,* esp. 63–93.

3. Fitzsimmons, "Privilege and the Polity in France," 294. See also the more general discussion of fraternity by Robert Darnton in "What Was Revolutionary About the French Revolution?" *New York Review of Books,* January 19, 1989, p. 10.

use of political space early in the fall of 1789. Deputies were still taking their seats in the hall mostly according to the estate that they represented. Such placement began to represent a statement of political alignment full of both ideological and personal enmity. For example, on September 9, during debate on permanence of the legislature and the limits of the royal veto, the comte de Virieu made a remark that was taken by the Third Estate as an insult. As the presiding officer, César Guillaume de La Luzerne, was trying to regain order a voice cried, "Nobles are no longer permitted to call deputies of the Commons demagogues, and the Commons are no longer allowed to call nobles aristocrats."[4]

After the popular intervention of women and national guardsmen from Paris in the château and National Assembly at Versailles on October 5 and 6 and the transfer of the royal family and the National Assembly to Paris, observers let go of the old language of estates and started classifying the deputies as either "patriots" or "aristocrats," a new vocabulary that developed as some issues—the royal veto, church lands, the Declaration of Rights—were resolved in constitutional decrees, while other issues— church governance, judicial power, reform of the army—instigated new battles. The radical journalist Armand Elisée Loustallot, writing in *Révolutions de Paris* in May of 1790, defined within the Assembly two kinds of patriots: true supporters of the people, and egotistical demagogues; equally, Loustallot saw two kinds of aristocrats: frank reactionaries, and the "impartials," who did not regret the Old Regime, many features of which were not in their interest, but who had much to gain from court favors such as pensions, ambassadorships, and other remunerative benefits.[5] Daniel Wick's study of deputies who belonged to the Society of Thirty in Paris makes the case for "four distinct parties" by November, 1789: a conservative right of aristocrats and clerical deputies, and three factions of the original patriot party, namely, Anglophile constitutionalists, centrist supporters of Lafa-

---

4. *Archives parlementaires*, VIII (September 9, 1789, morning session), 604.
5. *Révolutions de Paris*, Vol. IV, No. 43 (May 1–8, 1790), pp. 253–60. Readers may also be interested in Pierre Rétat's article on this journal: "Forme et discours d'un journal révolutionnaire: *Les Révolutions de Paris* en 1789," in Claude Labrosse, Pierre Rétat, and Henri Duranton, *L'Instrument périodique: La Fonction de la presse au XVIIIe siècle* (Lyon, 1986), 139–78, and in Keith Michael Baker, "'Revolution,'" in *The Political Culture of the French Revolution*, ed. Colin Lucas (New York, 1988), 41–62, Vol. II of *The French Revolution and the Creation of Modern Political Culture*, 3 vols.

yette, and a left led by Adrien Du Port and Alexandre Théodore Victor de Lameth.[6] Timothy Tackett presents a third description of alignment: a "two-party system" existing between February and mid–July, 1790, aligning 205 Jacobin deputies against 292 "Capuchins" (those deputies who signed the April 19 "Déclaration" protesting the failure to decree a state religion on April 13).[7]

By whatever label, this broad patriot/aristocrat division and narrower factional splitting deepened and polarized during debates on religious issues—the question of whether to declare a state religion, the Civil Constitution of the Clergy, and the clerical oath requirement—and on issues of royal legitimacy and popular participation that came to a head with the king's attempt to leave France for Belgium on June 21, 1791, and with the martial law decree and the violence on the Champ de Mars on July 17, when the National Guard followed orders to fire on a crowd of petitioners.

These events and debates, falling between the united Assembly's first vote by head, on July 4, 1789, and its last session, on September 30, 1791, shaped and consolidated deputy alignment throughout the National Assembly. No deputy in the fall of 1791 was politically in the same place he had occupied during the first sessions of the National Assembly, although he might have remained aligned stably relative to his colleagues. The problem for the historian is to fix in place the structure of alignment in the early sessions, so as to have a point of departure for alignment trajectories. In fact there is no way to trace the direction of alignment for every individual deputy. Even those who intervened frequently in debate did not speak about or publish their reactions to every event or issue, and many deputies never articulated their opinions at all. Furthermore, there is not even a sure way to know how many deputies were in attendance at the Assembly on a given day or how many resigned their posts. It does, however, seem to be the case that most blocs of deputies remained aligned in the same position relative to one another that they had established at the beginning of the Assembly: that is, for example, deputies on the right in the summer of 1789 remained on the right, unless they resigned, as the entire Assembly's agenda gradually moved to the left. To document this observation, we can begin with a look at the legislative minutes from sum-

6. Wick, *Conspiracy of Well-Intentioned Men,* 319.
7. Tackett, "Nobles and Third Estate," 294–96.

mer, 1789, to fall, 1791, for evidence about the number of deputies voting and the spread between majority and minority on roll calls.

Evidence from the minutes of the National Assembly on the number of deputies voting and on the breakdown of roll-call tallies does not show a linear progression toward increasing right-wing resignations and a shrinking group of voters more and more dominated by the left. There is, instead, considerable fluctuation in the number voting and the margin of victory. I have been able to locate seventeen tallies of roll-call votes taken during the life of the National Assembly (Table 21). Except for a partial list of names on a vote concerning rights of free blacks in the French colonies, there are no name lists for these roll calls, just a vote breakdown given in the *Archives parlementaires*. The total number of votes cast on different issues does not steadily decrease over time, nor is there a clear trend in the margins of victory issue by issue. Observers and historians have imposed a more ordered trajectory upon the National Assembly than that portrayed by the roll-call votes.

This is not to say that the political trajectory in the National Assembly was random. The tallies do give an accurate picture of which issues polarized the deputies and divided the Assembly most closely, with victory margins of less than 25 percent of the total votes cast. Yet care must be taken in interpreting this evidence. First, the tallies are not valid indicators of the total number of deputies in attendance at the Assembly at any given time. For example, considerable numbers of deputies resigned or at least asked for leave in the weeks following October 6, 1789, and yet the number voting on three different roll calls decreased only from 962 to 867 between September 21 and December. Another caution concerns the nature of the roll call as it was used in the National Assembly. Many of the roll calls listed in Table 21 were not substantive votes on issues, but procedural votes used as tactics to close debate, continue debate, or avoid a vote altogether. In other cases, the roll call was substantive, but on a relatively uncontroversial or uncontested issue tangential to the main conflictual issue. For example, the session of September 16, 1789, became very stormy over the issue of the succession in case of royal *défaillance*. The presiding officer proposed voting procedures that followed the rules established the previous July, with the Assembly to vote on the principles involved by sitting and standing, but to vote on *rédaction,* the actual formulation of the law, by roll call. Two voice votes were held on this proposal; the results

Table 21
Roll-Call Tallies, June 23, 1789, to September 24, 1791

Date	Issue	Left	Right	Not Cast	Total	Margin (% of Total)
1789						
June 23	Inviolability	493	34		527	87
July 8	Mandates	700	28		728	92
Sept. 10	Bicameralism	490	89	122	701	57
Sept. 11	Royal veto	673	325	11	1,009	35
Sept. 17	Succession	541	438		979	11
Sept. 21	Duration of veto	224	728	10	962	52
Nov. 2	Church property	568	346	40	954	23
Dec. 3	Active citizenship	428	439		867	1
1790						
April 12	State religion	495	400		895	11
April 29	President's oath	454	200	19	673	38
May 7	Royal authority	503	450		953	6
1791						
May 12	Colonies[a]	276	378		654	16
May 14	Colonies	354	488		842	16
June 18	La Rochefoucauld[b]	271	286		557	3
Aug. 25	Royal family's residence	267	180		447	20
Sept. 23	Colonies	307	191		498	23
Sept. 24	Colonies	389	276		665	17

[a] Vote totals are given in *Archives parlementaires,* XXVI (May 12, 1791), 17. The list of left-wing voters on pp. 25 and 26 includes 273 deputies' names, not 276.

[b] Cardinal de La Rochefoucauld had been accused by the district court of denying the powers of two parish vicars who had been elected. The vote in the Assembly was on the question of whether La Rochefoucauld should be accused of a violation of law. The vote was 286 "no" and 271 "yes." See *Archives parlementaires,* XXVII (June 18, 1791), 330.

were inconclusive. The president proposed a roll call, which the nobles and clergy opposed; the session was adjourned without one at the request of the curés. The next morning, September 17, a roll-call vote (no tallies given) produced the decision to vote by roll on royal inviolability and male heredity to the throne, traditional principles that had scarcely any opposition, and omitting altogether the centrally contested issue of *défaillance;* the results of *that* vote were 541 for royal inviolability and male succession and 438 against.[8]

On some of the most controversial issues, roll-call votes were never taken. There were none, for example, on the abolition of parlements (November 3, 1789), the Civil Constitution of the Clergy (November 26 and 27, 1790), or the decrees establishing qualifications for citizenship (October 20–22, 1789). The closest vote I was able to find did, in fact, concern citizenship, although not the fundamental constitutional articles that defined it. On December 3, 1789, the Assembly was debating articles on elections, and a voice vote was taken on whether a man could be granted active citizenship status if for two years running he paid a civic tribute that was equal to the amount of his tax. The proposal lost, and Alexandre de Lameth (consistent left), demanded a roll call. Despite opposition from the right, the roll call was held, but the proposal still lost by 11 votes, 439 against to 428 in favor.[9]

Bearing in mind these limitations on the use of vote tallies as evidence for ideologically based decisions, we can make some observations on the trajectories of deputy alignment in the aggregate. In the fall of 1789, the Assembly became much more evenly divided than it had been in its first two months. Margins of victory grew smaller after the vote on the royal veto on September 11. The left "won" more often than the right, with the exception of several votes during the complicated maneuvering on the question of rights of colonial deputies. The total number of deputies voting was highest in the opening months of the National Assembly, lowest in the summer of 1791; then it rose by more than 200 votes from its August low to the last tally recorded, on September 24. This is not conclusive evidence of mass disaffection and nonparticipation. The nature and number of resignations from the National Assembly are impossible to establish with cer-

---

8. *Archives parlementaires,* IX (September 16, 1789), 1–4, (September 17), 25.

9. *Ibid.,* X (December 3, 1789), 359.

tainty. Deputies took leaves of absence because of illness, to attend to their estates and personal business, to handle family emergencies, and for a host of other reasons, some of which were genuine and some of which masked their distress at the Assembly's conduct. Some of them returned, and some of them never did.

On July 12, 1791, a roll call of all deputies was held to determine the names of those absent; the roll call was submitted to the Committee on Verification (of deputies' credentials) and reported out to the Assembly on July 18, 1791. The list is printed in the *Archives parlementaires* and the *Procès-verbal,* and it was reprinted by Armand Brette in *Recueil de documents relatifs à la convocation des Etats généraux.*[10] The three versions are not identical, but among them they give a total of 128 names of absent deputies. I have used these names to form one alignment category, the resigning right, limited to the 51 deputies for whom I have no other evidence sufficient to classify them. The roll call of July 12 plus individual biographical information gives a total of 170 deputies who resigned, 55 others who were absent for long periods (probably for political reasons), 36 who died, and 1,057 who remained in the Assembly.

The uncertain nature of the information on resignations is compounded by a further political practice that developed during the National Assembly, that of attending sessions but refusing to participate in debate or to vote—a kind of silent protest bearing witness to one's opposition to the Assembly's declarations. This tactic was much publicized and is usually used to explain why the total number of votes cast on bills was often several hundred less than the number of deputies supposedly in attendance. A close reading of the minutes, however, shows that deputies did not always stick to their decisions not to participate. For example, ten deputies elected from the French colonies signed a letter to the president of the Assembly on May 16, 1791, declaring that they would "abstain from sessions" as a protest against the Assembly's legislation on the rights of men of color in the colonies. At least two of them did not honor their decision throughout the summer of 1791, although they did intervene in debates only on other unrelated issues. The deputy Louis de Curt asked to speak on July 15 on the inviolability of the king; he was not scheduled, and discussion was

10. *Ibid.,* XXVIII (July 18, 1791), 405–407; *Procès-verbal,* LXIII (July 18, 1791), unpaged following p. 42; Brette, *Recueil,* II, 571.

closed before he could speak, but his remarks were inserted in the minutes. Arthur Dillon spoke briefly on July 28 on uniforms for the National Guard.[11]

The somewhat shaky evidence on those who either resigned from the Assembly or sat silent in the meeting halls is the best available with which to trace the trajectories some of the individual deputies followed as the Constitution progressed and the Assembly's agenda became more and more radical. Nobles were the most likely to resign, but to resign later than the other two orders: 83 resigners were nobles (27 percent of all the noble deputies), 53 were clergy (16 percent of that category), and 31 were Third Estate (5 percent of that group). The largest number of clerical and Third Estate deputies who resigned did so after the October Days in 1789 and before the April 12 vote on a state religion. The single largest group of noble resigners left later, between April, 1790, and June, 1791.

Of the 170 deputies who resigned, only 2 sat with the consistent left: François Pierre Lasnier de Vaussenay and Jean Baptiste Viguier. Three were right center or contradictory; all the rest were right-wing. Six consistent-right deputies resigned, but none before April, 1790. The percentages suggest the political pressures on moderates: 6 percent of the consistent-right deputies resigned, 23 percent of the moderate-right, and 55 percent of the center-right. It is tempting to conclude that moderates like Mounier became quickly disillusioned in the National Assembly, whereas strict reactionaries from the beginning had never supported important parts of the Assembly's work, such as constitutional limits on royal prerogatives, the abolition of privilege, and legislation on religion, and therefore were more inclined to remain in the Assembly and oppose its agenda from within. Of the 81 center-right resigners, 30 left in the months between the October Days (after October 6, 1789), and April, 1790, and 20 more did so between April, 1790, and June, 1791, when the most divisive issues concerned legislation on the church. Such an interpretation of the high frequency of center-right departures is plausible, but not definitive. The center-right deputies, who signed but one protest and/or were perceived as right-wing only by a right-wing sympathizer, could really have been moderates by default, deputies whose acts of opposition were fewer than others'

11. *Archives parlementaires*, XXVI (May 16, 1791), 122, 123, XXVIII (annex to July 15, 1791), 348, 349, XXVIII (July 28, 1791), 730.

not because of different convictions, but because these men were no longer attending the Assembly.

Of all the 170 resigning deputies, 62 (36 percent) did sign at least one protest against the acts of the Assembly. Only 2 men who resigned before April, 1790, signed the April 19 protest against the Assembly's failure to declare Catholicism the state religion. Of the 170 resigners, 38 percent left the Assembly before April and their names do not appear on either the April 19, 1790, protest or the June 29, 1791, protest against the suspension of royal authority. Thirty-four percent had not left yet but did not sign either protest, and 28 percent signed one or both—an almost identical figure to the 29 percent of nonresigning deputies who signed one or both. Sixty-one percent of the resigners had gone before the August 31 and September 15, 1791, protests were published, and did not sign them; 31 percent were still available but did not sign, and only 8 percent did sign (compared with 26 percent signers among nonresigning deputies). These data suggest that leaving the Assembly early did not preclude signing a protest list, but that those who remained as deputies despite their opposition were more likely to sign. Differences between resigners and right-wing nonresigners were tactical rather than doctrinal. Motives can be determined only by individual biographical study, but the collective portrait does show that most extreme-right-wing deputies did not resign, but remained to oppose the left throughout the Assembly's existence.

As noted earlier, of the total of 170 deputies who resigned, I have classified a subgroup of 51 as the "resigning right." The names of these men (representing 4 percent of the Assembly) do not appear on any of the lists used to determine alignment, except for the fact of their resignation. By definition, they did not join clubs or sign protest lists. A disproportionate number of them were nobles: 15 out of 51, or 29 percent, compared with 23 percent nobles in the whole National Assembly. Another 13 (26 percent) were clergy, 22 (43 percent) were Third Estate, and 1 (2 percent) was elected after estates were abolished. Those of them who had previous political experience were most likely to have served in the royal bureaucracy; only 5 (including Mounier) had sat in a prerevolutionary political assembly.

The noble and clerical subdivisions of the resigning right were themselves divided at the beginning of the National Assembly: seven of the nobles and seven of the clergy were patriots; seven of the nobles and six of the clergy were conservatives (one noble member was not sitting in June).

About half of the nobles and clergy were early supporters of the Third Estate; about half were not. Thus the men of the resigning right do not appear to have shared many political convictions. Yet even had these 51 men all agreed and all remained in the National Assembly, they would not have been a large enough group to affect the outcome of many votes. Obviously, resignation from the National Assembly was not the only key to understanding how the left came to dominate the agenda. These resigners were probably moderates, divided at the beginning over the nature and task of the National Assembly, opposed to crowd interventions in legislative politics, yet not moved to join right-wing clubs or sign protests.

Deputies representing the two upper estates shifted their alignment in the aggregate to a greater extent than did members of the Third Estate. Several name lists can be used to trace their political trajectories between 1789 and 1791. If we classify clerical and noble deputies according to the choices they made in June, 1789, we can determine whether they changed alignment before the end of the National Assembly. The initial decisions taken by the nobility and clergy between June 17 and 27, 1789, about joining the National Assembly can be used to identify them as patriots. There were 155 patriot clergy who voted for common verification of credentials on June 19, 48 patriot nobles who answered the roll call in the Assembly on June 24, and 42 additional nobles classified with the patriots by James Murphy and Patrice Higonnet on the basis of additional acts and protests.[12] The other 192 nobles and 145 clergy I have labeled as conservatives in 1789 because they awaited the king's order before joining the National Assembly.

The first measure of opinion shifts among these four groups of deputies is resignation from the National Assembly. As we have seen, members of the first two estates were much more likely to leave the Assembly than were Third Estate deputies, only 5 percent of whom resigned. Conservative nobles were far and away the most likely group of deputies to resign;

12. Murphy and P. Higonnet, "Les Députés de la noblesse," 230–47; Murphy, P. Higonnet, and B. Higonnet, "Notes sur la composition de l'Assemblée constituante," 321–26. Murphy and Higonnet's criteria for liberal nobles, in addition to their names' appearing on the roll call of June 24, are as follows: voting for common verification of powers on May 6; signing a letter of secession presented to the nobles on June 25; protesting a May 28 or 29 decree within the Second Estate insisting on ancient precedence for the separation of orders and the vote by order; and having met with the Committee of Thirty.

46 percent of them did so, compared with 21 percent of the patriot nobles and 24 percent of the other liberal nobles. Meanwhile, 32 percent of the conservative clergy and 24 percent of the patriot clergy resigned. In other words, less than a quarter of the June, 1789, patriots in the two upper estates became sufficiently disturbed by the events of the Revolution to resign their seats, but their numbers were still much greater than those of resigners from the Third Estate.

The political careers of these four groups—patriot and conservative nobles and clergy—originated in distinct political backgrounds. The patriot nobles were highly public men, mostly urbanites, imbued with Enlightenment philosophy and devoted to the idea of limited constitutional monarchy. They were more than two and a half times as likely as their numbers would indicate to be authors of pamphlets and to come from the regions in the sample, particularly Paris and Dauphiné. *All* the noble deputies from Paris, in fact, were patriot supporters in June, 1789. Besides Dauphiné and Paris, most of the rest of them came from Touraine, Orléanais, Franche-Comté, and Ile-de-France. Among the forty-eight early noble joiners of the National Assembly, 29 percent had sat in prerevolutionary assemblies, three of them (6 percent) in the Assembly of Notables and seven (15 percent) in the Estates of Dauphiné. Six of the total of ninety patriot nobles had been in the Paris Parlement, and five in the royal court. Nobles of the sword were slightly more likely to be patriots than robe nobles (31 percent versus 25 percent). Finally, the forty-eight patriot nobles who joined the Third Estate before they were ordered to were much more likely than other nobles, clergy, or Third Estate deputies to be Freemasons (nineteen out of the forty-eight, or 40 percent). Only eight of the forty-two additional nobles whom Murphy and Higgonet classified as liberals had Masonic affiliations.

One hundred ninety-two deputies were conservative nobles in June, 1789. Their numbers were strong in the delegation from Normandy (eighteen) and Poitou (ten); otherwise there were some from every province except Touraine and the city of Paris. Twenty-three of them (12 percent, compared with 29 percent of the patriot nobles) had sat in Necker's provincial assemblies, and thirteen had served in the Assembly of Notables. In addition to these new assemblies, they had an institutional base in the court and the parlements, excluding the parlements of Paris and Dauphiné. The nature of the origin of their nobility did not differentiate conservative nobles: 59 percent of the sword nobles and 58 percent of the robe nobles were conservative in June, 1789.

Patriot clergy had very different backgrounds from conservative clergy. Twenty-one of the patriot clergy were nonauthors from Brittany, ten were authors from other sampled regions, and all the rest were proportionately distributed geographically. There was at least one member of the patriot clergy from every province except Aunis, Béarn, Foix, Roussillon, Alsace, and Corsica. Only 4 percent of them had sat in a political assembly before the Estates General. The humblest and least-privileged portion of the clergy, attuned to the daily lives of their parishioners, these parish priests were quite naturally likely to sympathize with demands for change. In two articles published in the 1950s, M. G. Hutt argued that the differences separating curés from the upper clergy were not extreme. He found that the curés were not fully in agreement with positions taken by the Third Estate, such as the vote by head, and were not necessarily immediately aware of the significance of the June 17 decision to declare the National Assembly.[13] Nonetheless, no matter how carefully nuanced their views were, the lower clergy did provide 85 percent of the patriot clergy who joined the Third Estate, and without their numbers it is unlikely that the supporters of the National Assembly could have stood up successfully to the king on June 23. Beginning May 8, radical leaders of the curés had organized evening caucuses to ensure that habits of deference toward church prelates did not result in clerical support for an aristocratic upper house in the new legislature.[14] Regardless of whether these patriot clergy were ignorant, intimidated, or indeed enthusiastic supporters of the patriot program, their collective action after June 17 was critical to the survival of the National Assembly.

More than half of the 145 conservative clergy had higher clerical rank than that of curé: 29 percent were upper clergy, 25 percent middle clergy, and 44 percent lower clergy. Conservatives were led by 42 of the highest officers of the church, such as Archbishop de Juigné in Paris—men who recognized how important a bulwark the Catholic church was to the legiti-

13. M. G. Hutt, "Role of the Curés in the Estates-General," 190–220, and "Curés and the Third Estate," 74–92.

14. Ruth F. Necheles, "The Curés in the Estates-General of 1789," *Journal of Modern History,* XLVI (1974), 433.

macy of the monarchy, and who had a stake in retaining the structures and political independence of the three orders. The conservative clergymen were somewhat overrepresented among the authors in the sample. They were also overrepresented among the Normandy delegation (13, compared with 5 patriots), Alsace (7, and no patriots), and Paris (10 conservative clergy and only 1 patriot). Only two were Bretons. As for experience, 22 percent of the conservative clergy had sat in a political assembly, compared with only 4 percent of the patriots; 11 conservatives had sat in provincial assemblies, 10 in provincial estates, 9 in the Assembly of Notables, and 2 in departmental assemblies. These princes of the church had been actively involved to a much greater degree than the curés in assemblies where members thrashed out the issues that produced the call for the Estates.

The institutions of the Old Regime contained nobles and clergy with coherent political beliefs—not necessarily formal ideologies, but convictions related to their station and career—and provincial politics determined which men expressing which beliefs would be preferred when delegates of the two upper estates chose their deputies. After the beginning of the National Assembly, these men made different political choices. Those who were initially conservative tended to remain conservative and sit on the right. Some of the patriot clergy of 1789 moved right. Patriot nobles became divided, with more than half of them remaining on the left. Protest signatures and evidence on resignations make it possible to determine, broadly, what issues disaffected those members of the first two estates whose alignment shifted between 1789 to 1791.

The data (Table 22) show, first of all, that both patriot nobles and clergy did not move overwhelmingly to the right by 1791. All three patriot groups (including the Murphy/Higonnet group) were less likely to be right-wing than were the initial conservatives. Conservatives, however, were even less likely to move leftward: only 8 percent of the conservative clergy ended up on the left, and only 1.5 percent of the conservative nobles. The patriots became more divided, especially the patriot clergy, 10 percent of whom moved to the far right by 1791, when 7 percent were consistent left; over half of them were center right or moderate right. Patriot nobles, especially the group who had joined the National Assembly by June 24, were less frequently on the right than the patriot clergy, although they were somewhat more likely to resign. One-fourth of them were classified ministerial left, supporters of a strong but constitutionally limited monar-

Table 22
June, 1789, Alignment of Deputies Relative to 1791 Alignment

	June, 1789						
	Patriot Clergy (N = 155)	Patriot Noble (N = 48)	Other Liberal (N = 42)	Conservative Clergy (N = 145)	Conservative Noble (N = 192)	Third Estate (N = 605)	Not Yet Deputy (N = 131)
1791 (%)							
Conservative right	10	2	2	20	23	1	6
Moderate right	32	17	31	50	44	10	24
Center right	20	17	14	11	21	6	6
Resigning right	4	10	5	4	4	4	1
Right center	3	2	0	1	0	1	1
Contradictory	4	0	0	2	3	4	5
Unclassifiable	10	6	5	4	4	20	15
Ministerial left	7	25	26	5	1	22	9
Shifting left	3	19	12	1	0	21	21
Consistent left	7	2	5	2	1	12	12
Total	100	100	100	100	100	100	100

chy; 19 percent shifted from Jacobins to Feuillants in 1791. The 42 additional liberal nobles from June, 1789, were more likely to move to the right; 26 percent of them, however, were ministerials.

These data suggest that patriot clergy were the most affected by events during the life of the National Assembly. They ended up with more than two-thirds of their number on the right (although not the extreme right), 16 percent in the center, and 17 percent on the left. Patriot nobles included few consistent-left and few consistent-right adherents; most were moderates. Nearly half (46 percent) remained on the left, 36 percent moved right, and 8 percent were in the center.

Signatures on the four protest lists may be used to determine what disaffected these members of the first two estates. Nearly two-thirds (64 percent) of the conservative clergy from 1789 signed the April 19 protest against the Assembly for its failure to declare a state religion; less than half (48 percent) of the conservative nobles signed it. In sharp contrast, 39 percent of the patriot clergy signed it, compared with 6 percent of the patriot nobles. That is a sizable proportion of the patriot clergy, a key group of initial supporters of Third Estate patriots in June, 1789. They were, nonetheless, much less likely to sign than the initially conservative clergy.

The two protests of the summer of 1791 against the Assembly's articles on executive authority similarly exhibit the least disaffection on the part of 1789 patriot nobles, only 17 percent of whom signed one or both. Among the patriot clergy, 27 percent signed—still a small proportion compared with 48 percent of conservative nobles and 51 percent of conservative clergy. Conservative clergy were the most likely of the four groups to sign all four protests.

The patriot nobles were the least likely to swing to the right during the course of the National Assembly, to the extent that we can determine their allegiances from protest lists. They were very significant contributors to the majority that produced the Constitution, and as will be seen in chapter 5, they held key leadership positions in the National Assembly out of proportion to their numbers. The patriot clergy were more likely to be disaffected than were patriot nobles, particularly by voting outcomes on religious issues. Although more than half of the patriot clergy did not sign any protest, a sizable minority of 39 percent did sign the protest on state religion, indicating a strong inclination to defend traditional religion even while voting with the left on other issues. Nobles and clergy who were conservative in May and June, 1789, contributed most of the protest-list signatures; they began on the right and remained on the right throughout the Assembly, if they did not resign early.

The Civil Constitution of the Clergy was a bitter experience for most of the clerical deputies, and the oath requirement put considerable pressure on them at the end of 1790. Of the 99 clerical deputies who took the oath, only 2 resigned, and 6 had lengthy absences (5 of the 99 died). Eighteen clerical deputies refused to take the oath at all; 11 of them resigned. In contrast, only 7 of the 142 deputies who retracted their oaths resigned. The oath requirement in and of itself does not appear to have been closely connected to the decision about whether a clerical deputy should resign. The oath, after all, concerned his functions as a priest, not as a deputy. The Assembly's refusal to declare Catholicism the state religion seems to have propelled more lower clergy into resigning than did the oath requirement; of the 34 resigners out of a total of 219 lower clergy, 19 left before April, 1790, another 8 during the peak of controversy over debates on the oath, and 7 more in the summer of 1791. Eleven of 50 upper clergy and 8 of 63 middle clergy left the National Assembly; there was no particular pattern to the timing of their resignations.

It is very difficult to determine opinion shifts for Third Estate deputies between the spring of 1789 and the fall of 1791. Although 90 Third Estate deputies voted on June 17, 1789, against the motion to declare the National Assembly, the list of all their names does not survive. We do know that Malouet, Mounier, Pison du Galland, Tronchet, Target, and Du Pont de Nemours were among them. Of these six deputies, Mounier was the only one who resigned his seat; he is classified as "resigning right" because he left the Assembly right after the October Days in 1789, signed no protests, and joined no clubs. Malouet and Pison du Galland are each moderate right; Tronchet and Target are ministerial left. Du Pont de Nemours is classified in the center on the alignment scale; the evidence used for his alignment is contradictory. These six men—well-known, active members of the Assembly in its opening months—all supported a constitutional monarchy with strong executive authority for the king and his ministers. They varied individually in their reactions to left-wing victories on constitutional questions and to interventions by Paris crowds in the fate of the Assembly. Their individual decisions put their names on different lists that I have used to classify deputies. Enough is known about them to conclude that they were not adherents of the extreme right, but moderates who lost the struggle to control the constitutional agenda. For the Third Estate in general, however, there is no measure from June, 1789, comparable to those for clergy and nobles that may be used to fix alignment and provide a benchmark for measuring political trajectories.

Several additional lists of deputies in various categories can help to determine opinion shifts and to test the validity of the alignment scale. In addition to the July, 1791, list of absent deputies, one roll call in the minutes of the National Assembly includes a partial listing of names that enables us to compare the alignment on this vote with the alignment scale. On March 8, 1790, the Assembly had given French colonies the right to take the initiative in drafting their own constitutions, but the deputies in Paris had never resolved the issue of who could participate in colonial assemblies. The debate on May 12, 1791, concerned whether or not to grant active citizenship to free black men in the colonies. The May 12 vote was actually procedural: 378 deputies favored the right-wing position, to continue debate on the bill as it had been presented by the committee on the Constitution; 276 favored the left-wing position, to oppose further discussion.[15] The issue divided some famous deputies usually placed on the left: Barnave, for example, voted with the right, to continue deliberations, while Roederer voted with the left, to stop discussion. Nonetheless, a cross-tabulation of all the names with the alignment scale indicates that 74 percent of those voting to stop debate were on the left, 20 percent were in the center, and 6 percent were on the right (Table 23).

The issue was bitterly fought in debates on May 14 and 15, and finally resulted in one of the Assembly's rare and noteworthy compromises—that free black men would be admitted to colonial assemblies if they met other property qualifications for citizenship. Right-wing deputies argued that granting active citizenship to blacks would destabilize the colonies, possibly produce revolts, and allow the English to intervene and even seize French colonies. One fervent right-wing deputy, the abbé Jean Siffrein Maury, feared "that these men of color, who would numerically dominate all elective assemblies once you have recognized them as active citizens,

---

15. *Archives parlementaires*, XXVI (May 12, 1791), 25, 26. There is a discrepancy between the vote count of 276 given *ibid.*, 17, and the 274 names listed (273 of which are names of deputies).

Table 23
Supporters of Active Citizenship for Colonial Blacks, May 12, 1791

Alignment	N 1,318	Alignment Category[a] (N = 273)		% of 273 Voters Taking Left Position[b]
		f	%	
Consistent right	108	1	0.9	0.4
Moderate right	315	5	2	2
Center right	147	8	3	3
Resigning right	51	2	4	1
Right center	13	2	15	0.7
Contradictory	44	6	14	2
Unclassifiable	173	46	27	17
Ministerial left	184	68	37	25
Shifting left	176	83	47	30
Consistent left	107	52	49	19

[a]Percent of each alignment category voting to stop deliberations on May 12, 1791. This was the left-wing position, supporting active citizenship for free blacks in the colonies.

[b]Alignment as a percentage of all deputies voting to stop deliberations. The vote total given on p. 17 in the minutes of May 12, 1791, differs, giving 276 votes to stop deliberations.

Source: *Archives parlementaires*, XXVI (May 12, 1791), 25, 26.

will unceasingly be the masters of your colonies, and they will soon have all the whites at their mercy." [16]

On May 13, the right succeeded in getting the Assembly close to a vote, but many left-wing deputies got up to leave when there were motions to adjourn. The presiding officer, Antoine Balthazar Joseph d'André, stood up to signal adjournment; the right protested; and the deputies exited in great disorder. The next day a deputation of persons of color from the colonies was, after objection, granted permission to enter the Assembly. Their spokesman asserted the rights of free black proprietors and stated that blacks comprised most of the police forces in the colonies. The Assembly then held another roll-call vote, deciding it would deliberate on

16. *Ibid.* (May 13, 1791), 55.

an article of the law on the colonies that would obligate colonial assemblies to advise the French legislature before it voted on free men of color. On May 16, by voice vote, the Assembly decided it would not deliberate on the political status of colonial blacks without first hearing the will of colonial assemblies, but it did decree that men of color born of a free mother and father would be admitted to colonial assemblies if they had other qualifications. The right wing claimed that the result of the voice vote was inconclusive and demanded a roll call, but the Assembly refused.[17]

As Table 23 makes clear, the deputies who supported the rights of free blacks in the colonies on the May 12 roll call were predominantly leftists. In fact, those men farthest to the left were the most likely to vote with the left on this issue, and the deputies farthest to the right the least likely. Lacking the names of the voters on the opposing side, we cannot correlate them statistically with the alignment scale. The colonial issue doubtless split off some deputies normally supporting the left wing. Of the total of 467 men on the left, 57 percent did not vote to stop discussion on May 12 (that is, did not take the leftist position), but without a full list of all deputies voting, there is no way to determine whether they abstained, were absent, or supported the right-wing position (to continue debate). Nonetheless, this issue did not redraw the lines of allegiance within the whole Assembly. Only 16 deputies, less than 3 percent of the total right, were supporters of colonial blacks, compared with 203 left-wing deputies, 43 percent of the total left.

Another approach to the puzzle of alignment trajectories in the National Assembly is to disassemble the categories of men in the center, an important group because neither the right nor the left could count on a reliable majority to win the vote on every issue. Of the total of 1,318 deputies, I have labeled 173 "unclassifiable" because their names do not appear on any of the lists I used to determine alignment. Large enough in number to make a difference on some of the closer vote tallies, this group cannot be discounted as insignificant in the politics of the National Assembly. There are several possible ways to characterize its members. They may have been quiet and unassertive men, fundamentally followers, who avoided clubs, protests, and other allegiances that would mark their political position.

17. *Ibid.* (May 13, 14, 1791), 41–75, (May 16, 1791), 97.

Some of them were curés who were not conservative and yet did not like the Assembly's decrees on clerical issues. Finally, as the attitudinal evidence from unclassifiable authors suggests, these deputies may have been ideologically centrist, constitutional monarchists inclined to create a constitution that left the king in a stronger executive position than the one defined by Chapter II of the Constitution of 1791.[18]

Three of the unclassifiable deputies (Charles Alexandre d'Arberg, Pierre Maujean, and Guillaume Florentin de Salm-Salm) had their elections nullified and thus never sat in the Assembly. On July 20, 1789, the Assembly decided that Arberg, who was bishop of Ypres, and Salm-Salm, bishop of Tournay, ought not to have been elected because they were foreigners.[19] Maujean, from Metz, supposedly a member of the Third Estate, had his election declared null on July 11, 1789, because he was a noble.[20] We may safely conclude that these three men's absence did not affect the pattern of political alignment in the National Assembly.

As for the unclassifiable deputies who did take their seats in the Assembly, the best evidence of their general alignment comes from the debates and actions surrounding the issues of the clerical oath and the colonies. For example, five unclassifiable deputies were curés who indicated their agreement with Armand Gaston Camus on November 27, 1790: Guy Boulliotte, Jean Louis Gouttes, Jacques Louis Guino, Jacques Arnaud de Labat, and René Le Cesve. In a speech to the Assembly, Camus criticized the "Exposition" of thirty bishops against the requirement of a clerical oath and accused them of causing disobedience and creating a schism in the Assembly.[21] The five unclassifiable curés who agreed with him were supporting the left-wing position on the oath. A dozen more unclassifiable deputies were members of the clergy who took the clerical oath and did not

18. Robert Howell Griffiths makes a case for the ideological coherence of the center from August and September, 1789, onward for a decade until the advent of Napoleon. However, as I demonstrate below, the deputies he lists by name are almost all classified with the right wing according to my measures. Only one deputy on his list is not—Faydel, whom I categorize as "contradictory." See Robert Howell Griffiths, *Le Centre perdu: Malouet et les "monarchiens" dans la Révolution française* (Grenoble, 1988), 10–16, 67, and chap. 5.

19. See Brette, *Recueil,* I, 42, for Arberg, and I, 304, for Salm-Salm.

20. *Ibid.,* 235.

21. *Archives parlementaires,* XXI (December 6, 1790), 103.

retract it. Finally, the names of forty-six unclassifiable deputies appear on the May 12 roll-call list of those who took the left-wing position on the colonies. If all these indications are accepted as solid evidence of alignment, then sixty-three unclassifiable deputies (36 percent) became willing to support the left, at least by late 1790. For the remaining two-thirds, there is simply no collectively applicable evidence on which to assign a classification.

In his study of Malouet and his center party, Robert Griffiths identified a central committee of a "party" of deputies who wanted to strengthen the king's executive role in the new constitution. He called these the key group in the political center. They came together during debate on the Declaration of the Rights of Man and were defeated politically within the National Assembly by mid-September. His book gives the names of twenty deputies in this central committee.[22] When I matched these names with my alignment classifications, I found that nineteen of the twenty were on the right and only one, Faydel, was really in the center; he was classified as contradictory. Seven were consistent right, eight were moderate right, two were center right, and two more were moderate right. Griffiths' research does illuminate partisan political practices within the National Assembly, and indicates that those deputies who supported the royal veto and bicameralism were firmly on the right by 1790.

Lists of deputies who were probably Freemasons and membership lists for six of the political clubs frequented by deputies yielded some additional evidence on alignment trajectories. Two hundred forty-four deputies may have been Freemasons. The idea that the Revolution was produced by a Masonic plot was first published in 1798 in Hamburg in a volume purporting to be a history of Jacobinism written by a conservative Catholic, the abbé Augustin Barruel.[23] Current interpretations of the political impact of Freemasons no longer consider them conspirators, but rather procreators of a new style of social conduct labeled "democratic sociability." Increasing membership in Masonic lodges after 1750 helped create and spread new values of advancement through merit, rather than by birth, and new rela-

---

22. Griffiths, *Le Centre perdu*, 67.

23. Augustin Barruel, *Mémoires pour servir à l'histoire du Jacobinisme* (Hamburg, 1798). See also Jacques Lemaire, *Les Origines françaises de l'antimaçonnisme: 1744–1797* (Brussels, 1985), esp. Introduction and chap. 3.

tionships of equality, rather than deference. The new standards fostered a cultural mentality hospitable to revolutionary ideas.[24] Data in chapter 3 indicated that deputies with Masonic affiliation were found in every alignment category from far right to far left, although they were somewhat overrepresented among the shifting left. This finding suggests a closer look at the political trajectories of deputies who were Freemasons.

As we have seen, Freemasons were disproportionately likely to be patriot nobles. Twenty-four percent of the deputies who were Masons became members of moderate and right-wing clubs, particularly the Société de 1789, with twenty-three Masonic members out of fifty-three, and the Club de Valois, with twenty-five out of sixty-one. Similarly, 27 percent of the Freemason deputies were Jacobins, and 30 percent of all the Jacobin deputies were probably Freemasons. Finally, 39 percent of the Freemason deputies joined the Feuillants in the summer of 1791. These data together fail to support any notion of revolutionary conspiracy among Freemasons. They were somewhat disproportionately likely to support liberal positions in 1789 and later to be Jacobins, but there is no overwhelming tendency for them to be on the left.

Political clubs frequented by deputies include the Society of Thirty, the Club de Valois, the Société de 1789, the Club Monarchique, the Jacobin Club, and the Club des Feuillants. The Society of Thirty began to meet regularly at the home of Adrien Du Port, councillor in the Paris Parlement, in November, 1788. Its reformist members, mostly Paris nobles, campaigned as leaders of the patriot party in Paris to secure doubled representation of the Third Estate, to influence elections to the Estates General, and to structure that body's agenda. These liberals supported the vote by head, the concept of the nation as a society of property-owning citizens, the transformation of the Estates General into a constituent assembly, the abolition of privilege, and a monarchy anchored in a legislature representing the national will.[25] Most of the members of the Society of Thirty joined the Breton Club in the spring of 1789. Daniel Wick has found some circumstantial evidence that the original group continued to meet until 1791, but he concluded that the society probably dissolved into factions in the National Assembly after the fall of 1789.

24. Halévi, *Les Loges maçonniques*, 9–16.
25. Wick, *Conspiracy of Well-Intentioned Men*, 251–70.

The Club de Valois, the first club to be located in the Palais Royal, was founded February 11, 1789, by the abbé Sieyès and twenty-five nobles and upper-bourgeois gentlemen. Its almanac of 1790 lists 616 members. The club reflected the shift in the early months of the Revolution from literary societies to political clubs. Its members subscribed to the philosophic and scientific canon of the high Enlightenment. Politically, they tended to be constitutional monarchists who advocated a strong executive role for king and ministers. The club dissolved in 1791; according to Augustin Challamel, many of its members moved to the right and joined the Club Monarchique; others became Jacobins or Feuillants.[26]

The Société de 1789 was established in January, 1790, by Lafayette, Marie Jean Condorcet, and other moderates who were beginning to feel excluded from the power center in the Jacobin Club, although they were not regarded as hostile to the Jacobins. Soon the Society had 413 members and began publishing a journal. In summer, 1790, its members began to quarrel over issues involving political stability, particularly the war-making powers of the monarch. Those members in favor of limiting the king's powers returned to the Jacobins, whereas those inclined toward the right who wanted a stronger monarchy joined the new Club Monarchique, founded in late 1790. Remaining moderates joined the Feuillants, who split off from the Jacobins in the summer of 1791.[27]

The Club Monarchique was a debating society with antecedents in meetings held ever since 1787 by certain nobles, parlementary magistrates, church leaders, and electors of Paris to discuss the political issues of the day. Its immediate forerunner was Malouet's Club des Impartiaux, which took credit for the election of the abbé François Xavier de Montesquiou to the presidency of the National Assembly on January 2, 1790. Stanislas Marie Adélaïde Clermont-Tonnerre and other nobles and members of the upper clergy produced a membership list in December, 1790, for the Club Monarchique. Its members were ardently royalist. In the paternalistic monarchical tradition, they organized distributions of food and clothing to the

26. Challamel, Les Clubs contre-révolutionnaires, 31–35.

27. Keith M. Baker, "Politics and Social Science in Eighteenth Century France: The 'Société de 1789,'" in French Government and Society, 1500–1850, ed. J. F. Bosher (London, 1973), 208–50; Charles Kuhlmann, "Relation of the Jacobins to the Army and Lafayette," University Studies (University of Nebraska), VI (1906), 153–92.

poor in order to capture their support and attempt to control their political mobilization.[28]

The most famous revolutionary club was popularly known as the Jacobin Club; its official name, adopted in January, 1790, was Société des Amis de la Constitution. Its origins have been traced to the Breton Club, the name given to those who joined the Breton deputation's meetings, begun in April, 1789, at Versailles before the opening of the Estates General and used to coordinate the actions of the Breton delegation. By the time the National Assembly was declared, more than two hundred deputies were meeting with the Breton Club.[29] After the Assembly transferred to Paris in October, that group disbanded, but some of its members began meeting regularly in November at a Jacobin convent hall. In the summer of 1791, the Feuillant Club was formed by moderate members of the Jacobins, who walked out rather than accept a petition asking that Louis XVI be replaced.

Historians have pointed to movement of members among these clubs as evidence of the leftward shift in revolutionary politics in the years before the overthrow of the monarchy. My evidence shows that these alignment shifts were complex and multidirectional, not linear and toward the left.

Twenty-seven future deputies had been meeting with the Society of Thirty in Paris before their election and during the spring of 1789. Thirteen of these men were also Freemasons; fourteen were not.[30] Nineteen were elected as deputies to the nobility, six to the Third Estate, and two as clergy. Following them through to the alignment evidence for 1791, I found the nobles the most fragmented, with five on the right, including three who were also Freemasons, one in the center (a Freemason), and thirteen on the left (six Freemasons). Clermont-Tonnerre, a Freemason, had become a founder of the Club Monarchique; he is classified as moderate right along with d'Eprémesnil, also a Freemason, and La Rochefoucauld. Anne Charles Sigismond de Montmorency-Luxembourg is center right, Trophime Gérard Lally-Tolendal (Freemason) had resigned, and Marie

28. Malouet, *Mémoires,* II, 47; Challamel, *Les Clubs contre-révolutionnaires,* 128–275.

29. Kuhlmann, "Influence of the Breton Deputation," 237. The major recent study is Michael L. Kennedy, *The Jacobin Clubs in the French Revolution: The First Years* (Princeton, 1982).

30. Daniel Wick, in *Conspiracy of Well-Intentioned Men,* 354, mistakenly includes Aumont of Boulogne as a deputy; he was not.

Charles César de Fay de La Tour Maubourg (Freemason) is unclassifiable because his name appears on none of the lists used. Six noble members of the Committee of Thirty became members of the ministerial left: Armand Louis de Gontaut Biron Lauzun, Boniface Louis André Castellane, de Stutt de Tracy (Freemason), Alexandre Frédéric François de La Rochefoucauld Liancourt, Louis Joseph Amable d'Albert de Luynes, and Fréteau de Saint-Just. Six more had joined the Jacobins and then switched to the Feuillants, thus qualifying as shifting left: Armand Désiré d'Aiguillon (Freemason), Du Port, Marie Joseph Du Motier de Lafayette (Freemason), Alexandre Lameth (Freemason), Charles Lameth, and Louis Marie de Noailles (Free-mason). Lepeletier de Saint-Fargeau, a Freemason, is classified consistent left. The six Third Estate deputies who were members of the Committee of Thirty ended up with two centrists, both contradictory (Du Pont de Nemours and François Louis Jean Joseph de Laborde de Méréville, a Free-mason), and four deputies on the left: Target became ministerial left, Sieyès shifting left, and both Mirabeau (a Freemason) and Pierre Louis Roederer consistent left. The two deputies for the clergy were Claude Maurice de Talleyrand-Périgord, a Freemason who became ministerial left, and Perro-tin de Barmond, moderate right.

This group of twenty-seven deputies were activists and leaders in the Assembly. All of them were among the earliest liberals whose affiliations we can document (seven months before the National Assembly), and two-thirds of them remained on the left. As early activists, they were very centrally involved in the Assembly's factional politics, in which the remain-ing third of them gravitated to the right and center. Within a small and intimate circle of friends like the Society of Thirty, the association of estate and alignment was considerably weakened. By 1791 a total of six (five nobles, one clergy) were on the right, three in the center (one noble and two Third Estate), and eighteen on the left (thirteen nobles, four Third Estate, and one clergy). The Third Estate and clergy members did later sit in the center or on the left, as we would expect, but almost three-quarters of the nobles in the society sat on the left. Masonic affiliation did not impel them toward the left; proportionately more Masonic nobles were on the right (three out of five) than on the left (six out of thirteen).

Of the 1,318 deputies, 211 (16 percent) were members of one or more of the three moderate to right-wing clubs, the Club de Valois, the Société de 1789, and the Club Monarchique. Only four deputies belonged at one time or another to all three, but 52 percent of the deputies in the Club de Valois, 38 percent of those in the Société de 1789, and 15 percent of those in the Club Monarchique were also members of one or both of the other two. Challamel's conclusion is confirmed for the Club de Valois: its membership split left and right after the first revolutionary year, with 23 percent of its deputy members on the 1790 list for the Société de 1789 and 23 percent on the list for the Club Monarchique. Seventy-five percent were never Jacobins.

The Société de 1789 had only six overlapping deputy members with the Club Monarchique; fourteen of its members had belonged to the Club de Valois. Because some well-known Jacobin leaders of the left—for example, Le Chapelier and Roederer—were members, the Société is often assumed to have had considerable overlapping membership with the Jacobins. Actually, only 14 percent of its fifty-three deputy members ever joined the Jacobins.

The Club Monarchique had the largest number of deputy members, 135, of whom only 25 belonged also to another club (14 to the Club de Valois). Ninety percent were never Jacobins. The Club Monarchique, founded in opposition to constitutional articles on executive power written in 1789 and also as a counterweight to Jacobin influence in 1790, stood farthest to the right of the three moderate to right-wing clubs and had the fewest multiple members.

Overlapping or sequential club memberships did not reflect alignment shifts for very many deputies. Relatively few deputies were members of more than one, and only the members of the Club de Valois became polarized after a year in existence, with nearly a quarter of the members moving left into the Société de 1789 and a quarter moving right into the Club Monarchique. Although all of these clubs functioned to debate and discuss issues before the National Assembly, they did not become nuclei of stable factions. Without names on roll calls, we cannot determine how often deputies in the same club voted together. We do know that not many deputies moved from one club to another, with the notable and significant exception of the Jacobin rupture in July, 1791.

I have used the membership lists for the Jacobin Club and the Feuillant Society to construct the two farthest-left alignment categories, labeled "shifting left" and "consistent left." Since the membership lists for the other three clubs are not part of the data for the alignment scale, they may be compared with it to generate further evidence on shifting alignment.

Of the sixty-one deputies whose names appear on the 1790 membership list for the Club de Valois, 39 percent are classified as right-wing and 53 percent as left-wing, with 8 percent considered unclassified. By my measures, more of this club's members had moved toward the moderate left by 1790 than toward the right. Seventeen of them (28 percent) were "ministerial left," and fifteen (25 percent) were "shifting left." These men, aptly described as constitutional monarchists, were more nearly split between left and right in 1791 than were the other two clubs.

Of the 135 deputies listed by the Club Monarchique in December, 1790, as members, 67 (54 percent) were classifiable as right-wing on the alignment scale. Only 3 were consistent left and 9 shifting left—a total of 9 percent left. The largest group of deputy members was moderate right.

Finally, the Société de 1789 could be considered a moderate-left club, judging by its deputy members, of whom 11 percent were classified as right-wing, 7 percent as centrists (contradictory evidence), 53 percent as ministerials, 21 percent as shifting left, and 8 percent as consistent left.

In summary, the deputies in the Société de 1789 were mostly on the moderate left, with only four of them moving farther left by remaining in the Jacobins in the summer of 1791. Six deputies ended up on the right; the majority remained moderate left. The farthest-right of the three clubs was the Club Monarchique, only 12 of whose 135 members were on the left by 1791. Again, these deputies tended not to realign; most of them stayed on the right. The Club de Valois was the most polarized of the three, its deputy members being divided fairly evenly between left and right.

These cross-tabulations of club members tend to confirm the conclusion that deputies who did not resign from the National Assembly remained where they began, whether left or right. Only a relative handful became markedly more radical or more conservative during the months that the Assembly was in session. This evidence from club membership must be qualified as tentative and suggestive, not definitive. There is no reliable way to fix the alignment of a club at any point in time, nor can we be certain that its members shared a coherent set of beliefs that could be placed on a left-to-right continuum. However, since the membership lists date from 1790, club membership offers an approximate standard of comparison with 1791 measures based on protest lists and Feuillant Club membership lists, used to construct the categories of right and left. By this standard, few deputies realigned drastically.

All of these clubs had subscriptions to political journals, and their members tried not only to keep informed of debate in the National Assembly but also to influence its outcome. Given the fact that relatively few of their members were also members of the Jacobin Club, the more moderate clubs may well have acted as a counterweight to the Jacobin influence in the Assembly. Malouet's *mémoires* confirm this tactic for the Club des Impartiaux. Another deputy, Lally-Tolendal, justified his resignation from the Assembly in late fall, 1789, on the grounds that the Assembly had become a creation of the Jacobins, that a "clubocracy" ruled France, and that he could not remain a deputy and continue to engage in debate without implying a freedom of opinion that did not exist.[31] To these observers, at least, clubs were acting as pressure groups to mold and control deputies' political opinions and their votes. This is doubtless too one-sided a view of influence; deputies tended to congregate with their like-minded colleagues both within and outside of the Assembly. Most of the members of these clubs were not Jacobins, nor were many of them extremely far to the right or to the left. Most of them did not appear to change their relative alignment between 1789 and 1791.

The final summer of the National Assembly was marred by the king's flight to Varennes and the violence on the Champ de Mars, two major crises that undermined the legitimacy of the new constitutional monarchy. The nearly completed Constitution of 1791 was based on the premise that the king would be transformed into the legally constituted chief representative of a nation of citizens, a premise that the actions of Louis XVI had called into question repeatedly since 1789. Furthermore, the nation of citizens had restricted the king's free will on at least two dramatic occasions. On October 6, 1789, Louis XVI had been carried to Paris against his own preferences, and in April, 1791, he had been prevented by a Paris crowd from going to Saint-Cloud for Easter. He had lost whatever trust and respect he had once enjoyed from his subjects. Nonetheless, he was the only monarch of the constitutional monarchy; for the deputies, his flight was a matter of

31. Trophime Gérard Lally-Tolendal, *Lettre écrite au très-honorable Edmund Burke, membre du Parlement d'Angleterre* (Geneva, 1791), 10.

the utmost gravity and a profound dilemma.[32] Their most immediately pressing question was practical: who would wield executive power?

On June 21 at nine in the morning, Alexandre de Beauharnais, then serving as president of the National Assembly, informed the deputies of the royal family's flight. His words were met by a "profound silence," followed by a decree ordering the arrest of anyone leaving the kingdom. The Assembly went into closed and permanent session (without adjournment and with gallery observers prohibited) and decreed that Louis' royal authority was provisionally suspended; ministers would carry out executive responsibilities overseen by committees of the National Assembly. On the twenty-sixth the deputies named commissioners to take the depositions of the king and queen, who had been apprehended and returned to Paris.[33]

This event and its aftermath brought about an irredeemable split between the National Assembly and the radicals of Paris, tested the unity of the leftwing constitutionalists in the Assembly, and split the Jacobin Club. The king's flight began after midnight the night of June 20–21 and became known in the city the next morning. Fearing riot and even civil war, the Paris city government moved to reassure people and maintain order. The Jacobins, meeting on that same day, named commissioners to attend sessions of the National Assembly, the Department of Paris, and the General Council of the Commune and return to the Jacobins with hourly reports.[34]

That night the royal family was recognized and apprehended at Varennes, and early on the morning of the twenty-second they began the journey back to Paris. For the next three weeks feelings ran high. Fear of foreign intervention and war, and mounting enthusiasm for republicanism, made a backdrop of tension for deputies wrestling with what to do about the king and the Constitution. On July 15 the National Assembly decreed that the king's flight did not represent a forfeiture of the crown, although

32. J. M. Thompson, in his *French Revolution,* 209, interprets this effect differently. Thompson grants that the political crisis was extreme but maintains that the "constitutional change . . . was almost insignificant." He reasons that for a long while the king had not been exercising real executive power. My data show that the king's attempted flight and its aftermath fractured the fragile unity in the Assembly as the Constitution neared completion.

33. *Archives parlementaires,* XXVII (June 21, 1791), 358, (June 25, 26, 1791), 520–44.

34. Printed address by P. Couedic to the Jacobin Club, following the minutes of July 3, 1791, in Aulard, *La Société des Jacobins,* II, 580.

Louis XVI could not be restored to his full executive authority until the Constitution was completed and he had freely ratified it. The temporary suspension of June 26 was continued until the king had given this endorsement. On July 16, a second decree reiterated that the Constitution would be submitted to the king; if he rejected it, the deputies would decide at that time what to do.

Meanwhile, the Paris crowds and their leaders had become more and more ready to acknowledge their influence and their sense that a king who deserted his people was hardly necessary even as a symbol of unity, let alone as a center of power. The pull between these left-wing pressures, proclaimed outside the Assembly in the Cordeliers Club and in other popular societies, and the moderate views expressed within the Assembly was more than the Jacobin Club could withstand.

On July 14, a parade to the Champ de Mars celebrated the second anniversary of the fall of the Bastille and the second Fête de la Fédération. Members of the Cordeliers published a petition calling for a plebiscite throughout France on the future of executive authority. The next day another petition was drafted. The National Assembly refused to accept either one, decreeing on the fifteenth that the extension of the king's suspension had settled the matter. The petitioners then went to the Jacobin Club, where, as the minutes state, the hall was "filled by a deputation of these citizens, men and women of all estates, showing in their eyes and exhibiting with their gestures the energy and tranquility which suit free men." The morning of the sixteenth the Jacobins read and approved the petition, the key phrase of which was that the National Assembly should provide a replacement for Louis XVI "by any constitutional means." This last phrase was not in the original Cordeliers' petition but was added to win the support of the Jacobins, who as friends of the Constitution feared their act would be read as an illegal acceptance of a republican government.[35]

As the petition was taken to the Champ de Mars, fifty-four deputies, led by Barnave, left the hall of the Jacobins and moved to the Feuillants, where they adopted the same title, "la Société des Amis de la Constitution," but added, "séant aux Feuillants." These deputies, sometimes called

---

35. *Ibid.*, III, 19, 20; Albert Mathiez, *Le Club des Cordeliers pendant la crise de Varennes et le massacre du Champ de Mars* (1910; rpr. Geneva, 1975), "Pétition du 15 juillet," 116, 117; see also Mathiez' note on the Jacobin petition, 123.

Table 24
Jacobins and Feuillants, 1791

	Jacobins: Dec. 1790, List (N = 180) %	Jacobins: Aulard Additions (N = 38) %	Never Jacobins (N = 1,100) %
Never Feuillant	16	34	83
July, 1791, Feuillant	30	24	8
Sept., 1791, Feuillant	3	5	2
Both lists	51	37	7
Total	100	100	100

constitutionalists, thought that the phrase "constitutional means" was merely wordplay and did not disguise what they believed to be the Jacobins' abandonment of the National Assembly and its decrees. In the session of July 16, the Assembly passed its second decree, stating that the Constitution, when completed, would be submitted to the king. That evening, the remaining Jacobins withdrew their support of the petition at the Champ de Mars, on the grounds that they existed to support the National Assembly and that once the Assembly had declared its decision to leave Louis XVI on the throne, petitioners had no right to demand his removal. The Cordeliers and other popular societies kept the petition in place on the altar of the Champ de Mars.

Of the 218 deputies whom Aulard listed as members of the Jacobin Club, only 42 never moved to the Feuillant Club. The membership lists provide an additional measure of alignment trajectories. Of the 180 deputies whose names appear on the December, 1790, Jacobin membership lists, 84 percent (151 men) joined the Feuillant Club, as did 66 percent (25 men) of the 38 not on the membership list but considered by Aulard to have been Jacobins (Table 24). Together, these are the 176 deputies I have categorized as "shifting left" on the alignment scale.

Deputies who left the Jacobin Club for the Feuillant Club were adamant supporters of the Constitution of 1791. That Constitution constructed a nation of equal citizens held together by a hereditary monarchy.

The king was the first among equals, the first representative of the nation. These underlying premises began to crumble when Louis XVI defected and the Cordeliers Club and Paris radicals openly advocated replacing him and even constructing republican institutions. The Feuillants rallied to isolate the radical Jacobins, to support the king on the throne until he accepted the Constitution, and to complete their work and adjourn with the new legislature and other political, administrative, and judicial institutions in place. The 176 members of the shifting left were not greatly different in background or experience from the 107 consistent-left deputies. The majority of both groups were Third Estate deputies somewhat less likely than the ministerial left to have had experience in a law court or in administration before the Revolution. One marked difference between the two groups was their experience in political assemblies: the shifters were more likely than the consistent left to have served in provincial assemblies or estates before 1789. The shifting left, in addition, contained more lawyers than any other alignment: of 176 deputies so classified, 52 (30 percent) were avocats. Extrapolating motives from these political backgrounds is pure speculation, of course; there is no obvious reason why lawyers with previous experience in political assemblies would be disproportionately inclined to switch to the Feuillants and separate themselves from the more radical Jacobins. It is possible that their adversarial experience as lawyers and deputies made them more concerned about the consequences of eroding or abolishing the Constitution before it was ratified, thus leaving France without effective government. The decision made by the shifting left was a significant step, in any event, in assuring the establishment of constitutional monarchy with Louis XVI still on the throne as the first constitutional king. For republican historians like Aulard, this step avoided republicanism in 1791, a mistake that helped to push politics in a more radical direction and ultimately into Terror.[36]

The pattern of alignment trajectories has two major dimensions. First, the relative left-to-right placement of individual deputies did not change for

36. F. A. Aulard, "La Formation du parti républicain, 1790–1791," *La Révolution française,* XXXV (1898), 296–347; "La Fuite à Varennes et le mouvement républicain," *ibid.,* 385–436; "Les Républicains et les Démocrates depuis le massacre du Champ de Mars jusqu'à la Journée du 20 juin 1792," *ibid.,* 485–529.

very many of them. The agenda of the Assembly did move leftward as constitutional articles were completed and more extensive changes in church and state were debated. But with a few notable exceptions, deputies tended to remain aligned the same way relative to one another. In May and June, 1789, most of the movement was within the Third Estate as the political maneuvering over the structure of the vote gradually produced a majority in favor of declaring the National Assembly and committing it to write a constitution. Small but significant numbers of clerical deputies also shifted to support of the National Assembly; there was less movement among the nobility, where the number of patriots was not much augmented over the first six weeks of the Estates General. Once the Assembly was in place, the evidence from roll-call tallies fails to demonstrate a clear pattern of alignment shifts.

The second key point about alignment trajectories concerns those deputies who *did* realign significantly. These men made choices that determined constitutional outcomes and structured political conflicts beyond 1791.

The largest number of deputies who resigned from the National Assembly were nobles, many of whom had not supported the transformation of the Estates General in the very beginning. The evidence from protest-list signatures suggests that they were most disaffected by constitutional decisions limiting the power of the monarchy. The patriot clergy were more likely than the nobles to be pulled in two directions; by 1791 they had split, left and right. Furthermore, their political decisions were shaped mostly by legislation on the church, particularly the Assembly's refusal to declare Catholicism the state religion.

Evidence from the pamphlets that was presented in chapter 3 suggests that the most significant trajectory was the one followed by deputies whose pamphlets expressed centrist opinions between 1789 and 1791. The decline in frequency of expressions of trust in the king and the rise in concern about popular violence reflect a greater magnitude of change than occurred in opinions farther to the left or right. Data on centrist and unclassified deputies, presented earlier in this chapter, support this interpretation. Particularly noteworthy is the fact that 55 percent of the center-right deputies resigned.

Club membership lists indicate relatively little movement from one club to another or from left to right, with the exception, of course, of the Jacobin fissure in July, 1791. The Society of Thirty was the initial organization of patriots to accomplish a specified political purpose; two-thirds of that original group remained on the left up to 1791. Three-quarters or more of the members of the Société de 1789, the Club Monarchique, and the Club de Valois were never Jacobins, and there was not much overlapping membership among the three. Deputies in the Société de 1789 were mostly moderate left, those in the Club de Valois more divided, and those in the Club Monarchique moderate right.

The split in the Jacobin Club in July, 1791, was the most important alignment shift because it guaranteed that the Constitution of 1791, and particularly its articles on the king, would remain in place and that the National Assembly would finish its work more or less on schedule. By reputation, the Jacobins were the most influential "pressure group" affecting deputies. Pressures from more radical clubs, radical journalists, and Paris crowds did not succeed in pulling the Jacobin Club into alliances with the Cordeliers, let alone in removing Louis XVI from the throne. The leftward movement of revolutionary politics external to the National Assembly fragmented the Jacobins and carried only a few deputies along with it.

Majoritarian politics did not develop in the National Assembly. Contemporary commentators used terms such as *patriot* and *aristocrat* and *left* and *right,* but there is no evidence that these categories were structured like formal political parties. The men of the National Assembly were in fact establishing precedents for partisan politics by their spatial placement left to right, their language of collective affiliation to indicate insult, abuse, or support, and their practice of coordinating legislative tactics at the meetings of their clubs. But these practices did not develop into an "in" and an "out" party, much less a government and an opposition. Politics in the National Assembly were factional politics, not majoritarian politics. By looking closely at the numbers presented in this chapter, we can indeed discern a left and a right, and patterns of individual alignment that were quite remarkably stable. Furthermore, the left did achieve a Constitution that was close to the design envisioned by Paris patriots in 1788 and 1789. Nonetheless, supporters and opponents of this Constitution did not structure a stable and organized political party system. The patriots succeeded not by producing a cohesive majority, but by capturing the leadership of the National Assembly.

Chapter 5

Roles in the National Assembly

Deputies on the left were not a decisive majority in the National Assembly. They succeeded in dominating the agenda and producing a Constitution generally to their liking partly because some right-wing deputies resigned or withheld their participation, but as the numbers cited in chapter 4 demonstrate, such defections were not frequent enough to account for left-wing victories.

It is commonly asserted that the left-wing deputies began with a stronger organization among their adherents, orchestrated support from political clubs such as the Jacobins outside the Assembly, and practiced parliamentary tactics more effectively than did their right-wing counterparts. This interpretation is not unchallenged: Timothy Tackett has suggested that the right was in fact more organized than the left in the fall of 1789, when moderate and extreme right-wing deputies attempted a coalition, and that between February and July, 1790, the signatories of the April 19 declaration (protesting the Assembly's failure to declare a state religion) actually constituted a right-wing "Capuchin" party of nearly three hundred deputies, quite strong enough to challenge the numerically fewer Jacobin deputies.[1] Tackett's evidence on the place of origin, residence, occupation, and age of the "Capuchins" compared with the Jacobins does

---

1. Georges Lefebvre emphasized the organization of the patriot party in *The French Revolution from Its Origins to 1793*, trans. Elizabeth Moss Evanson (London, 1962), 139. See also Simon Schama, *Citizens: A Chronicle of the French Revolution* (New York, 1989), 479. Tackett's data come from "Nobles and Third Estate," 276–96.

indeed describe a unique group of deputies. Tackett, however, does not refer to the actual outcomes of votes in the Assembly, which the left wing was consistently winning. Robert Griffiths' study of centrist deputies points out that Malouet and his supporters did not intend to form an official opposition and were too weak to mount more than a symbolic resistance on most issues in the winter and spring of 1790.[2] Furthermore, intense pressure on the deputies from spectators attending sessions, from crowds in the Palais Royal, and from the deputies' constituents was mostly on the side of revolutionary change.

From the opening session, attentive constituents, electoral committees, and people in the galleries from Paris and Versailles all followed proceedings in the Estates General very closely. The Third Estate's meeting rooms admitted up to 3,000 spectators, and many hundreds attended. In the first six weeks most of the spectators were well-dressed bourgeois or aristocrats, many of them wives, relatives, and friends of deputies.[3] On May 28, a deputy who kept a diary made special mention of women in the galleries: "We noticed with pleasure that all the citizen spectators, notably the women, listened to all discussions with great attention and did not leave until the end, despite the boring prolixity of a great many wordy orators who abused their right to speak until silenced by the Assembly."[4] In May and June, most of the people in the galleries of the Third Estate were patriot sympathizers supporting demands for common verification of powers, common sessions, and the vote by head. Pressure from the galleries was significant in creating a majority in favor of declaring the National Assembly on June 17.

The nobles and clergy did not have to contend with the galleries because their meeting rooms were closed to the public, but whenever they adjourned they were greeted by throngs of spectators in the antechambers. Their resolutions were circulated and discussed by the crowds and especially in the cafés of the Palais Royal in Paris. Supporters of the patriots criticized the deputies of these two orders for their closed sessions.[5]

The political questions with which deputies struggled in the weeks

2. Griffiths, *Le Centre perdu*, 87–95.

3. Rouanet, "Les Débuts du parlementarisme française," 188–91.

4. Creuzé-Latouche, *Journal des Etats-Généraux*, 11.

5. *Ibid.*, 38–42; Rouanet, "Les Premiers Leaders parlementaires en France," *Annales révolutionnaires*, IX (1917), 12.

before June 17 were discussed in chapter 3. As deputies contested over the immediate question of the voting method and the larger issue of the purpose of the Estates General, they were also defining their own roles as representatives. Noble supporters of the vote by order argued on the basis of an organic view of the nation that the king was the head of the body politic, and that the three estates of the realm were of equal importance to the health of the whole regardless of disproportionate numeric weight. This theory found no spokesmen within the Third Estate. Mounier opposed the separation of the three estates and the vote by order, although he felt strongly that the aristocracy must retain a voice in the new constitution through an institution of an upper house. The nobles' adamant refusal to compromise at the beginning doomed the chances that Mounier's English-model constitution would find much support. The June 17 vote on the National Assembly amounted to a claim that the Third Estate could constitute the nation without the other two orders. As Creuzé de Latouche put it, "The will of the Third Estate, when it is unanimous, when it conforms to general principles of equity, will always be called the national will."[6]

The rejected conservative view held that the nation took concrete form as a body of three corporate estates whose electors chose and empowered deputies. The June 17 vote and the Tennis Court Oath nullified that conception; deputies did not represent their electors, but an abstraction called the nation, the will of which they alone could formulate and articulate.[7] These official collective acts therefore created a dilemma for individual deputies, particularly those required to keep in close communication with their electors: who or what articulated the will of the sovereign nation? This fundamental question of political legitimacy went to the heart of the representative institution they were trying simultaneously to work within and to invent.

If this abstract nation was to guide deputies' actions in the Assembly, they had to give it a somewhat more concrete meaning. The pamphlets treat of two specifications of role: deputies' views on their own primary function and on factions inside and outside of the Assembly. Given that pamphlet authors were drawn not from a random sample of all the deputies

6. Creuzé-Latouche, *Journal des Etats-Généraux,* 73.

7. This point is also made by Ran Halévi, "La Révolution constituante: Les ambiguités politiques," in *Political Culture of the French Revolution,* ed. Lucas, esp. p. 73.

Figure 4

Deputies' Role Perceptions over Time: Information Versus Opinion

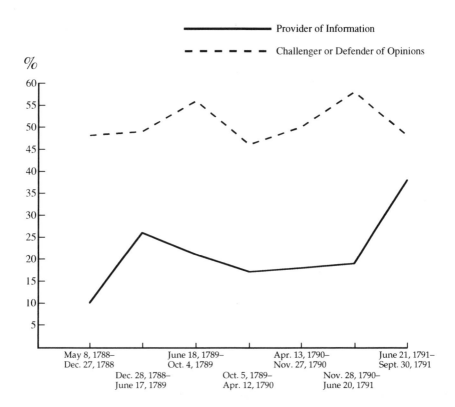

but instead from a regional sample, their views on representation may very well not reflect those of all the deputies, particularly those less experienced and less active. Therefore, these data should be considered to reflect regional differences. Deputies who wrote pamphlets were much more likely to speak of themselves as challengers and defenders of certain groups of opinions than as providers of information. This view of themselves as challengers peaked after two crises: the formation of the National Assembly and the flight to Varennes. Only in the summer of 1791, when the Constitution was nearly complete and deputies felt obligated to explain it, did as many as 38 percent of the pamphlets emphasize deputies' roles as communicators of information (Figure 4). Before the Estates General sat, between a third

Figure 5
Deputies' Attitudes Toward Factions over Time

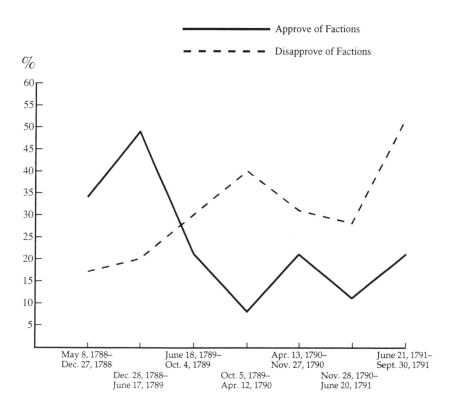

and a half of the pamphlets stated approval of factions, but during the first six weeks approval dropped to 21 percent and never went any higher; disapproval increased and peaked at 52 percent the summer of 1791 (Figure 5). As for deputies' attitudes toward their colleagues, consistently, more pamphlets spoke of defending interests than of cooperating. In May and June, 39 percent of the pamphlets stressed cooperation, compared with 46 percent stressing defense of group interest, and thereafter the proportion favoring conciliation fell dramatically (Figure 6).

Attitudes toward role varied not only over time but also according to province. The Bretons were the most frequent defenders of group interests, coming as they did from a year of struggle with noble interests in their

Figure 6

Deputies' Role Perceptions over Time: Group Defense Versus Conciliation

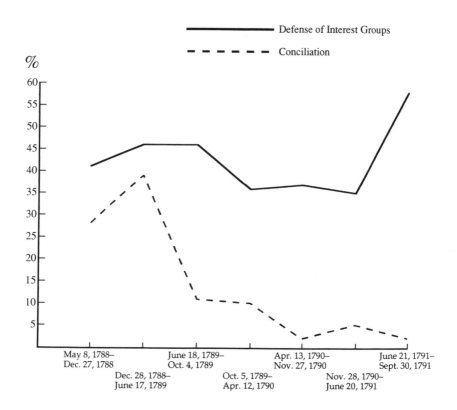

provincial estates. The Parisians were the most conciliatory, followed by the Dauphinois.

Group defenders were overrepresented among Third Estate lawyers who had sat in provincial estates, many of them Bretons (Table 25). Those writing pamphlets recommending conciliation were most likely to be nobles or judicial officers and to have sat in the Assembly of Notables or estates of Dauphiné. As with the other attitudes, these role perceptions cannot be assumed to apply to the whole membership of the National Assembly, and they do reflect the inclusion of the radical views of Breton deputies and the more conciliatory efforts of the Dauphinois.

Table 25
Authors' Role Perceptions by Background Characteristics

	% Pamphlets Advising Group Defense N = 158	% Pamphlets Advising Conciliation N = 48
Estate, Occupation		
Clergy	15	23
Nobility	16	38
Third Estate		
Judicial Officer	20	21
Lawyer	30	12
Professional	9	4
Other	4	2
Clergy in Third Estate	6	0
Totals	100	100
Prerevolutionary Assembly		
Assembly of Notables	2	11
Provincial estates	27	4
Estates, Dauphiné	9	23
Provincial assembly	11	8
Departmental or municipal assembly	2	2
None	49	52
Totals	100	100
Province		
Brittany	44	14
Paris	26	42
Dauphiné	10	23
Bourges	0	2
Auxerre	0	0
Bourbonnais	6	2
Orléanais	14	17
Totals	100	100

Deputy authors, then, expected divisiveness, disapproved of factions, and yet saw their function as defending their group's interests rather than looking for a basis of compromise and conciliation. Most of the deputies blamed others for not being more conciliatory; a few, especially if they wrote memoirs later in their lives, criticized themselves for not having been more cooperative.[8]

Debates about mandates provide a specific example of the definition of representatives' roles. Along with his cahier, each deputy brought to Versailles a mandate containing instructions. There were three types of mandates: *general,* as specified by the king's instructions of January, 1789, which left the deputy full responsibility for his own votes in the Estates General; *special,* which required that he take a specified stand on certain issues; and *imperative,* which ordered him to vote according to the positions set forth in his cahier, under pain of recall if he did not.[9] On June 14, during review of deputies' election credentials, Du Pont de Nemours protested that the Bretons had a mandate prohibiting them from voting for anything contrary to provincial privileges or provincial decrees. Du Pont called upon the Breton delegation to state whether they intended any such opposition, in which case they could not be admitted. Le Chapelier protested that this inquiry was out of order and that the king had ruled his consent to Brittany's electoral procedures.[10] On the other hand, once the National Assembly was formed, some deputies explained their delay in joining it on the basis of their mandates, arguing that they represented their electors directly, that their mandates were expressions of those electors' wills, and that they therefore could not act contrary to instructions.[11] Writing retrospectively in 1808, Pierre Victor Malouet stated cogently the

---

8. Malouet, *Mémoires,* II, 10, 11.

9. Beatrice Fry Hyslop, *A Guide to the General Cahiers of 1789* (New York, 1936), 38, 39, 99–103. Hyslop's table on the general cahiers lists mandates for each electoral district, pp. 116–42. As they crafted the Constitution of 1791, deputies worked out a theory of national representation. See Jean-Claude Masclet, *Le Rôle du député et ses attaches institutionnelles sous la Ve République* (Paris, 1979), 1–8.

10. Creuzé-Latouche, *Journal des Etats-Généraux,* 105, 106.

11. See, for example, Trophime Gérard Lally-Tolendal, *Pièces justificatives, contenant différentes motions de M. le comte de Lally-Tolendal* (N.p., 1789), 42; Claude Benjamin Vallet, *Mémoire présenté à l'Assemblée nationale, 25 juin 1789* (N.p., 1789); and Vallet, "Souvenirs," *Nouvelle Revue rétrospective,* XVI (1901), 239, 240.

conservative view of mandates, that they articulated "the limits of our duties and powers." Malouet bitterly condemned the king and his ministers for not deciding to verify deputies' powers themselves and for giving insufficient importance to mandates, "which formed all our titles, all our powers, without which we were nothing, and which we could neither go against nor pass over without being traitors to the oath we took before our constituents to execute our duties faithfully." [12]

There were 232 imperative mandates assigned to deputies, and 150 of them (65 percent) went to the first two estates, 112 to the nobles and 38 to the clergy. Sixty general cahiers are still available for the electoral districts chosen as the sample for the analysis of deputy attitudes; twenty-seven of the sixty had imperative mandates. When I matched deputies' mandates with their pamphlet opinions, I found that 57 percent of those assigned general mandates described their roles as information giving and only 27 percent saw themselves as challengers, whereas 63 percent of those with imperative mandates and 53 percent of those with special mandates saw themselves as challengers. On the other hand, 63 percent of holders of general mandates stressed defense of group interests, compared with 45 percent of the holders of imperative mandates and 32 percent of those with special mandates. These data reflect the impact of estate as a political determinant; mandates were associated with role perceptions because the majority of the restrictive mandates belonged to the nobles and clergy, who in general tended to see themselves as challengers, albeit sometimes willing to compromise. As Norman Hampson has noted, imperative mandates could have been seen as a mechanism of popular sovereignty holding deputies absolutely accountable to their electors—although such a practice would have made it virtually impossible to legislate. [13] The deputy Jérôme Pétion de Villeneuve understood this conundrum. In a speech on September 5, 1789, during debate on mandates, he opposed binding mandates for "normal" legislative circumstances but recommended the use of "assemblées élémentaires" (similar to modern referenda) to be used to form laws on major issues, known in advance, where citizens' approval was required. [14]

12. Malouet, *Mémoires*, I, 250.
13. Hampson, *Prelude to Terror*, 189.
14. *Archives parlementaires*, VIII (September 5, 1789), 581–84. Pétion's speech was cited in Halévi, "La Révolution constituante," 78, 79.

The data just cited show the unacceptability of that position. Imperative mandates were closely connected to the traditional form of the Estates General as the representation of a society of orders, and as such, were soon to be nullified.

Whether they were group defenders or conciliators, passionate and enthusiastic or intimidated and apprehensive, the deputies on June 24 found themselves no longer representing the estates of the realm coming together to be instructed by the king, but henceforth representing the sovereign nation of France and undertaking to limit the powers of that king and to make him the nation's first representative, no longer an absolute ruler by divine right. From this point on, parliamentary leaders and their supporters determined the contents of the Constitution and the relationships of deputies with revolutionary activists, the king, and his council. Pamphlets and biographical information can be used to investigate the attitudes and behavior of leaders and followers.

Establishing Leadership Positions

I defined five categories of deputies' roles, ranging from least to most active, in terms of seven different variables concerning participation in debate, service on committees, and election as secretary or president of the Assembly. Information on these role definitions is fully presented in the Methods and Sources section. The remainder of the present chapter is devoted, first, to developing the evidence that men in each of the five role categories shared common background characteristics, such as region, estate, and prerevolutionary experience, and second, to illuminating through role analysis the development of left-wing dominance, the importance of several dozen liberal nobles, and the erosion of the center in 1790 and 1791.

In a deliberative body as large as the National Assembly, with 1,318 members, it is perhaps surprising that 875 men were at least minimally active (Table 26), addressing the floor at least once, sitting on at least one committee, or serving as an officer, in addition to attending sessions and voting on motions. Relatively few of the deputies were personally acquainted with

Table 26
Role Frequencies for All Deputies

	Frequency	%
Debate		
Never spoke	332	25
Not indexed (in *Archives parlementaires*)	228	17
Spoke once	175	13
Spoke 2–5 times	222	17
Spoke 6–19 times	173	13
Spoke 20–49 times	86	7
Spoke 50–99 times	38	3
Spoke 100–200 times	29	2
Spoke over 200 times	35	3
	1,318	100
Officership		
Not officer	1,127	86
Secretary once	137	10
Secretary 2 or more times	1	0
President once	15	1
Secretary and president	29	2
President 2 or more times	9	1
	1,318	100
Committees		
Not on any	773	59
On 1 committee	307	23
On 2–3	174	13
On 4–5	51	4
On 6–7	8	1
On 8–9	5	0
	1,318	100
Role Scale		
Listeners	443	34
Participants	240	18
Active participants	325	24
Leaders	166	13
Dominant leaders	144	11
	1,318	100

more than a handful of colleagues before they came to Versailles.[15] Meeting halls were crowded, noisy, and filled with sometimes thousands of spectators. It was not easy to communicate in them, either in Versailles or in Paris. Speeches had to be made without any form of voice amplification; some deputies complained that they could not be heard because they were not endowed with a carrying voice. Others whose native tongue was Bretonne (Celtic) were hesitant about addressing such a large assembly in French.[16] Moreover, deputies were very aware that their votes and opinions could cause them to be singled out for praise, blame, or threats by journalists, orators, club members, electors, and those in local assemblies. Real personal risk was not uncommon. One is often struck by these men's personal courage and sense of mission—as well as by their occasional foolishness and pettiness. We might remark the wry comment of the marquis de Ferrières: "There are among the Third [Estate] men of merit; but it is impossible that 1,200 assembled persons have common sense, were it the Areopage of Athens or even the Senate of Rome."[17]

Rules governing the determination of officers were drawn up after the formation of the National Assembly. During the Estates General, the eldest deputy from each order was named presiding officer of the meetings of that order; official secretaries were not designated. In the Third Estate, not all those who wished to speak were able to be recognized by the chair, so on June 7 all deputies were placed in bureaus—a total of twenty, with thirty members each. Deputies from the same electoral circumscription were assigned to different bureaus to weaken the impact of regional and collegial groups. The bureaus were not standing committees; any issue remanded to them was to be debated in all of them, with one spokesman from each bureau designated to present its collective opinion on the floor of the full Estates. Such a scheme obviously made it easier for more deputies, espe-

15. We can document the unfamiliarity by looking at misspellings of deputies' names in journals such as that of Creuzé de Latouche, who wrote Piozat for Biauzat (p. 9), Blezen for Glezen (p. 100), and Robert Pierre for Robespierre (p. 117); he also mistook Kauffman of Colmar for Reubell (pp. 117 and 280).

16. Jean Joseph Mounier, *Exposé de la conduite de . . . dans l'Assemblée nationale et des motifs de son retour en Dauphiné* (Paris, 1789), 30, 31; Guillaume Le Lay de Grantugen, *Motion présenté à l'Assemblée nationale* (N.p., 1789), 2, 3.

17. Charles Elie, marquis de Ferrières, *Correspondance inédite (1789, 1790, 1791)*, ed. Henri Carré (Paris, 1932), 78.

cially the shyer ones, to air their opinions, but it also weakened the impact of spectators' reactions to dramatic oratory. Moderates quickly evolved the tactic of proposing that controversial issues be returned to the bureaus for discussion. [18]

When the National Assembly was constituted, bureaus were retained, although after September 12 their members ceased to discuss motions and kept only their function of counting votes for the election of officers and committee members. Issue-specific committees, like parliamentary standing committees, took over the political function of discussing substantive issues.

The first important committee to be instituted was the Committee of Thirty on the Constitution, elected following a decree on July 6 to begin plans for drawing up a constitution. The committee was formed by the selection of one member from every bureau. [19] It was replaced by a Committee of Eight, elected on July 14, with proportionate representation of deputies from the three estates.

The first committees were filled with deputies whose names had been widely known before the opening of the Estates General or who had played a leading role during the first six weeks. A systematic inquiry into the leadership patterns in the National Assembly can begin with the deputies who were the first chosen for a designated responsibility, the thirty-two men named as commissioners to try to resolve the impasse between the three orders over common sessions and the voting method (Table 27). The clergy on May 11 named their eight commissioners: four members of the upper clergy (two archbishops, a bishop, and a canon) and four curés. On the same day the nobles named six military nobles, one parlementary magistrate, and the lieutenant-général of Alsace. Eight days later the Third Estate selected their sixteen commissioners, mostly well-known and highly influential deputies, some of whom also secured nominations for less-familiar colleagues from their home regions. [20] No single province, however, predominated among the thirty-two commissioners. They came from

18. Oliver J. Frederiksen, "The Bureaus of the French Constituent Assembly of 1789: An Early Experiment in the Group-Conference Method," *Political Science Quarterly,* LI (1936), 418–37; Creuzé-Latouche, *Journal des Etats-Généraux,* 68, 175, 176.

19. Fredericksen, "Bureaus of the French Constituent Assembly."

20. Rouanet, "Les Premiers Leaders parlementaires en France," *Annuales révolutionnaires,* IX (1917), 624–25.

Table 27

Early Leadership: Conference Commissioners in the Estates General

	Occupation	Province	Role	Alignment
Clergy (named May 11)				
Champion de Cicé, Jérôme Marie	Archbishop	Bordeaux	Dominant leader	Center right
Coster, Sigisbert Etienne	Canon, vicar	3 Bishoprics	Active participant	Consistent right
Dillon, Dominique	Curé	Poitiers	Leader	Ministerial left
Le Franc de Pompignan, Jean Georges	Archbishop	Dauphiné	Leader	Center right
Le Cesve, René	Curé	Poitiers	Listener	Unclassifiable
La Luzerne, César Guillaume de	Bishop	Châlons	Dominant leader	Center right
Richard de La Vergne, Pierre	Prêtre	Marches Communes	Listener	Moderate right
Thibault, Anne Alexandre Marie	Prêtre	Ile-de-France	Dominant leader	Shifting left
Nobles (named May 11)				
Crussol d'Uzés, Anne Emmanuel François Georges, marquis	Army lieutenant-général	Poitiers	Participant	Unclassifiable
Lachastre, Claude Louis	Maréchal de camp	Berry	Listener	Moderate right
Lemulier de Bressey, Jean	Magistrate	Burgundy	Listener	Moderate right
Levis-Mirepoix, Marc Antoine	Maréchal de camp	Burgundy	Listener	Consistent right
Montmorency-Luxembourg, Anne Charles Sigismond de	Lieutenant-général of Alsace	Poitiers	Participant	Center right
Escars, François Nicholas René de Pérusse, comte	Colonel	Poitiers	Participant	Moderate right
Montboissier, Charles Philippe Simon de	Maréchal de camp	Orléanais	Participant	Center right
Mirabeau, André Boniface Louis, vicomte	Colonel	Limousin	Leader	Moderate right

Third Estate (named May 19)

Ailly, Michel François	Conseiller d'état	Ile-de-France	Leader	Unclassifiable
Barnave, Antoine Pierre Joseph Marie	Avocat	Dauphiné	Dominant leader	Shifting left
Bergasse, Nicolas	Avocat	Lyonnais	Active participant	Moderate right
Du Pont de Nemours, Pierre Samuel	Conseiller d'état	Ile-de-France	Dominant leader	Contradictory
Garat, Dominique	Avocat	Gascony	Dominant leader	Unclassifiable
Le Chapelier, Issac René Guy	Avocat	Brittany	Dominant leader	Shifting left
Le Grand, Jérôme	King's avocat	Berry	Leader	Ministerial left
Milscent, Marie Joseph	Royal judge	Anjou	Leader	Resigning right
Mounier, Jean Joseph	Royal judge	Dauphiné	Dominant leader	Resigning right
Rabaut de Saint-Etienne, Jean Paul	Protestant minister	Languedoc	Dominant leader	Shifting left
Redon, Claude	Mayor, sheriff	Auvergne	Dominant leader	Moderate right
Salomon de La Saugerie, Guillaume Anne	Avocat	Orléanais	Dominant leader	Ministerial left
Target, Guy Jean Baptiste	Avocat	Ile-de-France	Dominant leader	Ministerial left
Thouret, Jacques Guillaume	Avocat	Normandy	Dominant leader	Ministerial left
Viguier, Jean Baptiste	Avocat	Languedoc	Leader	Consistent left
Volney, Constantin François Chasseboeuf de	Director-général	Anjou	Dominant leader	Ministerial left

a total of eighteen provinces; only among the eight nobles was there much regional grouping, with three commissioners from Poitiers, two from Burgundy, and one each from Berry, Orléanais, and Limousin. The eight clergy came from seven provinces and the sixteen members of the Third Estate from eleven. Mounier was the leader of those who put their faith in compromise among the orders. He and Barnave were commissioners from Dauphiné for the Third Estate, and his former associate from the provincial estates, Le Franc de Pompignan, the archbishop of Vienne, was a clerical commissioner. The fact that none of the liberal nobles from Dauphiné was selected commissioner dashed Mounier's hopes of replicating the 1788 political revolution in Dauphiné through unified efforts of strategists from all three orders.

Seventeen of these thirty-two men went on to active roles in the National Assembly. Eleven of the sixteen Third Estate commissioners became dominant leaders, four more were leaders, and one was an active participant. Among the clergy, only two were listeners; the remaining six played active roles. Their rate of activity far surpassed that for all the clerical deputies, of whom 46 percent were listeners and 54 percent active in some way. In contrast, commissioners for the nobility did not go on to participate in the entire Assembly as fully as the whole noble delegation. Three of the eight were listeners, four were participants, and one was a leader, whereas for the whole delegation 26 percent were listeners, 17 percent were participants, and 15 percent were leaders.

The Third Estate commissioners included four who became right-wing deputies, two who emerged as centrists, and ten who ended up on the left. Half the clerical commissioners were later on the right, two in the center, and two on the left. The eight nobles did not include any representative on the left; seven were right-wing and one unclassifiable. The nobles chose as their delegates men highly unlikely to support any concessions to unity or the vote by head. The forty-six noble patriots who initially supported common verification had no spokesman among the commissioners.[21]

These data suggest the futility of Mounier's hopes of uniting the three

21. These findings contradict the thesis of Guy Chaussinand-Nogaret, who argues for commonality of interests between noble and Third Estate deputies. See his article "Aux origines de la Révolution: Noblesse et bourgeoisie," *Annales: Economies, Sociétés, Civilisations*, XXX (1975), 265–78, and his book *La Noblesse au XVIIIe siècle*.

estates. Whether by accident or by design, the nobles selected eight men not very likely to work toward compromise, most of whom were army officers, not experienced administrators or magistrates. The commissioners from the other two orders were much more broadly representative of the alignment developing among the deputies and included a good many men already experienced in leadership, well known to other deputies, and destined to play active roles in the National Assembly.

Leaders and Followers: Backgrounds and Experience

Among the deputies from the sampled regions, authors were much more likely than nonauthors to participate in the National Assembly. Half of the nonauthors were listeners, compared with 11 percent of the authors; 2 percent of the nonauthors were dominant leaders, compared with one-third of the authors. Writing pamphlets was a political activity, part of a whole set of behaviors engaged in by deputies who wanted to influence the course of events.

As it was with alignment, estate was an important determinant of deputies' roles in the National Assembly (Table 28). The Third Estate was disproportionately represented among the leaders, especially the dominant leaders, but its deputies by no means monopolized control over the important posts. Noble deputies were dominant leaders proportionate to their numbers among the total membership. The clergy and especially the lower clergy were disproportionately inclined to be listeners. Substantial pluralities of both clergy and nobility were listeners, compared with a quarter of the Third Estate.

Level of participation also proved to be associated with deputies' previous political experiences, occupations, and June, 1789, alignment (Table 29). Listeners were disproportionately drawn from the clergy, royal administrators, and the conservative nobility, whereas men with previous political experience in an assembly or a prerevolutionary political institution were disproportionately unlikely to fall into that quiet category. Participants—those whose only activity was occasional intervention in debate (one to five times)—included somewhat more clergy than would be pro-

Table 28
Deputies' Estates by Role, Roles by Estate

	Listeners N = 443	Participants N = 240	Active Participants N = 325	Leaders N = 166	Dominant Leaders N = 144
Estate (%)					
Clergy	34	30	21	16	10
Nobility	25	23	21	23	25
Third Estate	39	45	55	58	64
Not elected by estate	2	2	3	3	1
	100	100	100	100	100

	Clergy N = 332	Nobility N = 311	Third Estate N = 645	Not by Estate N = 30
Role (%)				
Listeners	46	36	26	27
Participants	22	18	17	23
Active participants	20	22	28	30
Leaders	8	12	15	17
Dominant leaders	4	12	14	3
	100	100	100	100

portionate, but were quite representatively distributed in the other two estates. Active participants, who were either committee members, officers, or frequent debaters, were likewise proportionate. Among the two leadership categories, there is a marked decline in proportionality. Leaders and dominant leaders were drawn substantially from the Third Estate and from among those with political experience before they came to the Assembly, and lawyers were strikingly overrepresented among the dominant leaders. (The leading roles played by lawyers in the Revolution have long been remarked. This index reveals, in addition, the importance of prerevolutionary political experience. Clearly the men who had practicated before law

Table 29
Index of Proportionality for Role

	Listeners N = 433 (33%)	Participants N = 240 (18%)	Active Participants N = 325 (25%)	Leaders N = 166 (13%)	Dominant Leaders N = 144 (11%)
Clergy	1.4	1.2	.8	.6	.4
Lower Clergy	1.4	1.3	.7	.6	.2
Middle Clergy	1.4	1.0	1.0	.4	.8
Upper Clergy	1.0	.8	1.0	.8	.8
Nobility	1.0	1.0	.9	1.0	1.1
Third Estate	.8	.9	1.1	1.2	1.3
No Estate	1.0	1.5	1.5	1.5	.5
In pre-1789 assembly	.6	.8	1.1	1.6	1.4
Not in	.9	1.0	1.0	.9	.9
Lawyers	.6	1.0	.8	1.3	1.9
Judicial Officers	.6	1.1	1.3	1.4	1.2
Royal Administrators	1.3	1.0	.7	1.3	1.3
In prerevolutionary institution	.3	.9	1.1	1.3	1.5
Not in	1.1	1.0	1.0	.9	.8
June, 1789, Alignment					
Patriot clergy	1.2	1.2	1.0	.7	.1
Patriot nobles	.5	0	.9	1.7	3.9
Conservative clergy	1.5	1.3	.6	.5	.4
Conservative nobles	1.3	1.2	.6	.5	.4
Other liberal nobles (Murphy/ Higonnet)	.8	.5	1.3	.6	2.4

courts, administered government enterprises, or served previously in political assemblies had the knowledge, the talent, the experience, and the interest to be singled out by their fellows in a very large Assembly.)

Noble deputies were proportionately distributed across the categories of leaders and followers, but when the patriot nobles from June, 1789, are separated out, their central role in producing the Constitution in 1791 is immediately obvious. They were nearly four times more likely than their numbers would indicate to be dominant leaders. Their reputation and influence are critical to understanding how the left-wing deputies were generally able to win votes on constitutional motions even though their numbers did not add up to a reliable majority. Conservative nobles, on the other hand, were disproportionately inactive. For the clergy, there is no comparable split between the patriots and the conservatives; both were about equally predisposed to be among the less-active deputies.

Some contemporary observers reported that deputies tended to exhibit certain characteristic forms of activity. Some were said to be orators who sought recognition from the chair to address the Assembly as often as they could. Others were reluctant to speak before the whole Assembly but took active part in committees. Yet others were repeatedly elected to serve as officers.[22] The data on roles contradict this interpretation. Those who were active in one way in the Assembly tended to be active in other ways as well. A total of 191 men served as officers, presidents, or secretaries in the National Assembly. A total of 545 served on at least one committee, and 758 debated at least once. Only 10 of the 560 men who never debated were ever elected secretary or president, and only 26 of the 773 men who were not on committees were officers. Frequent debaters were most likely to have served on four or more committees. Of the activists, the 13 men who served on six or more committees were all officers, and all but 12 of the 64 men who debated a hundred or more times were officers.

Although not all frequent debaters were officers or committee members, officers and committee members were overwhelmingly drawn from frequent debaters. Except for those few deputies whose reputations preceded them to the Estates General, most men used oratory to win recognition and support for election to leadership posts. Not just debating but debating frequently was what facilitated election. Out of all 1,318 deputies, 43 percent never debated, 43 percent debated from one to nineteen times, and 14 percent debated twenty or more times. Of the nondebaters, 2 percent were officers; of the infrequent debaters (one to nineteen times), 11 percent were officers; of the frequent debaters, 63 percent were officers.

22. Adrien Cyprien Duquesnoy, *Journal d'Adrien Duquesnoy, député du Tiers état de Bar-Le-Duc, sur l'Assemblée constituante* (3 mai 1789–3 avril 1790), ed. Robert de Crèvecoeur (Paris, 1894), 488–94. The notion of specialization is also accepted by Dawson, *Provincial Magistrates*, 234.

Roles and Political Alignment

The left did not monopolize the leadership of the National Assembly, but it did indeed dominate it. The left had by far the smallest percentage of listeners and the largest percentage of dominant leaders, whereas the right had the largest percentage of listeners and the smallest percentage of dominant leaders (Table 30). Of the listeners, 60 percent sat on the right, compared with 18 percent of left-wing deputies. The opposite relationship obtains for the dominant leaders, who included 12 percent from the right and 78 percent from the left. The pattern of leadership, however, is more complex than this general statement indicates. To clarify the dynamics of politics within the National Assembly, we must look more closely.

Listeners—those who never intervened in debate—were drawn disproportionately from the consistent right, the center right, and as we would logically anticipate, from the resigning right. The right, however, were not silent and inactive. Participants, active participants, and leaders included men of the right in proportion to their numbers; participants, in fact, were disproportionately moderate-right deputies. Most striking about the findings in Table 31 is the profile of the dominant leaders, which proved to be dramatically underrepresentative of the consistent right and the entire right, and overrepresentative of the left, especially the shifting left, who became Feuillant Club members in 1791.

The collective influence of the consistent right was reduced by a number of factors: resignation, silent inactivity as a protest, or downright intimidation by their colleagues on the left and the noisy and often threatening gallery audience. Although by no means totally excluded from such posts as secretary or president or from membership on key committees, right-wing deputies on the whole were less frequently elected to leadership positions than leftists. In particular, the consistent right had very few of their number elected to leadership positions. Clearly, however, they were not defeated by their opposite number, the consistent left. Nearly the same size as the consistent right, the category of extreme left-wing deputies made up only 10 percent of the dominant leaders; altogether they were distributed quite proportionately across the range of levels of activity within the Assembly. The real contest for top leadership was among the deputies of the center left, both categories of which were heavily overrepresented among the 144 dominant leaders.

Table 30
Alignment by Role, Role by Alignment

Alignment Scale

Role Scale	Consistent Right (N = 108) %	Moderate Right (N = 315) %	Center Right (N = 147) %	Resigning Right (N = 51) %	Right Center (N = 13) %	Contradictory (N = 44) %	Unclassifiable (N = 173) %	Ministerial Left (N = 184) %	Shifting Left (N = 176) %	Consistent Left (N = 107) %
Listener	43	39	47	57	38	39	42	16	11	31
Participant	18	26	17	14	15	23	15	15	10	21
Active Participant	25	24	25	17	31	20	28	29	21	24
Leader	13	7	9	8	8	4	11	19	24	11
Dominant Leader	1	4	2	4	8	14	4	21	34	13
Total	100	100	100	100	100	100	100	100	100	100

Role Scale

Alignment Scale	Listener (N = 443) %	Participant (N = 240) %	Active Participant (N = 325) %	Leader (N = 166) %	Dominant Leader (N = 144) %
Consistent Right	10	8	8	9	1
Moderate Right	28	35	23	13	8
Center Right	16	10	11	9	2
Resigning Right	6.5	3	3	2	1
Right Center	1	1	1	1	1
Contradictory	4	4	3	1	4
Unclassifiable	16	11	15	11	5
Ministerial Left	6.5	12	16	22	26
Shifting Left	5	7	12	25	42
Consistent Left	7	9	8	7	10
Total	100	100	100	100	100

Table 31
Index of Proportionality for Alignment and Role

	Listeners (N = 443)	Participants (N = 240)	Active Partipants (N = 325)	Leaders (N = 166)	Dominant Leaders (N = 144)
Right					
Consistent	1.3	1.0	1.0	1.0	.1
Moderate	1.2	1.4	1.0	.6	.3
Center	1.4	.9	1.0	.8	.2
Resigning	1.7	.7	.7	.6	.4
Center					
Right	1.1	.8	1.2	.6	.7
Contradictory	1.2	1.3	.8	.4	1.0
Unclassifiable	1.2	.8	1.2	.9	.4
Left					
Ministerial	.5	.8	1.2	1.6	1.9
Shifting	.3	.5	.9	1.9	3.1
Consistent	.9	1.1	1.0	.9	1.2

Journalists and observers with rightist sympathies commented that it was sometimes difficult to obtain recognition to address the Assembly, and some implied that once their conservative views were known they were deliberately kept from speaking.[23] The evidence shows that right-wing deputies were not exactly silenced but were significantly less likely to debate than the left wing, albeit somewhat more likely to do so than the center (Table 32). Only four men sat on the right out of a total of thirty-five who debated more than two hundred times.

Additional data, not presented in Table 32, refine these generalizations and reinforce the pattern of roles and alignment. These data show, first of all, that the extreme left wing did not debate much: 36 percent of its members never spoke, and only 16 percent spoke twenty or more times. The largest proportion of frequent debaters came from the shifting and ministerial left. Second, the total left-wing predominance over the right on

23. See, for example, Pierre Quéru de Lacoste, *Lettre de MM. les recteurs de Saint-Jean de Rennes et de Retiers à leurs confrères, messieurs les recteurs, curés, et autres ecclésiastiques du diocèse de Rennes* (Paris, 1790).

Table 32
Participation in the National Assembly by Alignment

	Left (N = 467) %	Center (N = 230) %	Right (N = 621) %
Debate			
Never	28	52	50
1–19 times	46	39	42
More than 20 times	26	9	8
Committees			
None	40	60	72
1	28	25	19
2–3	21	11	8
4–5	8	3	1
6–7	2	0 (1 man)	0
8–9	1	0	0
Officership			
Never an officer	68	94	96
Secretary once	24	5	3
Secretary twice	0	0	0 (1 man)
President once	1	0 (1 man)	1
Secretary and president	6	1	0 (1 man)
President twice	1	0 (1 man)	0 (2 men)

committees and as officers was even stronger than the left's share in debate. All thirteen men who served on six or more committees were ministerial or shifting left, and a total of 60 percent of the leftist deputies served on at least one. Again, the relative lack of influential voice for the consistent left, compared with the center left, is noteworthy: 60 percent of the consistent-left deputies did not serve on any committee, and 40 percent served on from only one to four.

When colleagues assessed the relative influence of their fellow deputies, their views were obviously colored by political sympathies and antipathies. To avoid similar biases, I have used independent measures to tabulate the alignment of deputies serving on committees that drafted constitutional articles or handled sensitive inquiries. The first constitutional committee, the Committee of Thirty, elected July 6, was made up of twenty left-wing deputies, three in the center, and seven on the right. The second committee, trimmed to eight members (July 14, 1789), had three left-wing deputies on it, Sieyès, Le Chapelier, and Charles Maurice Talleyrand, the bishop of Autun. These three were the sole advocates of a unicameral legislature, which would deny aristocrats an institutional base; the remaining five members—J. M. Champion de Cicé, Clermont-Tonnerre, Lally-Tolendal, Mounier, and Nicolas Bergasse—all desired an upper house representing the aristocracy. The third constitutional committee, also with eight members, was elected on September 12. Sieyès, Le Chapelier, and Talleyrand were reelected; Jacques Guillaume Thouret, Target, Démeunier, Rabaut de Saint-Etienne, and Tronchet were added. All were on the left.[24]

When the initial constitutional committee was reduced in size on July 14, Mounier won a temporary strategic victory over his rival and fellow member Sieyès and secured a rightist majority. That vanished when the committee was replaced on September 12. From July through September, the majority in the Assembly had come to agree on a set of constitutional principles. The jockeying for position on the constitutional committee reflected the major constitutional decisions made in the National Assembly in August and September. A corporatist and religiously traditional construction of the Declaration of the Rights of Man and of the Citizen was revised to represent an individualistic and secular social philosophy. An aristocratic upper house and an absolute royal veto were rejected in favor of a nearly unchecked unicameral legislature and a mere delaying veto. As we have seen in the previous chapter, all the deputies were not becoming radical; the leftists among them were undergirding their own position under pressure coming from the strength of their conservative colleagues and concern over the popular unrest of the summer of 1789.[25]

Leftists kept the majority in the Comité des Rapports and the Comité des Recherches, but the contributions of right-wing deputies were not insignificant. The thirty-member Comité des Rapports, formed on July 28, 1789, to receive, evaluate, and report on all communications sent to the

24. *Archives parlementaires*, XXXII, Annexes, 549.

25. Philip Dawson, "Le Sixième Bureau de l'Assemblée nationale et son projet de Déclaration des droits de l'homme," *Annales historiques de la Révolution française*, L (1978), 161–79.

National Assembly, was dominated by a four-to-one left-wing majority. Late in August, Malouet enlisted the aid of fifteen or more like-minded deputies to meet regularly, to coordinate tactics, and to resist what they considered to be the erosion of monarchical authority.[26] Although they were unable to produce an absolute royal veto and a bicameral legislature, they were partially successful in securing representation for their conservative views on the twelve-member Comité de Recherches, charged with looking into accusations of conspiracy against the state or citizens. The sixty-three members who served on the committee during one or more of its six renewals included a small majority of thirty-six on the left, with five in the center and twenty-two on the right.

Presidents and secretaries of the Assembly were considered by deputies to be very influential, particularly in agenda setting, curbing the galleries, and controlling debate. When the results of voice votes were not clear, a strong president could sometimes dictate the outcome by announcing it and moving on to the next item on the agenda. Deputies on the left dominated but did not monopolize these leadership positions. Of the 138 men who served as secretaries but not president, 18 were on the right (13 percent), 12 were in the center (9 percent), and 108 (78 percent) were on the left. More than three-quarters of the presidents were also on the left, and there is a significant chronological pattern: after April 28, 1790, *all* presidents were on the left save for one unclassifiable (center) deputy, Anne Pierre Montesquiou-Fezensac, and one right-wing deputy, Charles François de Bonnay, first elected on April 12, 1790, and elected again on July 5 and December 21 of that year (Table 33). In 1791 the left had enough votes, whether because of absences, silent protests, or manipulative tactics, to keep right-wing deputies out of the presidency. Control of the president's chair brought strategic strength in the form of recognition of speakers and a better chance than any other individual had of controlling the Assembly. After Varennes, that strength saved the completed Constitution.

Roles in the National Assembly were associated with membership in revolutionary clubs. Those deputies who were most active in the Assembly were the most likely to be members of revolutionary clubs. Large majorities of listeners, participants, and active participants never joined the Jacobins, the Feuillants, the Société de 1789, the Club de Valois, or the Club Mon-

26. Griffiths, *Le Centre perdu,* 67.

Table 33
Estate and Alignment of Presidents of the National Assembly

Date Elected	Name	June, 1789, Alignment	Alignment Scale
1789—June 12	Bailly	Third Estate	Consistent left
July 3	Orléans	Patriot noble	Shifting left
July 3	Le Franc de Pompignan	Patriot clergy	Center right
July 18	La Rochefoucauld-Liancourt	Patriot noble	Ministerial left
Aug. 3	Le Chapelier	Third Estate	Shifting left
Aug. 27	Clermont-Tonnerre (marquis)	Patriot noble	Moderate right
Aug. 31	La Luzerne	Conservative clergy	Center right
Sept. 14	Clermont-Tonnerre	Patriot noble	Moderate right
Sept. 28	Mounier	Third Estate	Resigning right
Oct. 10	Fréteau	Patriot noble	Ministerial left
Oct. 28	Camus	Third Estate	Consistent left
Nov. 12	Thouret	Third Estate	Ministerial left
Nov. 23	Boisgelin de Cucé	Conservative clergy	Moderate right
Dec. 5	Fréteau	Patriot noble	Ministerial left
Dec. 22	Démeunier	Third Estate	Ministerial left
1790—Jan. 4	Montesquiou (l'abbé)	Conservative clergy	Contradictory
Jan. 18	Target	Third Estate	Ministerial left
Feb. 2	Bureaux de Pusy	Patriot noble	Ministerial left
Feb. 16	Talleyrand-Périgord, C. M.	Conservative clergy	Ministerial left
Feb. 28	Montesquiou (l'abbé)	Conservative clergy	Contradictory

Mar. 15	Rabaut de Saint-Etienne	Third Estate	Shifting left
Mar. 27	Menou	Patriot noble	Shifting left
Apr. 12	Bonnay	Not yet admitted	Moderate right
Apr. 27	Virieu	Patriot noble	Consistent right
Apr. 29	Gouttes	Patriot clergy	Center, Unclassifiable
May 8	Thouret	Third Estate	Ministerial left
May 27	Briois de Beaumez	Conservative noble	Ministerial left
June 8	Sieyès	Third Estate	Ministerial left
June 21	Lepeletier de Saint-Fargeau	[a]Murphy/Higonnet liberal	Consistent left
July 5	Bonnay	Not yet admitted	Moderate right
July 20	Treilhard	Third Estate	Ministerial left
July 31	André	Patriot noble	Ministerial left
Aug. 16	Du Pont de Nemours	Third Estate	Contradictory
Aug. 30	Jessé	Not yet admitted	Ministerial left
Sept. 11	Bureaux de Pusy	Patriot noble	Ministerial left
Sept. 25	Emmery	Third Estate	Shifting left
Oct. 9	Bureaux de Pusy	Third Estate	Shifting left
Oct. 25	Barnave	Third Estate	Shifting left
Nov. 8	Chasset	Third Estate	Ministerial left
Nov. 20	A. de Lameth	Patriot noble	Shifting left
Dec. 4	Pétion de Villeneuve	Third Estate	Consistent left
Dec. 21	Bonnay	Not yet admitted	Moderate right
Dec. 21	André	Patriot noble	Ministerial left

Continued

Table 33
Continued

Date Elected	Name	June, 1789, Alignment	Alignment Scale
1791—Jan. 4	Emmery	Third Estate	Shifting left
Jan. 18	Grégoire	Patriot clergy	Shifting left
Jan. 29	Mirabeau, G. H.	Third Estate	Consistent left
Feb. 14	Du Port	Patriot noble	Shifting left
Feb. 26	Noailles	[a]Murphy/Higonnet liberal	Shifting left
Mar. 14	Montesquiou-Fezensac	Conservative clergy	Unclassifiable
Mar. 26–29	Tronchet	Third Estate	Ministerial left
Apr. 9	Chabroud	Third Estate	Shifting left
Apr. 23	Reubell	Third Estate	Shifting left
May 7, 9	André	Patriot noble	Ministerial left
May 23, 24	Bureaux de Pusy	Patriot noble	Ministerial left
June 4, 6	Dauchy	Third Estate	Ministerial left
June 18, 19	Beauharnois, A. (vicomte)	Patriot noble	Shifting left
July 2, 3	C. de Lameth	[a]Murphy/Higonnet liberal	Shifting left
July 18, 19	Defermon	Third Estate	Shifting left
July 30	Beauharnois, A. (vicomte)	Patriot noble	Shifting left

	Aug. 13	de Broglie	[a]Murphy/Higonnet liberal	Shifting left
	Aug. 27	Vernier	Third Estate	Shifting left
	Sept. 10	Thouret	Third Estate	Ministerial left

Totals by June, 1789, Alignment

	N	%
Third Estate	26	42
Conservative clergy	6	10
Patriot clergy	3	4
Conservative noble	1	2
Patriot noble	22	36
Not yet admitted	4	6
Totals	62	100

Totals by Alignment (Condensed)

	N	%
Left	48	77
Center	4	7
Right	10	16
Totals	62	100

[a] Counted as patriot noble in Totals.

Table 34
Club Membership and Deputies' Roles, Index of Proportionality

	Listeners (N = 443)	Participants (N = 240)	Active Participants (N = 325)	Leaders (N = 166)	Dominant Leaders (N = 144)
Jacobins	.4	.6	.9	1.7	3.1
Not Jacobins	1.1	1.1	1.0	.9	.6
Feuillants, both	.4	.7	1.0	1.5	2.8
Feuillants, Sept.	.8	1.4	.9	1.4	1.0
Feuillants, July	.5	.6	1.0	1.8	2.2
Not Feuillants	1.2	1.1	1.0	.8	.5
Other clubs					
Member	.5	1.0	1.0	1.4	2.1
Not member	1.1	1.0	1.0	.9	.8

archique, but roughly a quarter of the leaders and more than half of the dominant leaders belonged to one or more of these clubs. The index of proportionality shows that Jacobins were more than three times as likely, the Feuillants just under three times as likely, as their numbers would suggest to be classified as dominant leaders (Table 34).

Profile of Leaders and Dominant Leaders

An analysis of the background of the 310 deputies classified as leaders and dominant leaders can give us a direct measure of routes to political influence in the National Assembly. As has been shown (Table 31), all political alignments were represented fairly proportionately among the active participants, but the left was disproportionately strong among the leaders. Nearly two-thirds (65 percent) of the leaders and dominant leaders together were classified as left-wing, with only 23 percent right-wing and 12 percent centrist. The Third Estate, with 61 percent of the total of 310 leaders and dominant leaders, contributed to the leadership of the Assembly out of proportion to their numbers; conversely, only 37 percent of the 310 were nobles and clergy (the remaining 2 percent were not elected by estate).

Besides tending to be leftists and members of the Third Estate, a fairly large number of this group of leaders and dominant leaders had considerable political experience before their election as deputies: 24 percent of them had sat in a prerevolutionary assembly (compared with 16 percent of the total 1,318 deputies), and 41 percent (compared with 29 percent of the total) had been associated with a court or administrative institution. Many of these deputies had judicial backgrounds, 16 percent of them being judicial officers (compared with 13 percent of the whole National Assembly), and 26 percent lawyers (compared with 15 percent of the Assembly). Liberal nobles were a significant subgroup; 14 percent of the leaders and dominant leaders were patriot or other liberal nobles in June, 1789, whereas 9 percent were conservative nobles, 11 percent were patriot clergy, and 11 percent were conservative clergy.

If we divide the 310 leaders and dominant leaders into left, center, and right alignment, differences in political experience appear even more clearly (Table 35). The left-wing leaders were disproportionately from the Third Estate, with lawyers and men in all other occupations slightly more overrepresented than judicial officers, royal administrators, and professionals. Among the leftist leaders who were not Third Estate, lower clergy and robe nobles were slightly overrepresented. Centrist leaders were something of an anomaly, disproportionately made up of middle clergy, nobles not classified as robe or sword, and Third Estate professionals and royal administrators. The upper clergy were the predominant group composing the right-wing leaders.

Men from the upper two estates who were left-wing leaders tended to have been early joiners of the National Assembly in June. Nobles identified by Murphy and Higonnet as liberals were more inclined to become centrist leaders. June, 1789, conservative clergy and nobles who became leaders were likely to be right-wing.

The geographic distribution of these leaders reflects prerevolutionary politics in Paris and the provinces. Perhaps the only surprising finding is that Breton deputies were not particularly likely to take on leadership roles. There are probably two reasons. First, the Breton deputation did not include any nobles at all, and therefore did not include any June, 1789, patriot nobles, who in other provinces molded reputation and experience into leadership. Second, as we have seen, the Bretons were considered to be extremists from their first days in Versailles, and hotheadedness was not

Table 35
Index of Proportionality for Leaders and Dominant Leaders (N = 310)

	Left (N = 202 = 64%)	Center (N = 35 = 13%)	Right (N = 73 = 23%)
Estate			
Clergy, all	.8	.8	1.7
Upper	.3	0	3.8
Middle	.6	1.8	1.7
Lower	1.2	.8	.6
Nobility, all	.7	.9	1.8
Sword	.7	.7	1.9
Robe	1.1	.9	.8
Other noble	.3	2.0	2.3
Third, all	1.2	1.1	.5
Judicial officers	1.1	1.0	.7
Lawyers	1.2	.9	.4
Royal administrators	.9	2.2	.7
Professionals	1.0	2.0	.6
All others	1.3	1.7	.4
June, 1789, Alignment			
Patriot clergy	.7	.9	1.8
Patriot nobles	1.0	.6	1.3
Murphy/Higonnet liberals	1.2	.6	.6
Conservative clergy	.5	1.2	2.3
Conservative nobles	.1	1.3	3.3
Pre–June, 1789, Public Institution			
In	1.1	1.0	.7
Not in	.9	1.0	1.2

likely to make them popular candidates for leadership posts. Dominant leaders were drawn disproportionately from Paris, with a total deputation mostly positioned on the left, and from Dauphiné, on the right. Franche-Comté also contributed a disproportionate number of leaders, as did the small deputations from Aunis, Corsica, and Artois.

Club membership was the most distinguishing characteristic of the leaders/dominant leaders. Deputies with Masonic affiliations were disproportionately likely to hold office in the National Assembly; 41 percent of the probable Freemasons were leaders or dominant leaders. Clubs founded during the Revolution also contributed substantial numbers of their members to the 310 officeholders in the National Assembly: 55 percent of them were Feuillants, 39 percent Jacobins, 25 percent members of the Club Monarchique, 12 percent members of the Société de 1789, and 11 percent members of the Club de Valois. As we saw in chapter 4, there was some overlapping membership in these clubs, especially between the Feuillants and Jacobins, so these percentages cannot be totaled. All of the clubs had considerable success in getting their members elected to leadership positions in the National Assembly. Nearly 70 percent (37 out of 53) of the Société de 1789 became leaders or dominant leaders, three times as many as would be proportionate. Other clubs also contributed many of their members to leadership in the Assembly: 56 percent for the Jacobins, 54 percent for the Club de Valois, 47 percent for the Feuillants, and 25 percent for the most right-wing of these clubs, the Club Monarchique.

Revolutionary clubs did not control the leadership of the National Assembly; a small majority (55 percent) of the leaders/dominant leaders were Feuillants, but for all other clubs considered here, a majority of officeholders were not members. Yet, if we assess the impact of clubs by the percentages of their deputy members who were elected to offices, their influence was considerable. Lacking roll call votes, we cannot measure the weight of that influence in terms of bloc voting, and therefore are unable to document the power of revolutionary clubs to determine decisions in the National Assembly. The evidence does suggest that club membership was a significant dimension of deputies' lives outside of the Assembly, especially for those who were elected as officers and especially for the moderate and shifting left-wing officers who affiliated with the Feuillants in 1791.

To summarize, almost two-thirds of the most powerful men in the National Assembly, as measured by incumbency among the leadership, were those who sat on the left. Furthermore, those leftist leaders were mostly drawn from the Third Estate delegations, from members of the Jacobin Club and (in 1791) the Feuillant Club, and from the June, 1789, patriot nobles. Right-wing leaders had been elites in the church and aristocracy of the Old Regime: bishops and archbishops and members of old noble families. Leaders aligned in the center were disproportionately middle clergy, nobles who were neither robe nor sword, Third Estate professionals, and moderately liberal nobles who had been willing to compromise in June, 1789.

Summary and Conclusions

Analysis of the roles deputies played in the National Assembly produced a significant finding: the Assembly was indeed dominated by leftists, lawyers, and Jacobins, but they confronted opposition from right-wing activists who very often had strong and well-organized institutions behind them. Deputies of very different political persuasions often expressed a sense of being threatened by their own disunity. Their moments of accord were genuine but fleeting, and generally reflected very real fears. The Tennis Court Oath, for example, did not come until virtually all the Third Estate deputies had given up on the possibility of any compromise from the nobles or the bishops and had come to fear dissolution enforced by a show of military power.[27] Such a perceptive deputy as Creuzé de Latouche was apprehensive about the effects that bringing in the nobles and clergy might have on the fragile unity of the Third Estate.[28] After the king's flight to Varennes in 1791, deputies emphasized unity against a background of fears of aristocratic and foreign intrigue and concern over developing republicanism in the Cordeliers Club and popular societies in Paris. A man whose political views were nearly opposite Creuzé de Latouche's, but who was an equally coolheaded and keen observer, was the marquis de Ferrières. At the close of the National Assembly he was ambivalent. He wrote his wife expressing simultaneously his confidence that the constitutional monarchy

27. See, for example, the speech by Glezen on June 23: "Absolute power is in the mouth of a sovereign who recognizes that a people must make its own laws. A *lit de justice* is held in a National Assembly; a sovereign speaks as a master, when he should be consulting." *Archives parlementaires,* VIII (June 23, 1789), 146.

28. Creuzé-Latouche, *Journal des Etats-Généraux,* 150.

would survive and his sense of the uncertain degree of support for the new Constitution.[29]

Questions about legitimacy and participation were central in developing the roles deputies chose within the National Assembly. The deputies' attitudes toward these roles varied in part according to their institutional backgrounds. Most of the pamphlet authors portrayed themselves as challengers of other views and defenders of their group interests, although they also disapproved of factions—presumably those to which their opponents belonged. The men holding these attitudes had sat in provincial estates, practiced before courts, or served as high-level church officials. They were accustomed to adversarial struggles and competition for power. Those deputies whose writings stressed conciliation tended not to have had such institutional affiliations and were disproportionately nobles and curés.

The estates represented by the deputies were of fundamental importance in separating leaders from followers. Listeners were drawn from the ranks of the curés, leaders from the Third Estate and—to a lesser but politically significant extent—noble deputies. Leaders were also likely to be drawn from among men with experience in Old Regime political institutions; they became the debaters, the committee members, and the officers of the National Assembly.

Deputies did not tend to specialize in one form of active involvement in the affairs of the Assembly, such as debate or committee membership. Those very involved in one activity were highly likely to be involved in another. Although certain individuals may have gained recognition in the Assembly through taking an active role in their bureaus or through close attachment to a famous colleague (such as Barnave with Mounier), the more typical route to election to committees or leadership positions was probably through oratory—debating often and dramatically enough to be considered a statesman.

The contention that the left-wing dominated the Assembly by silencing its opposition and keeping the right out of leadership needs to be somewhat modified. For one thing, the right was not silenced: although half of the right never engaged in debate (compared with 28 percent of the left),

29. The marquis de Ferrières to his wife, October 2, 1791, in Ferrières, *Correspondance inédite,* 432–35.

42 percent did debate from one to nineteen times. Left-wing deputies *were* much more inclined than right-wingers to debate twenty or more times (25 percent against 7 percent), but again the right minority had opportunities to air their views. Left-wing dominance of committees and leadership positions was stronger, but not total: 59 percent of the left, compared with 28 percent of the right, sat on one or more committees; 32 percent of the left and only 4 percent of the right were officers. As extreme-right deputies resigned from the Assembly, other men on the right remained active—not enough to change the direction of the Constitution, but enough to fuel rumors of court intrigue and aristocratic plots.

When leaders and dominant leaders are grouped by alignment, estate and political experience complicate the explanation of leadership. Taken all together, clergy and nobles were right-wing, but the clergy were just slightly more likely than the nobles to be left-wing leaders and somewhat less likely to be rightists. There were internal divisions within the first two estates. Lower clergy were somewhat overrepresented among the left wing's leaders and underrepresented among the right wing's. As for the nobility, men of the sword strengthened the right, whereas robe nobles strengthened the center. These differences were greater than the occupational distributions among the Third Estate. Lawyers were the most overrepresented among the left's leaders, but not significantly more so than the rest of the Third Estate.

Patriot nobles in June of 1789 were a key group in shaping the politics of the National Assembly. They were almost four times as likely as their numbers would indicate to be dominant leaders. The whole category of nobles who were liberals in June, 1789, had become polarized by 1791, with 46 percent of them remaining on the left, 47 percent having gone to the right, and 8 percent having settled in the center. Those who remained on the left filled important leadership positions in the Assembly. Fifteen members of the Society of Thirty in Paris in 1788 went on to serve as president one or more times in the National Assembly; ten of those were patriot nobles in June, 1789. These are the men to whom the "converging elites" thesis really does apply. They were allies and friends of leaders of the Third Estate, particularly those from Paris like Sieyès and Target, and they helped to formulate the patriot political agenda from the moment that the Estates General was announced.

The National Assembly was led but certainly not controlled by the men of the left, and not by the most consistently and extremely radical left at that, but by the moderate left who were ambitious for influence in a constitutional monarchy and who abhorred republicanism. They came out of active political careers and institutional connections, but their road to power was not automatic. They faced organized opponents who were certainly not absent from positions of influence in the Assembly.

Chapter 6

Deputies' Public Careers After 1791

In June, 1791, the deputies saw their long and often tedious responsibilities winding down after two years. Regardless of whether they sat on the left or the right, many must have been glad to know that in only one or two more months they could return to their families, their professions, and the management of their properties. Elections were under way at the district level to begin the selection process for deputies to the new Legislative Assembly; the Constituents had already disqualified themselves from reelection on May 16. Then, on June 21, the deputies learned of the king's unannounced departure the night before; they voted to suspend his executive authority temporarily until they could learn the facts.

Abstract constitutional questions became immediately pressing and occasioned much intense debate on the floor of the Assembly and in the Jacobin Club. The Constitution decreed that unless he abdicated, the king could be removed from the throne only if he were declared insane. Did attempting to cross the frontiers secretly and in disguise constitute abdication? The Constitution decreed that the king's person was inviolable. Did that mean that he could not be brought to trial or even reprimanded for his flight? The French monarchy was hereditary, but the heir of Louis XVI was a young boy. The deputies debated naming a regent or a committee of regents and declaring Louis' son the king, but there was much apprehension about the uncertainty and disagreement that would result from having a "regent, a dethroned King, and an infant King all at the same time." [1]

1. Speech delivered by P. Couedic before the Jacobin Society, printed after the minutes of July 3, 1791, in Aulard, *La Société des Jacobins,* II, 580.

Finally, the king had been given the right to sanction the Constitution, but his behavior and the letter of explanation he left behind, thinking he was sure to escape, was an address to the French people making it unmistakably clear that he opposed many constitutional decrees to which he had previously assented.[2]

When Louis was brought back to Paris, fear of foreign military intervention on his behalf and mounting enthusiasm for republicanism in the Cordeliers Club, in some popular societies, and in radical Paris sections created a backdrop of tension for deputies wrestling with what to do about the king and the Constitution. In the summer of 1791 deputy opinion in pamphlets tended to rally around support for the National Assembly and the Constitution, to criticize the king more often as untrustworthy, and increasingly to mention that violence was destabilizing. After Varennes, those who spoke or published their views seemed to come closer together regardless of remaining differences of opinion and political alignment, out of recognition that if they failed to work together, there was little hope of salvaging two years' worth of effort. The marquis de Ferrières, whose signature on the protest of June 29 classifies him as a partisan of the moderate right, was quick to praise his colleagues for their firmness on the Tuesday morning after the king's flight was discovered. On June 23 he wrote to his wife: "All the deputies returned to the meeting hall of the Assembly, and it must be said in eternal praise of this same Assembly, that [the deputies] conducted themselves with wisdom and firmness worthy of the most beautiful days of the Roman Senate."[3] A similar concern for unity is contained in the letters that Le Gendre and Moyot wrote to their correspondence committee on June 21, 22, and 24, exhorting their constituents to remain calm and follow the example of the Parisians in rallying around the National Assembly.[4]

Two hundred eighty-six of the deputies did not, however, rally around the Constitution but signed the June 29 declaration protesting the Assembly's decision to suspend the king's authority after his flight. They

2. Thompson, *French Revolution,* 213.
3. The marquis de Ferrières to his wife, June 23, 1791, in Ferrières, *Correspondance inédite,* 360.
4. François Laurent Le Gendre and Ildut Moyot to correspondence committee, June 21, 22, 24, 1791, in Le Gendre and Moyot, "Correspondance, 28 avril 1789 à 30 décembre 1791," ed. A. Corre and Delourmel, *La Révolution français,* XL (1901), 68–71.

vowed not to leave the National Assembly but to refuse to partake in any of its business as a silent protest. If we compare the signatures on this protest with the names on the April, 1790, protest against the Assembly's refusal to declare Catholicism the state religion, we can demonstrate yet again that deputies' reactions were conditioned by the estate they had been elected to represent. The index of proportionality for estate and protest signing (Table 36) reveals that the clergy were more disaffected by the religious decree than by the aftermath of Varennes, and the upper clergy were more likely to sign than the lower. The nobles were more upset by the Assembly's decision after Varennes than by the religious issue. Whereas 50 percent of the signers of the June protest were clergy, only 38 percent were nobles and a mere 12 percent were Third Estate. But of those who signed only the June, 1791, declaration and not the April, 1790, religious protest as well, 53 percent were nobles and only 29 percent clergy. These signatures are a clear indication that even though estate, along with hereditary nobility, had been abolished as a legal category, and even though the clergy were being compelled to take an oath to a temporal power, deputies who had been delegated by estates still saw themselves as representing those corporate interests. The clergy were defending the church as an institution allied with temporal constitutional authority but superior to it, and the nobles were adamant that a king could not be suspended by his legislature or even by his constitutional convention.

This conclusion is even more strongly supported by evidence from the performance of patriot clergy and nobles who in June, 1789, wanted a unified Assembly and the vote by head. As Table 36 indicates, although the June, 1789, conservatives were the most strongly overrepresented among the protestors of 1790 and 1791, the patriot clergy were nearly twice as likely as their numbers would indicate to sign the April, 1790, protest, and the patriot nobles were more than twice as likely to sign the June, 1791, protest. Many of the nobles still remaining in the Assembly during its final months were among those who could support a declaration of rights and a constitutional monarchy, but not the suspension of the king.

The arguments behind these protests, and the opposing position that finally triumphed, were laid out in pamphlets and in speeches before the Assembly and the Jacobin Club. I coded all available pamphlets written by deputies from the sampled provinces for the time period from June 21, 1791, to the end of the Assembly. There were forty-eight pamphlets writ-

Table 36

Index of Proportionality for Estate and June, 1789, Alignment by Signatures on Protests of April 19, 1790, and June 29, 1791

	Signed Both (N = 207)	Signed Apr., 1790, Only (N = 85)	Signed June, 1791, Only (N = 79)	Signed Neither (N = 870)	No Longer in Assembly (N = 77)
Estate					
Clergy (upper)	2.9	3.1	.7	.2	2.4
Clergy (middle)	2.5	2.1	1.2	.5	1.5
Clergy (lower)	2.1	1.6	1.1	.7	1.2
Nobles (sword)	1.2	1.8	2.3	.7	1.5
Nobles (robe)	2.2	2.6	—	.7	.7
Nobles (other)	1.4	1.8	2.1	.7	1.5
Third Estate	.2	.1	.4	1.4	.5
Patriot clergy	1.7	1.9	1.0	.7	1.3
Patriot nobles	.1	.3	2.1	1.2	1.1
Conservative clergy	3.2	1.9	.9	.3	1.9
Conservative nobles	1.9	2.8	2.2	.4	2.0
Third Estate	.2	.1	.4	1.4	.6
Not Yet in Assembly	.6	.8	1.5	1.2	—
Nobles (Murphy/ Higonnet liberals)	.3	.4	2.0	1.2	.8

ten by twenty-four different deputies, who represented the entire spectrum of political alignment from right to left. Four were on the right, four were unclassifiable, and sixteen sat on the left. Eight were Parisians; nine were Bretons. Fourteen of these authors represented the former Third Estate, nine had been patriot nobles in 1789, and one had been conservative clergy. All of these men took some active role in the National Assembly; more than half of them (thirteen) were dominant leaders. These authors were activist deputies moved by the dramatic events of the summer of 1791 to print their views and recommendations to direct the Revolution toward whatever ends they saw fit.

Of the forty-eight pamphlets, twenty-five did not mention the flight to Varennes. Seventeen did, and their authors presented the position that the Assembly decreed on July 15 and 16: the Constitution was strong enough to withstand the king's obvious unreliability. Six of the pamphlets took the right-wing position that the National Assembly had usurped the king's executive authority by suspending him from his functions. Only Bailly and Pétion printed pamphlets on the incidents on the Champ de Mars. Bailly's tract was an extract from the official statement of the municipal government of Paris exonerating the National Guard and the authorities of all blame for the tragedy and fingering conspirators as the instigators of the incident.[5] Pétion disassociated himself from the petition signers coming to the Champ de Mars and denied that he had urged on the crowd.[6]

Most of the pamphlets supported the Assembly's actions, but several of them articulated points of view farther to the right or the left. Lally-Tolendal, who had resigned as a deputy and was writing from exile, expressed the extreme right-wing position. He still approved of the achievement of civil liberty but insisted that the Assembly had annulled the legitimate authority of the throne, which the king had been attempting to regain by his departure. Lally insisted that the king could still rally support among French landowners, farmers, merchants, capitalists, and manufacturers. This hope could be realized if the king, supported by General Bouillé, would convoke a new national assembly representative of these

5. Jean Silvain Bailly, *Extrait du régistre des délibérations du corps municipal du dimanche 17 juillet 1791* (Paris, 1791).

6. Jérôme Pétion de Villeneuve, *Lettre . . . à ses commettans sur les circonstances actuelles, 18 juillet 1791,* rpr. Pétion de Villeneuve, *Oeuvres* (4 vols.; Paris, 1792–93), III, 419–33.

interests. Failing that, the king should recall his ministers and refuse to sanction any laws, then guard his family and wait for the nation to reject the Constitution and the existing Assembly.[7]

None of the right-wing deputies in the sample who had remained in the National Assembly were as extreme as Lally-Tolendal and were closer to the Assembly's majority view. Clermont-Tonnerre, founder of the Club Monarchique, wrote that he found no fault with Louis XVI for his attempted flight, saying that the king had not intended to leave France but had sacrificed himself to save the Revolution from the excesses being committed by the National Assembly, especially the decrees on religion. Once the Constitution was achieved, the king would support it, and ambitious politicians would be thwarted by a calm and free people.[8] In another pamphlet deposited with the National Assembly, Clermont-Tonnerre said he had taken an oath of loyalty to a Constitution consecrating monarchical government, establishing separation of powers, and guaranteeing the inviolability of the king. "Before his departure, the monarch was the dividing line between two views: locating the Revolution in the National Assembly, and the Constitution in the [king]. Thus, he was the fear of the one group, and the hope of the others. His withdrawal has confused everything. Constitution—Revolution: everything is reunited in the legislative body, and the nation, without approving [the Assembly's] work, is cast into its arms with unrestricted confidence."[9] This total reliance on the Assembly, Clermont believed, was only a temporary contingency. It was absolutely essential to have a king to lead the nation and direct executive power. Should Louis XVI refuse to accept the Constitution, the deputies would wait for his son to become king.

Clermont-Tonnerre criticized individual deputies and deplored what he saw as an unnecessary alienation of the clergy through decrees on religion. He emphasized that separation of powers was the structural key to the entire Constitution, and men like Du Port and Barnave echoed this conviction when they defended the reasoning behind the Assembly's decision to

7. Trophime Gérard Lally-Tolendal, *Post Scriptum d'une lettre . . . à M. Burke* (N.p., 1791).

8. Stanislas Marie Adélaïde Clermont-Tonnerre, *Le Secret de la coalition des ennemis de la Révolution française* (N.p., n.d.).

9. Stanislas Marie Adélaïde Clermont-Tonnerre, *Déclaration . . . remise à M. le Président de l'Assemblée, le 5 juillet 1791* (N.p., n.d.).

perpetuate the king's suspension until he had "freely" consented to the completed Constitution. Only the Jacobin left wing gave up on the separation between an executive monarch and a legislative assembly. Pétion and Maximilien Robespierre were the most popularly acclaimed of the relatively few deputy members of the Jacobin Club who opposed both the king and the Assembly's decision, and remained members of the club when their colleagues abandoned it for the Feuillants. They did not accept a republican government, refusing to go as far as the Cordeliers and some of the popular societies. They wanted a king—although not necessarily Louis XVI—on the throne as a powerless symbol, monitored, restricted, and guided by advisers responsible to the people. Pétion elaborated a proposal for an elected executive council of about ten men, to be chosen from among eighty-three candidates, themselves selected, like the new deputies, by those men who qualified as electors in each of the eighty-three departments. Pétion argued that kings always try to aggrandize their power, so that there is "a perpetual state of war between them and legislators. This conflict could be prevented by surrounding the King with the people's representatives." [10] Robespierre did not propose any such structural solution, but he dared to use the much feared word *republic* in a speech to the Jacobins on July 13, 1791. He said: "What is the real French Constitution? It is a republic, with a monarch. It is thus neither monarchy, nor republic; it is both." [11]

The majority of deputies believed that proposals like these undermined a central premise of their Constitution: that the king would head an executive council of ministers appointed from outside the legislature, while the legislature would make the law and represent the people. Du Port asserted that the monarch was not only the chief executive, but also a checkrein on the legislature to prevent arbitrary decisions and educate popular opinion. The Constitution required a monarch who freely accepted it; if Louis XVI decided to reject the Constitution, he would be replaced. [12] Barnave argued

10. Jérôme Pétion de Villeneuve, *Opinion sur un conseil d'exécution électif et national,* rpr. in Pétion de Villeneuve, *Oeuvres,* III, 403.

11. Maximilien Marie Isidore de Robespierre, speech delivered on July 13, 1791, in Aulard, *La Société des Jacobins,* III, 12.

12. Adrien Jean François Du Port, *Opinion . . . prononcée à la séance du matin 14 juillet* (Paris, 1791).

that France was a large and complex nation with powerful neighbors, which therefore required a monarch to act as a powerful center, creating unity. The king's suspensive veto was a necessary check on the legislature. The Revolution had to come to an end with the Constitution of 1791, lest the ambitions of demagogues inflame the people.[13]

Parisians who had been attending the Cordeliers, popular societies, and section assemblies were already inflamed. When the Cordeliers' leaders placed on the altar of the fatherland on the Champ de Mars their petition asking for a national vote on the future of the king, thousands of people gathered to sign it. With rumors of violence flying, Bailly—who was the mayor—and the municipal government decreed martial law and brought up troops of the National Guard. The evening of July 16, the guard marched to the Champ de Mars and ordered the crowd to disperse, which it did not. When some in the crowd began to throw stones, the guardsmen panicked and opened fire. A number of petitioners were killed and many others wounded trying to flee. Bailly's official statement underreported the deaths at eleven or twelve. He claimed the National Guard had been insulted and the people stirred up by paid foreign plotters conspiring to destroy the Constitution.[14] Jean Paul Marat reacted with a violent diatribe against the municipal government and the deputies, claiming that the erstwhile friends of the people had massacred hundreds of those whom they supposedly represented. The actual number of casualties will never be known, but the best estimate is about fifty.[15]

For the days that followed, there is no record of even a single deputy's expressing any comprehension of the aims of the petitioners, any sympathy for the victims, or any possibility that the municipal government and the National Guard might have overreacted and used excessive force, with tragic results. The municipal government and the Comité des Recherches interrogated participants and arrested many, including some women. Particularly targeted were journalists and members of the printing trade—the

---

13. Antoine Pierre Joseph Marie Barnave, *Opinions de M. Barnave et Salle sur les événemens du 21 juin 1791, prononcés à la séance du 15 juillet* (Châlons, 1791).

14. Bailly, *Extrait du registre;* George Armstrong Kelly, "Bailly and the Champ de Mars Massacre," *Journal of Modern History,* on-Demand Supplement, LII (1980), D1021–D1046.

15. Mathiez, *Le Club des Cordeliers,* 149.

authorities knew what they had to fear from an aroused and an informed citizenry.[16]

Debates within the Jacobin Society on July 17 and the days following portray a group of men scrambling to disassociate themselves from both republican opinion and the violence on the Champ de Mars. They had lost a significant proportion of their membership to the Feuillants and were dismayed by accusations that they were in conflict with the National Assembly. Admitting their differences with committees of the National Assembly over the decree of July 15, they repeated their assurances that once the further clarification on July 16 had signaled the Assembly's intention to retain Louis XVI, they supported and would continue to support all decrees.[17]

The flight to Varennes and the massacre on the Champ de Mars etched indelibly the left and right ideological boundaries for the men about to end forever their careers in the National Assembly. The extreme-right-wing monarchists saw the king's attempted escape as a tragic indication of his weakness and proof of the wholesale abandonment of his cause by those who had a political and a moral obligation to undergird his throne. Most of these monarchists were, like Lally-Tolendal, no longer deputies. Some of those who remained signaled their disapproval by announcing that they would cease participating in debate. One hundred fifty-one deputies signed the protest of September 15, 1791, claiming that the king's acceptance of the Constitution could not be free and was therefore invalid.

The extreme left of the Assembly was represented by men like Robespierre, Pétion, and Louis Jacques Hippolyte Corroller de Moustoir, who had remained with the Jacobins and had been willing, for a time at least, to recommend the king's removal from the throne. They were not at that time republicans, and they were not the champions of the popular movement. They must have been acutely aware that the 7,000 signatories of the Cordeliers' petitions were overwhelmingly not scoundrels, foreigners, paid informants, and common criminals, but bakers, cooks, printers, brewers, and shopkeepers—men and women of the same class that had saved the National Assembly at least twice before when they conquered the Bastille

16. *Ibid.* Also see Darline G. Levy, Harriet B. Applewhite, and Mary D. Johnson, *Women in Revolutionary Paris* (Urbana, 1979), 64.

17. Aulard, *La Société des Jacobins,* III, 25–31.

and brought the king to Paris in 1789. There is no evidence of any feeling of guilt or remorse in the scanty number of pamphlets and records of debates that followed events on the Champ de Mars. The radicals in the National Assembly spoke in the name of the sovereign people, but not the flesh-and-blood women and men of Paris.

There is a curious similarity between the first and the last six weeks that these elected deputies spent as colleagues. In the initial six weeks a majority in favor of declaring the National Assembly had gradually coalesced within the Third Estate as other alternatives appeared to be forestalled. In the closing weeks the majority view came to be that the Constitution ratified by the king's assent was all that could prevent two unthinkable alternatives: a monarchical and aristocratic resurgence that would destroy newly granted civil liberties and restore the reign of privilege, or a republican Revolution that would unleash undisciplined mobs and discordant factions. Jean Marie Baudoüin de Maisonblanche, who sat on the left, wrote to his correspondence committee in Brittany about the "solidarity" of the Constitution on September 17.[18] Ferrières, a member of the moderate right, also felt the necessity of drawing together around the Constitution. He wrote his wife that he was very critical of émigrés, would not sign the protest against the king's acceptance, and felt that his work as a deputy had been well concluded. He doubtless spoke for a good many colleagues when he advised, "Let us march along with events."[19]

On September 13, Louis XVI notified the Assembly that he had accepted the Constitution. The next day he came to the meeting hall to swear his allegiance. The document was promulgated on September 15. The following Sunday there was a mass of thanksgiving at Notre Dame and a public festival with a balloon ascent on the Champ de Mars. The Assembly met for the last time the last day of September.

In his memoirs, Malouet acknowledged his exhaustion and relief at having his duties as a deputy finished but criticized the dissolution of the Assembly at that time and regretted his earlier support of the decree making the deputies of the National Assembly ineligible for the new Legislative

18. Jean Marie Baudoüin de Maisonblanche, Letter No. 43, *Mémoires de la Société d'émulation des Côtes-du-Nord,* XXVII (1889), 62.

19. The marquis de Ferrières to his wife, October 2, 1791, in Ferrières, Charles Elie, marquis de, *Correspondance inédite (1789, 1790, 1791),* ed. Henri Carré (Paris, 1932), 434.

Assembly. He claimed that the ineligibility decree was supported by the left as a tactic to hasten republicanism (an inaccurate reading) and was acceptable to the right as a means toward the destruction of the Constitution. Had the men who created the constitutional monarchy stayed assembled to husband it, it might have had a chance of success and the king might have remained true to the constitutionalists.[20] But these were afterthoughts written down years later; most of the deputies were glad to be finished in September, 1791. Many of them were to have a chance to support their Constitution when they were elected to judgeships and departmental administrative posts.

Many of the conceptualizations that historians apply to the Revolution delineate stages and time periods according to the particular social group or political faction in power: the revolt of the nobles, followed by the bourgeois Revolution and then the popular Revolution, or the Triumvirate followed by the Fayettistes, the Brissotins, and then the Robespierristes. Such an approach suggests that as one group fell from influence its members disappeared from the political stage, either moving into private life or being eliminated by their triumphant successors. Political reality proved to be less clear. Quite a large minority of the deputies to the National Assembly continued to hold political office throughout dramatic changes in regime. Indeed, at the close of the National Assembly, deputies recognized that although they had disqualified themselves for the next legislature, many of their colleagues had no intention of retiring from public life. The marquis de Ferrières commented wryly to his wife that he hoped for an early adjournment of the Assembly because so many of its lawyer-deputies were being elected to judgeships and would be eager to assume their new careers.[21]

I collected information on all 1,318 deputies as to whether they were ever involved in political violence and whether they were elected to the National Convention. For the 247 men in the sample, I collated all available information on the remaining years of their political careers until their deaths. Eighty-three former members of the National Assembly (6 percent)

20. Malouet, *Mémoires,* II, 137–63.

21. Thompson, *French Revolution,* 223. See also Cobban, *Social Interpretation of the French Revolution;* the marquis de Ferrières to his wife, November 30, 1790, in Ferrières, *Correspondance inédite,* 223.

were elected to the National Convention in 1792 or later. They are part of the total membership analyzed by Alison Patrick in her study of political alignment in the Convention. She categorized deputies according to their roll-call votes, protest-list signatures, and other political activities between the vote on the king's fate on January 15, 1793, and Thermidor.[22] I have used her classifications for the former deputies to the National Assembly, to investigate whether their earlier political experience predicted their political alignment in the Convention.

Given the ideological limits of the men of 1789, we might expect the left wing of 1791 to have been more likely to hold public office through the period of Girondin and Jacobin dominance, whereas their more moderate colleagues would reemerge politically after Thermidor and the fall of Robespierre. Because of their political activism, left-wing deputies would be more likely than right-wing deputies to be victims of the Terror. These expectations are generally borne out by the membership rolls of the National Convention and accounts of victims of revolutionary violence.

A deputy's former estate remained a strong predictor of the likelihood of his election to the Convention. Third Estate deputies were disproportionately likely to be Conventionnels. Of the eighty-three Conventionnels who had been in the Assembly, sixty-eight had been Third Estate; eight had been elected to the Estates General as clergy and six as nobility, and one was not elected by estate. Former estate, however, did not play much of a role in determining a deputy's *alignment* in the Convention. Former clergy and Third Estate deputies were equally likely to be Girondin, Montagnard, or to sit with the Plain. Of the six former nobles not one was a Girondin, three were Montagnards, one sat with the Plain, and two were not classified.

By way of contrast, there was a strong connection between Convention alignment and prerevolutionary membership in a provincial assembly; undoubtedly the locus of Girondin strength in the provinces and Montagnard strength in Paris underlay this connection. Among the eighty-three former members of the Assembly at the Convention, fourteen had sat in a prerevolutionary provincial estates or assembly. Of these fourteen, only two were Montagnards; six sat with Girondins and six with the Plain. (These latter fourteen men make an interesting small study in revolutionary politics; the

22. Patrick, *Men of the First French Republic.*

two Montagnards aligned with Jacobin centralizers trying to tighten control over French politics and administration from Paris, whereas the twelve Girondin and Plain supporters sought to defend provincial points of view in assemblies that spanned the Old Regime and the First Republic.)[23]

To understand the opinion trajectories of former members of the National Assembly, we can investigate the relationship between their political alignment of 1791 and that of 1793–1794. The left-wing deputies were indeed more likely than their colleagues to follow the political shift to republicanism and serve in the National Convention. Seventy-eight of the eighty-three Constituents had been on the left in 1791; only three had sat on the right, and two were unclassified. But the former left-wing Constituents did not all belong to the extreme left of the Convention; they were about evenly distributed among the Mountain, the Plain, and the Girondins and their supporters.

Following Patrick's classifications, we find two former right-wing Constituents classified with the Plain and one with the Mountain.[24] The Gironde drew its twenty-four former deputy supporters from the left wing; the Mountain drew all but two of its twenty-five from the left (one of the remaining two was unclassified and one was right-wing). Fourteen of the Plain deputies had been left-wing; one had been right-wing. One unclassified deputy sat with the Plain, and the other with the Mountain.

These relationships augment our understanding of the complexity of deputies' alignment trajectories in the First Republic. Clearly, being left-

23. Once again it is important here, in view of the small number of men involved, to remember that I am not sampling deputies, but looking at the entire membership of the National Assembly. These are not estimates of probabilities, but real numbers of actual men in a unique institutional setting.

24. Alison Patrick places the Conventionnels in three groups: the Gironde, the Mountain, and the Plain. Following Sydenham, she defines the Gironde as including known supporters of Jacques Pierre Brissot de Warville, along with men who protested against the June 2 decree expelling Girondin leaders, 8 deputies suspected of aiding federalist revolts, and 18 more who were reported to have sympathized with the Girondins. Besides Jacobin Club members, the Mountain included a number of deputies who sat with the Mountain but were not on the Jacobin Club lists, and an additional group of "regicides" who voted for the king's death. The Plain contained the remaining 250 deputies who continued to work for the Jacobin government or perform service on committees in the Convention or who withdrew from political activity between June, 1793, and Thermidor. See Patrick, *Men of the First French Republic,* esp. chap. 2, Table 1, p. 30, and Appendix IV, pp. 340–58.

wing in 1791 made it considerably more likely that one would be returned to national political office a year later. The left-wing deputies had indeed "marched along with events" and now had to confront a vote on the king's guilt or innocence and his sentencing, as well as to engage in the complicated political struggles over the nation's reaction to the developing alliance between the Paris Jacobins and the popular classes. The deputies' left-wing views in 1791 do not predict their alignment on these issues in January, 1793, and after.

Having been a member of a left-wing club in 1790 or 1791 greatly increased a former deputy's chances of being elected to the National Convention. Members of the other clubs included in this study were not nearly as likely to serve in the Convention—only five of them did. One of those became a Gironde supporter, two sat with the Plain, one was *en mission*, and one was not classified. In contrast, 27 percent of the 218 Jacobins from the National Assembly and 16 percent of the Feuillant deputies were sent to the Convention, compared with only 6 percent of the total membership of the National Assembly. Membership in a left-wing club also made it somewhat more likely that a man would vote with the Mountain in the Convention. This tendency was similar for both groups: 34 percent of the Jacobins supported the Mountain, as did 34 percent of the Feuillants. The Gironde party also received some support from Jacobin and Feuillant former deputies: 22 percent of the Jacobins sat with the Girondins, and 19 percent of the Feuillants. The split in the ranks of Jacobins from the National Assembly who were elected to the Convention is yet another illustration of the complicated issue of alignment trajectories followed by deputies. Men who had been Jacobin deputies in 1790 and 1791 did not uniformly move left with the Jacobin Club to support the Mountain in 1792 and 1793.

I have relied for the most part upon information contained in biographical dictionaries to tabulate the extent to which designers of the constitutional monarchy of 1791 met the same fate as the monarch: to be condemned to the guillotine or to become a victim of popular revolutionary violence. A total of 94 out of 1,318 deputies died as a consequence of their involvement in the Revolution. Fifty-six were guillotined or otherwise executed, 11 were prisoners who died in the September Massacres in 1792, 15 died in other incidents of revolutionary violence, and 12 more lost their lives while trying to escape or were assassinated by the enemies they had made during their public careers. In general, deputies in the center were the least likely to die a violent death. Only nine (4 percent) out of 230 deputies in the categories right center, contradictory, or unclassifiable were guillotined or died in revolutionary violence. Seven percent of all the deputies on the right met violent deaths, with the worst odds for those classified as moderate right, 9 percent of whom died in the Revolution. Actually, it was not quite as dangerous to have sat on the right as those percentages make it appear—unless one were a deputy for the clergy; the victims of the September Massacres included eleven right-wing clergy. The 467 left-wing deputies lost 9 percent of their number in the Revolution, and including twenty (11 percent) of the 176 members of the shifting left. The consistent left, who had remained with the Jacobins in the summer of 1791, were relatively unscathed; only 6 of 107 were victims of the Revolution.

Analysis of the leaders of the National Assembly in the previous chapter showed them to have been disproportionately left-wing and more likely to have been affiliated with political clubs than were their followers. These were men who in 1791 had national reputations. Left-wing leaders of the National Assembly were in fact much more likely than anyone else to be elected to the Convention. Of the 202 leftist leaders and dominant leaders, 52 (26 percent) became deputies again. Only one centrist leader and one right-wing leader were elected to the Convention. Nineteen of the left-wing leaders of the National Assembly became Girondins or Girondin supporters in the Convention; sixteen were with the Plain, fifteen were Jacobins, and two were not classified. The left-wing affiliation of these men in 1791 provided no basis for a prediction of their political alignment in 1793.

The prominence of these early revolutionary leaders put them at greater risk from revolutionary violence than the other deputies. Just as their salience made them more likely to continue in national office and thereby retain some political influence, so too it made them likely targets of political rivals and of popular vengeance. Among the total membership of the National Assembly, 7 percent died in the Revolution; 11 percent of the leaders died. The leaders were disproportionately likely to be victims of the Terror and its aftermath, arrested and condemned by the Jacobins in the Year II or by counterrevolutionaries after Thermidor; twenty-three of the thirty-four leaders who were killed were guillotined, and twenty of those were former leaders of the left wing. In sum, of all the former Constituents, those who had sat on the left, those who had been leaders, and especially those who had been left-wing leaders were the most likely to remain active at the national political level by being elected to the National Convention, but they also ran the greatest risk of dying in the Revolution.

That risk—even though the great majority of leaders survived the years of revolutionary conflict—was by no means negligible. Besides the figures just cited, there are some revealing data on the 247 deputies from the regions sampled in this book—that is, Brittany, Dauphiné, Berry, Bourbonnais, Paris, Orléanais, and Auxerre. These deputies were not representative of the entire membership of the Assembly but were more inclined to be active and to sit on the left. The authors of pamphlets among them exhibited these characteristics to an even greater degree. The sampled deputies were slightly more likely than their unsampled colleagues to die in revolutionary violence, and the authors among them were markedly more likely to meet such a fate (Table 37).

There were, of course, many positions below the national level, such as judgeships and local or departmental administrative offices, from which a man could influence the course of the Revolution. (It was these middle-level positions, in fact, that Alfred Cobban had most in mind when he contended that continuity in public service perpetuated the transformation in France from the rule of privilege to the rule of bureaucrats.)[25] The 247 sampled deputies were likely to extend their public careers beyond 1791, including in middle-level offices. All the way to the Bourbon restoration, they were quite likely to have a public role. These were extraordinarily political men. Because they had made themselves ineligible for the Legislative Assembly, 39 percent of them were in private life from September, 1791, to September, 1792—more than at any later date.

The following descriptions are accurate for the 247 men, but should not be extrapolated to all Constituents. At the close of the National Assembly, 23 percent of the sampled deputies were elected to departmental or district offices. The percentage decreased only slightly in the period of Girondin and then Jacobin ascendancy. During the Directory, there were somewhat fewer men in office at the municipal and departmental levels, but more in the legislature. After the radical phase of the Revolution, nationally prominent deputies were increasingly more likely to be elected to

25. Cobban, *Myth of the French Revolution.*

Table 37

Victims of Revolution: Sampled Authors, Sampled Nonauthors, and Remaining Deputies

	Authors in sample (N = 114)	*Nonauthors in sample* (N = 133)	*Remaining deputies* (N = 1,071)
Cause of death	(%)	(%)	(%)
Executed	6	2	4
Died in September Massacres	3	2	1
Killed in revolutionary violence[a]	4	2	1
Died other non-natural death[b]	1	2	1
Died natural death	86	92	93
Totals	100	100	100

[a] Deputies included in this category died in revolutionary uprisings, in the civil war against the Vendeans in the west, or in the revolutionary and Napoleonic wars. For example, some, like Louis Jean Baptiste Le Clerc de Lassigny de Juigné, were killed defending the Tuileries on August 10, 1792 (or, like Clermont-Tonnerre, were killed on that day by republicans who recognized them and identified them as royalists); others, like Pierre Suzanne Deschamps, died in 1793 in the Federalist rebellion at Lyon against the National Convention; and a few more were killed by *chouans,* peasant rebels in Brittany. Louis Charles César Maupassant, Antoine Alexandre Méchin, and Laurent François Rabin died in the Vendean war.

[b] This category includes anyone whose death was directly connected to political involvement, for example, Lepeletier de Saint-Fargeau, stabbed by a royalist incensed by Lepeletier's vote to condemn the king to death in 1793, or François Nicolas Léonard Buzot and Jérôme Pétion, who both committed suicide in the Gironde while trying to escape capture and trial before the Revolutionary Tribunal (their bodies were found partially eaten by wolves).

successive national legislatures, but at local and departmental levels they were being replaced by the next generation. Under the Consulate, the pattern reversed again; the number of former deputies in lower-level offices increased and the number in the legislature decreased.

Political alignment in 1791 proved to be the best predictor of a deputy's further political career. To 1814, left-wing Constituents were overrepresented among those still active in political roles, especially at the national and departmental levels. Both centrist and right-wing deputies were underrepresented, the latter more so. Only in 1814 was there some resurgence of surviving right-wing deputies into political office at the departmental level.

Eighty (32 percent) of the sampled deputies remained in public life in 1791, 57 of them in administrative and judicial posts, 7 in the army, and 16 as constitutional clergy who had sworn their civic oaths. Ten had died (4 percent), 6 (3 percent) were in prison, 31 (13 percent) had emigrated, 97 (39 percent) were in private life, and there is no information on 23 (9 percent). Most of the right-wing deputies either emigrated or retired. Left-wing deputies classified as ministerials and shifting left were most likely to be elected to departmental or district level office. In the first Republic, shifting-left and consistent-left Constituents were the most likely to be elected to the Convention, to departmental offices, and to district offices. This pattern continued through the Consulate and Empire. By the time of Napoleon's defeat, 54 percent of these 247 men had died, and there is no available information on an additional 13 percent, but of the remaining 80 former deputies, 41 (51 percent) still had political roles, 9 were clergy (11 percent), 4 (5 percent) remained outside France, and only 26 (33 percent) were in private life. The return of Bourbon monarchy in no way eliminated the left wing of twenty-three years earlier from political life.

Besides alignment, four additional variables—estate, occupation, role, and province of origin—also help to characterize the political careers of the Revolution's first generation. Alfred Cobban's case for continuity in office was based upon the 35 percent of former Third Estate deputies he found holding political office under Napoleon. Data here corroborate his finding. To the ends of their lives, deputies from the Third Estate were more likely than clergy and nobles to hold political office, although at each revolutionary period, a handful of the 70 clergy and 46 nobles from the sampled provinces did have political posts.[26]

A pattern of political officeholding was formed in 1791, lasted through the period of Jacobin dominance and the Directory, and changed with the advent of Napoleon in 1799. Among the Third Estate the largest occupational categories were lawyers (41 deputies), judicial officers (31), and other professionals (28). From the constitutional monarchy of 1791 through the Directory, lawyers were overrepresented by a factor of two or more in posi-

26. Thirty-nine percent of the nobles emigrated in or before 1791, compared with 34 percent of the clergy. During the Directory, those percentages dropped only slightly, to 35 percent for the nobles and 30 percent for the clergy. Only two members of the Third Estate emigrated. Note that these numbers apply only to the deputies from the sampled geographic regions.

tions at the departmental level. Judicial officers also held a disproportionate number of departmental jobs, but their greatest strength was at the district level. When Napoleon came to power, former judicial officers were returned to a more extensive number of posts, especially in the national legislature and the departments. After 1799, lawyers were still more likely than their numbers would suggest to serve in political office, but to a lesser degree than judicial officers. Other professionals moved more strongly into district-level posts after 1799. Leaders of the National Assembly became more likely than the dominant leaders to hold departmental political office, although dominant leaders continued to be overrepresented in national legislatures until their deaths.

This pattern of change in 1799 did not apply to the alignment configurations formed by 1791. The left wing of 1791 retained its dominance of political offices through the Restoration. Apart from a resurgence into departmental office in 1814, the right-wing former deputies were the least likely to continue their political careers. Centrist former deputies did not fall into any particular pattern.

Constituents' political careers after 1791 were not as demarcated by revolutionary epochs as we might anticipate from the abrupt and drastic changes of regime at the top. The Jacobins' rule and their fall from power ended the lives of some famous former deputies and diminished the political significance of Paris' first national representatives, but these events did not reduce the likelihood that lawyers, the National Assembly's leaders, and especially its left-wing deputies would continue active political roles. Napoleon's advent did reduce the numbers of lawyers in politics compared with former judicial officers, and the Assembly's dominant leaders compared with its leaders. But the left remained the most politically active group into the period of the Restoration.

The shifts in ideological direction of revolutionary policy were not mirrored in the political careers of the first revolutionaries. One possible interpretation would hold that these men had no coherent ideologies, that they were simply adept at tacking in variable political winds. But evidence presented earlier in this book does not support that conclusion. Furthermore, if they were merely opportunists there would be complete individual variation in their careers after 1791 instead of career patterns that proved to be shared by men with similar occupational, regional, and leadership classifications.

For right-wing deputies, with few exceptions, the collapse of monarchy brought an end to public life. The resigning right had quit the Assembly sometime after October, 1789, shocked and saddened by passage of the Declaration of the Rights of Man and of the Citizen unaccompanied by a declaration of duties, as well as by the suspensive veto and manifestations of popular violence. Their view of legitimate government was a monarchy with the king's supremacy guaranteed by his absolute veto and regularized by civil liberties sufficient to protect citizens from arbitrary acts. Political participation would be very narrowly based and limited by indirect elections to a legislature, perhaps no longer representing a society of three orders but certainly providing an upper house to articulate the two largest corporate interests, those of the aristocracy and those of the church. Men who held these beliefs had generally emigrated or returned to private life in 1791. (The fifty-one members of the resigning right included fifteen nobles, half of whom were liberals in June, 1789, and half conservative; thirteen clergy, likewise nearly evenly divided between patriots and conservatives in June, 1789; and twenty-three members of the Third Estate. Forty-six out of the fifty-one had not had experience in a prerevolutionary assembly.)

Members of the more moderate right were willing to wait and see whether France would function under the Constitution of 1791, although they protested against parts of it. These men were not very likely to die in revolutionary violence. They tended to disappear from public view to a greater degree than their colleagues to the left. An increased proportion of them did return to national government under the Bourbon restoration, but even then they were less likely than former left-wing deputies to hold other offices.

Deputies who sat on the left in 1791 were for the rest of their careers the most likely to remain in public life, but they did not move together into a particular political alignment if they were elected to the Convention. The issue of royal legitimacy that polarized them in 1791 was not so much settled as tabled once the king accepted the Constitution and the Legislative Assembly was in session. The new issue of regicide in 1792 and 1793 once again polarized left-wing deputies, but their 1791 decisions on constitutional questions did not turn out to be very strong predictors of their 1793 alignment. However they may have decided their views on the issues of legitimacy and participation that were raised by the events at Varennes and on the Champ de Mars in 1791, the questions were differently posed once the nation was at war, subsistence crises had returned to Paris, the common people were politically organized, and republicanism was a reality. Their alignment on these new questions could not be predicted from their 1791 alignment, but their activism could. A similar career pattern propelled them into political office: a "model" left-wing deputy was a lawyer, a leader in the National Assembly, and originally elected from Paris or Brittany. Many of these men were eliminated during the Terror. Those who survived remained the most political of former deputies until Napoleon's regimes. The events and aftermath of 1799 reduced the frequency of political officeholding by lawyers, the consistent left of 1791, and dominant leaders, and increased the preponderance in office of judges, the center left, and leaders. The right-wing deputies were not restored to disproportionate officeholding by the collapse of elected government, nor were the left-wing deputies eliminated.

The data here confirm and expand the thesis that bureaucrats and other officeholders created and then took advantage of the Constitution of 1791. Lawyer-deputies did consolidate their political influence, but so did those of other occupations and political backgrounds, most of them in the Third Estate. The political influence of the men of 1791 outlasted that of their Constitution.

Conclusion

Alignment in the National Assembly:
The Political Legacy

By the time they disbanded at the end of September, 1791, the deputies had abolished or radically transformed all the arenas where political power struggles took place in the Old Regime. Parlements, seigneurial courts, provincial estates and assemblies, provinces, the Assembly of the Clergy: all were gone. New institutions were put into place by the Constitution of 1791 and accompanying legislation. The National Assembly had established the legislature as the political center of the nation, especially after the crisis following the king's flight to Varennes. New modes of political discourse were in fashion, and new symbols stood for and legitimated the institutions. These developments add up to considerable political change. Nonetheless, how much of a watershed was the Revolution? This question, which Franklin Ford posed a generation ago, still does not have a universally agreed upon answer. Was the main work of revolution what Tocqueville believed it to have been, to continue and strengthen centralized administration and national politics manipulated by elites in Paris? Or was the Revolution a much sharper break, creating electoral and participatory politics, executive-legislative power struggles, and new national political resources, like public opinion, that ushered in eighty-six years of violence and recurrent crises, with no regime lasting longer than eighteen years?[1] In a century of faith in progress and enlightenment, why were French

1. Maurice Duverger, *La République des citoyens* (Paris, 1982), Introduction, 9; Franklin L. Ford, "The Revolutionary and Napoleonic Era: How Much of a Watershed?" *American Historical Review*, LXIX (1963), 18–29.

political elites unable to construct a system of majoritarian politics and a lasting liberal republic?

Marxist interpretations of the Revolution saw it as historically necessary, the antithesis of aristocracy and monarchy based on privilege that had to clear the way for bourgeois dominance based on capitalist accumulation. Postwar political theories, such as Robert R. Palmer's constitutionalist argument, also saw the age of revolution as a necessary stage in the progress toward political liberty and civic equality, the foundation of modern democracy.[2] Recent revisionist theories understand the Revolution not as a historical necessity, but as contingent upon political power struggles, a transformation of the corporate state based upon a hierarchy of privilege into the sovereign nation based upon property rights and competition among free and equal active citizens. These theories have called our attention to the centrality of discourse in political power struggle. Human acts were the motors that drove the Revolution—voting to create a constituent assembly and binding deputies by oath to produce a constitution—but words and symbols assigned meanings to those acts: the Estates General became the National Assembly; the sovereign king became the first of the sovereign nation's representatives. Winning the political struggle required the creation of citizens (people with new identities) whose loyalties bound them to an abstraction called "the nation," and those bonds were forged by those who succeeded at capturing the discourse of modern politics, giving citizens a vocabulary of meanings with which to understand political events. Those bonds were also forged by constitutions and laws that included some in the nation of citizens and excluded others. In my analysis of deputies' political alignment, I have looked both at their public discourse in printed pamphlets and at their actions and careers in order to understand their contributions to shaping the struggle that transformed the nation's constitutional structure and redrew not its geographic but its political boundaries.

In *The Old Regime and the French Revolution*, Tocqueville contended that the Revolution originated in enmities between social groups, enmities produced by resentment of the heavy hand of centralized government and the arbitrary and quixotic use of rewards and punishments to compel compli-

2. R. R. Palmer, *The Challenge* (Princeton, 1959), 3–24, and *The Struggle* (Princeton, 1964), 572–75, Vols. I and II of Palmer, *The Age of the Democratic Revolution*, 2 vols.

ance. When I compared attitudes of deputies grouped according to their province of origin, I did not find a direct correlation between relative administrative, judicial, and political centralization in a province and the attitudes of its deputies on issues involving participation and legitimacy. The long process of centralization did indeed create resentments, but the impact was enormously complex. The most administratively centralized provinces, like Berry or Bourbonnais near Paris, did not have the most radical deputies, nor were they uniformly the most conservative. The most autonomous provinces, Brittany and Dauphiné, had deputies with radical claims but differing grievances, related to their particular prerevolutionary experiences.

Furthermore, when all the provinces were ordered according to the proportionate alignment of their deputies, based on behavioral measures, the relative centralization or autonomy of a province did not affect the probability of its electing deputies with any particular alignment proclivities. These findings should not be taken to mean that Tocqueville's insistence on the importance of centralization was misplaced. Electoral politics as they were played out in 1788 and 1789 often turned on the reaction of local elites to a government initiative or, even more complex, their response to a national government reaction to a provincial action. Degrees of centralization and autonomy were not single variables but extremely complicated processes involving taxation; judicial politics; the registration, publication, and execution of royal laws; food distribution and the policing of markets; transportation; printing, distribution, and censorship of books, tracts, *affiches,* and pamphlets; water and forest administration; police and public safety; public health; and all the myriad other areas in which government and subjects came together. It was Tocqueville's great insight to see how these processes fostered rivalry and resentment and foreclosed the possibility of developing organizations and habits of thinking that could produce compromises within a larger consensus on the nature of legitimate and sovereign rule.

François Furet claims that Tocqueville's analysis never clarified why continuous political centralization produced a revolution because Tocqueville never really grasped the revolutionaries' commitment to political action as a process to shape human destiny.[3] This criticism is somewhat over-

3. Furet, *Interpreting the French Revolution,* 23, 24.

stated. Tocqueville argued that continuing centralization, and particularly the cessation of the Estates General in the seventeenth century, transformed the nobility from a governing aristocracy to a hereditary caste, and thus engendered resentment over unearned privileges. Resentment alone may not be a sufficiently compelling motivation to account for revolutionary energy, but that energy was certainly fueled by acts and events taking place once the Estates General began to meet. Tocqueville never finished the analysis he intended to extend into the revolutionary decade. His understanding of the psychological and political ramifications of the long survival of a society of orders in a bureaucratic monarchy remains the soundest explanation of the determining effect of estate on deputies' attitudes and behavior. The centralizing political processes in the immediate prerevolutionary period were simply too complicated and regionally variable for the degree of administrative centralization to determine directly and specifically the many provincial and local variations in deputies' attitudes and behavior.[4]

Tensions between the communitarian values of a corporate society and individualistic values developed in Enlightenment thought also produced certain kinds of direct participatory experience that proved to be inimical to acceptance of legitimate political competition. Principles of equality applied within small social units could work to exclude and devalue others outside the group. Freemasons, for example, were voluntary adherents who established their rules on the basis of harmony and advancement through merit and achievement, but the lodges excluded less-well-off, ill-educated men with little leisure time.[5] On the governmental level, the administrative units of a modernizing corporate society did not foster the growth of national consensus. David Bien has suggested that the impact of royal centralization was not so much to alienate Frenchmen from one another as to establish a kind of political equality circumscribed within small organizations that would not work in a national legislature. Venal officeholders participating as equals in setting goals and procedures in their *corps* were practicing Rousseauistic direct democracy on a small scale that was inappropriate for the whole nation because it set a standard of unanimity that

4. Tocqueville, *Old Regime and the French Revolution,* 82–89.
5. Chartier, *Cultural Origins of the French Revolution,* 162–66.

could not be achieved in a large legislative body.[6] Patrice Higonnet has argued that monarchical centralization did not destroy communal practices and values but made them defensive, protectionist, and parochial. Had the reforms begun in the 1770s continued to the point of uprooting the structures of privilege and expanding opportunities for non-noble elites, the French state might have fostered a political consensus and deflected revolutionary pressures.[7] Habits of deference and aspiration to aristocratic life styles might have given way to attitudes of competitiveness and ambition among social equals. Instead, the conflicts of the 1780s between parlementary magistrates and reforming absolutist bureaucrats weakened the state and produced not only bankruptcy but a full-blown crisis of legitimacy.[8]

As for the revolutionary changes that began in 1789, Tocqueville's perspective draws us away from seeing the patriot party as representative only of a rising bourgeoisie. The converging-elites thesis in a sense extends Tocqueville's general analysis of the origins and outcome of the Revolution. Its proponents contend that the Revolution was mostly made by and for better-off property owners, noble and bourgeois, who agreed on a program of careers open to talent, constitutionally defined and protected civil liberties, and laws to protect and encourage the ownership of property, and who disagreed only—and for no longer than a year or so—on the strictly political issue of the structure of voting in the Estates General.

This general challenge to the Marxist concept of bourgeois revolution is not completely contradicted by my findings, but it must be nuanced and modified to account for the correlates of deputy political alignment. Most centrally, the converging-elites thesis does not account for the consistent association between estate and alignment. All but 2 percent of the deputies were elected by assemblies of the First, Second, or Third estate, to a considerable extent economically and functionally obsolete institutions in the eighteenth century, but surviving in law and civic status. Estate functioned as a strong predictor of deputies' attitudes on issues of participation and legitimacy. Noteworthy especially was the early polarization in pamphlets

6. David D. Bien, "Offices, Corps, and a System of State Credit: The Uses of Privilege Under the Ancien Régime," in *Political Culture of the Old Regime,* ed. Baker, 109–12.

7. Higonnet, *Sister Republics,* 152–58.

8. Harriet B. Applewhite, "Political Legitimacy in Revolutionary France," *Journal of Interdisciplinary History,* IX (1978), 245–73.

printed before the declaration of the National Assembly divided deputies along lines of issues involving legitimacy and participation. Estate was strongly associated statistically with this polarization, with Third Estate deputies more likely to favor mobilization of popular participation, to fear excessive authority, and to question the king's traditional legitimacy. This evidence from pamphlets does not support George V. Taylor's conclusion, based on his reading of *cahiers de doléances,* that the French political nation was quite conservative in the spring of 1789 and that revolutionary radicalism was formed out of the political struggles at Versailles, the controversies over royal troops, the conquest of the Bastille, and the Grande Peur, all events of the summer of 1789. These diverging interpretations arise from the use of different sources from which one can glean political attitudes, and illustrate the danger of generalizing about national politics from the cahiers. My evidence comes from the pens of many future deputies who were in the thick of political maneuvering in Brittany, Dauphiné, Orléanais, Paris, and elsewhere, and who were doubtless ahead of "national" opinion as it can be aggregated from the cahiers.[9]

Estate of deputies was equally strongly associated with their left-to-right alignment in the National Assembly. More than three-quarters of the left-wing deputies were elected by the Third Estate, as were more than two-thirds of the center, but only a little more than a fifth of the right. The clergy contributed 11 percent of the left, 17 percent of the center, and 39 percent of the right. The nobles were the least likely to be left-wing or center (8 percent of the left and 12 percent of the center), and also constituted 39 percent of the right. The strength of estate as a variable to predict deputy attitudes and behavior continued long after estates were abolished as legal/political entities, and in fact continued to correlate with the future political careers of those surviving deputies whom I traced as long as they remained politically active.

The political significance of estate appears most strongly when the entire membership of the National Assembly is studied. As Alison Patrick

9. George V. Taylor, "Revolutionary and Nonrevolutionary Content in the *Cahiers* of 1789: An Interim Report," *French Historical Studies,* VII (1972), 479–502. See also John Markoff and Gilbert Shapiro, "Consensus and Conflict at the Onset of Revolution: A Quantitative Study of France in 1789," *American Journal of Sociology,* XCI (1985), 28–53. They found less consensus on program and agenda in noble cahiers than in Third Estate cahiers, and relatively low levels of consensus altogether.

found for the National Convention, alignments appear more deeply etched and partisan commitments stronger when viewed from a perspective on a whole legislature than they do when the historian focuses on one particular group and sees others only in relation to it. [10] Estate proved to be associated with sharper divisions among all the deputies than it seems to be in the work of those who have concentrated only on nobles, clergy, or Third Estate and have emphasized similarities rather than differences between the category of deputies analyzed and all the others.

The meaning and significance of this strong relationship between estate and other dimensions of deputies' politics require cautious interpretation. Estate did not determine the material interests of deputies, and certainly estates were not organized by the 1789 electoral system to operate as constituencies for their deputies or interest groups to "lobby" the National Assembly. What estates did do was channel initial political careers for future deputies and condition their opportunities and hence their responses in power struggles that became part of the repertory of their political behavior.

To understand revolutionary dynamics, the historian must also consider divisions *within* estates. I want to emphasize three such divisions that seem especially important in this study: first, the sharp divisions between patriot and conservative nobles; second, the early breech between patriot and conservative clergy (later narrowed); and third, the less-marked but still real contrasts among occupational groups within the Third Estate.

The ninety patriot nobles who supported the Third Estate at the beginning of the National Assembly between June 17 and 23 were of central political importance. They were the sort of men on whom Mounier pinned his hopes for a resolution of the voting issue in the early days of the Estates General. Most of them were in the delegations from Dauphiné and Paris. Many had served in the Estates of Dauphiné, in other provincial estates, or in the new provincial assemblies; only 6 percent of them had been in either the first or second Assembly of Notables. Thirty percent of them were

---

10. Patrick, *Men of the First French Republic,* 6–11. The same overview appears from the artful use of cluster analysis on six roll-call votes in the National Convention in Michael S. Lewis-Beck, Anne Hildreth, and Alan B. Spitzer, "Was There a Girondist Faction in the National Convention?" *French Historical Studies,* XV (1988), 519–36. In contrast, Michael J. Sydenham focused his study on the Girondin supporters and contended that they were not a cohesive party; see Sydenham, *Girondins* (London, 1961).

Freemasons. Vote totals from the first six weeks of the Estates General establish that their numbers did not change very much; they were not able to persuade other nobles deputies to cooperate with the Third Estate. Even when the patriot nobles from Paris arrived, the patriots could not outvote the conservatives in the Second Estate.

Career differences between patriot and conservative nobles continued to be marked until the end of the National Assembly. Patriots were much less likely to resign and much more likely to remain on the left in the Assembly. Those who did defect from the left in 1791 appear to have been critical of the constitutional structuring of executive power and disillusioned over the king's prevarication and secret departure from Paris. Patriot nobles tended to be very active deputies, much more likely than conservatives to take on leadership roles. Thirty-six percent of the presidents were patriot nobles.

Ideological divisions within the clergy, long remarked by observers of the Estates General/National Assembly, were likewise of considerable political significance. Divisions between patriot sympathizers (mainly lower clergy) and conservatives (mainly higher clergy) were instrumental in encouraging patriot leaders in the Third Estate in May and June of 1789 to risk the declaration of the National Assembly. Later, the shift to the right of many patriot clergy who were distressed by decrees on religion weakened the left, intensified rancor among deputies, and pushed further toward what ultimately became a complete break between the church and political radicals, one of the most tragic and enduring splits in the revolutionary period.

More patriot clergy became disaffected and moved to the right than did patriot nobles (69 percent compared with 48 percent). The Assembly's refusal to declare Catholicism the state religion in April, 1790, became the determining event for these men. Patriot clergy were nearly twice as likely as their numbers would indicate to sign the protest against this decree, and they did so in the same proportion as the conservative clergy, who had not hastened to join the Third Estate in the National Assembly on or right after June 17, 1789. Furthermore, 13 percent of the patriot clergy resigned early from the National Assembly, almost identical to the 14 percent of conservatives who resigned. Patriot and conservative nobles differed from one another to a much greater extent than patriot and conservative clergy. Only

4 percent of the patriot nobles resigned early from the National Assembly, compared with 43 percent of the conservative nobles.

Differences among occupational groupings within the Third Estate were not so all-encompassing as the patriot-conservative split within the nobility. More royal administrators did tend to sit in the center of the Assembly, and fewer of them sat on the left than did judges, lawyers, and those earning their livings in agriculture. Opinions expressed in pamphlets showed lawyers more likely than judges to take radical positions on legitimacy and participation. That finding is, of course, nothing new; lawyers have been considered the radicals of the National Assembly ever since 1789. I did not find occupational cleavages to be closely associated with leadership or other career patterns.

Because estate differences predicted varied and recurrent differences in deputies' attitudes and behavior, my study modifies the converging-elites thesis and suggests that Higonnet's bourgeois universalism in the first months of the Revolution was based more in rhetoric than in voting and political behavior. With the significant exception of the liberal patriot nobles, deputies within one estate tended more often than not to align themselves from left to right the same way as their colleagues.

All these political contrasts among and within estates do not fit very neatly with the converging-elites thesis. For the first revolutionary deputies, estate appears to have been one form of continuity from Old Regime to Revolution. Because it established prerevolutionary political opportunities and experiences in general, and structured elections to the Estates General in particular, estate was related more strongly than any other variable to deputy alignment in the National Assembly. The men elected in 1789 had already had formative political experiences in a government and society politically structured along lines of estate, and their attitudes and actions carried over into new institutional settings. Yet divisions within estates are also an important element of the explanation of revolutionary change. The gulf between patriots and conservatives in the nobility was wide, and was of great political significance because of the leadership roles of patriot nobles, especially as contrasted with the greater likelihood of early resignation by conservatives. Patriot nobles strengthened the left both numerically and politically, helping it to dominate the writing of the Constitution and the making of laws. The clergy, initially divided, became much more likely than the nobility to converge toward the right in 1790. These fissures within the first two estates helped create great changes in national politics by 1791.

The meaning of estate at the beginning of the Revolution can also be interpreted in the context of theories about representation. Keith Baker has demonstrated a progression that began with a theory of corporate representation based in a system of privilege, moved through social representation based in property, and culminated in the abbé Sieyès' doctrine of revolutionary representation in which an undifferentiated mass of equal citizens is represented by a national assembly that alone can express the unitary will of the nation.[11] Sieyès seems to have grasped as clearly as any of his contemporaries the political potency of the privileged orders that would be manifest if the elections to the Estates General were organized by estates. In *Vues sur les moyens d'exécution dont les représentans de la France pourront disposer en 1789,* published in January, 1789, Sieyès argued for a national representation based on elections in several stages, starting with town assemblies. He felt that members of all three orders had developed an interest in public affairs sufficient to allow them to cooperate.[12] In his famous pamphlet *Qu'est-ce que le Tiers-état?* published a few months later, he was less sanguine about the public-mindedness of the privileged. An extraordinary assembly ought to have been convened to draw up a constitution, he said, and deputies to this assembly ought to have had a special mandate from the nation, which he defined on the basis of population and geography: "Where is the nation? Where it is; in the forty thousand parishes that embrace the entire territory, all its inhabitants, and all contributors to the commonweal; without a doubt, the nation lies there. A territorial division would have been designed to form 'arrondissements' of twenty to thirty parishes each, from which the first level of deputies would have been chosen. Under such a plan the 'arrondissements' would have formed provinces; and the provinces would have sent to the capital genuine special representatives with extraordinary powers to decide upon the form and composition of the Estates General."[13] Thus the inimical effects of privilege could be nullified by a

11. Baker, *Inventing the French Revolution,* chap. 10 ("Representation Refined"), 224–51.

12. Emmanuel Joseph Sieyès, *Vues sur les moyens d'exécution dont les représentans de la France pourront disposer en 1789* (Paris, 1789), 93, 123–34.

13. Emmanuel Joseph Sieyès, *Qu'est-ce que le Tiers-état?* (Paris, 1789), 86.

geographically based system of representation that would allow each citizen to stand absolutely equal to every other, subject to a national will expressed only by the national assembly.

Since Sieyès knew that his electoral plan would not be accepted, he advocated other strategies, beginning with the abolition of privilege: "Therefore, if in France we want to reunite the three orders into a single one, it is first necessary to abolish all forms of privilege. The noble and the priest must have no interest other than the common interest, and by force of law they must enjoy only the rights of a simple citizen." [14] Second, he said that those with privileges should be ineligible for election by the Third Estate. If there were no such limits, representatives might end up being from only one order, and in fact all votes could even hypothetically go to only one man. [15] Finally, he indicated that the Third Estate was in fact the nation, because its efforts made up the entire productive capacity of the nation.

Sieyès' whole argument hinged on unity and fear of the divisive effects of unearned and undeserved privilege, which defined the politics of the three estates. Before the Estates General began to sit, he predicted the political significance of estate—so clearly demonstrated in this study—and he feared that significance. He envisioned a nation of citizens bound together only by their common membership in the nation, acting solely on their reason and not on their particular economic interests, local loyalties, or ascriptive castelike qualities. The representatives they would elect would come together to form the only body that could articulate the will of the entire nation. Imperative mandates or any other form of responsibility to particular constituents would be disallowed, and each deputy would consider himself a representative of the entire nation. [16]

Some of the decisions of the National Assembly pointed in the direc-

14. *Ibid.*, 62.

15. *Ibid.*, 24, 25.

16. David Bien considers that the impact of estate on elections was fatal for any chance for national representation. "The deputies from two of the orders represented small constituencies confined to specific occupational and social interests; they did not represent the public broadly. . . . Probably the exact same persons, if elected to the Assembly by the people as a whole, rather than by states, would have had a much better chance for establishing a stable democratic order." David D. Bien, "François Furet, the Terror, and 1789," *French Historical Studies* (Forum II on Furet's *Interpretation of the French Revolution*), XVI (Fall, 1990), 782, 783.

tion of this model—for example, the rejection of imperative mandates, the abolition of estates and noble status, and the repudiation of many privileges—but as Keith Baker concludes, the debates on the Declaration of the Rights of Man and of the Citizen in August and September, 1789, moved away from locating national unity firmly and exclusively in the national legislature. When the National Assembly approved the National Guard's fusillade against the petitioners on the Champ de Mars in July of 1791, the deputies made a tragic return to the principle that the Assembly alone could exercise the sovereign power; the majority of deputies could live with the use of armed force rather than accede to the extralegislative national expression of will on the nature of the executive power. But it was too late for any return to national representation along the lines Sieyès had drawn. The language of popular sovereignty and nonelite power bases in popular societies and section assemblies had overleaped constitutional monarchy.

Estate, with its continuing influence on deputies, is one thread of continuity between the Old Regime and the Revolution, just as its structural abolition was a key revolutionary change. The weakness of the center in the National Assembly, another significant finding documented here, also had implications for both continuity and change. There were only 173 unclassified deputies, 13 percent of the total, and only a few of them had leadership positions in the Assembly. They do appear to have been in the center out of conviction and not just narrow or opportunistic disagreement with the deputies to their left and right. Evidence from their pamphlets suggests that they shared a belief in strong executive authority and, indeed, lost their coherence as a faction in the Assembly after the king's flight to Varennes. Just under one-third of them voted with the left on the colonial question in 1791. Their lack of coherence may have been related to the career patterns characteristic of many of them. They tended to be bureaucrats and other professionals and had mostly administrative experience in the Old Regime. Not many of them had sat in provincial estates or provincial assemblies. Even more than the other factions, the centrists lacked experience with political maneuvering in some kind of representative institution, whether provincial estates or assemblies. Their numeric and political weakness in the National Assembly accounts in part for the centrifugal push of national politics in France from the Revolution onward. There simply was no preponderant group of deputies with moderate views and an inclination to compromise who might have been able to lay the groundwork for consensus.

The intransigence of right-wing deputies provided another centrifugal impetus. These men were on the defensive from the opening of the National Assembly and became a counterrevolutionary force in the summer of 1789. Resignations reduced the overall number of right-wing deputies but weakened the center right, 55 percent of whom resigned, much more than the extreme right, of whom only 6 percent resigned.

Of course, legislative politics was not the only determinant of French political culture, given the complexity of revolutionary behavior and institutions. The king's prevarications, international challenge, the rise of political clubs and later popular societies, the formation of the National Guard, changes in municipal leadership, *journées*—all these developments fostered political polarization and foreclosed the possibility of developing a national consensus on a legitimate constitution and political process. Furthermore, over against some deputies' belief that they were opening a wholly unprecedented epoch in their nation's history, French political development since the end of the Wars of Religion in the seventeenth century had not produced a unitary political culture or fostered a shared world view among the politically aware. Patrice Higonnet, comparing the American and French revolutions, has argued that during the course of more than a century before the Revolution the two French cultural strains, corporatist and individualist, developed a Manichean world view.[17] French political cultures never placed a high value on consensus or on the majoritarian politics necessary to achieve it, and legislative politics did contribute some major force to the movement away from the center and toward polarized extremes.

My reading of deputies' political trajectories differs somewhat from Timothy Tackett's. Tackett contends that the center of gravity in the National Assembly moved toward the right from the summer of 1789 to November, back toward the center after the October Days, and toward the left after February, 1790. From the late winter of 1790 to July, he maintains, there were two identifiable parties in the Assembly: 205 Jacobins on the left and 292 Capuchins on the right.[18] Tackett bases these numbers on

17. Higonnet, *Sister Republics,* esp. 163–70.
18. Tackett, "Nobles and Third Estate."

the Jacobin lists and the signatories of the April 19, 1790, declaration on religion. According to him, the left moved to a dominant position in the summer of 1790 with the passage of bills abolishing noble status and establishing the Civil Constitution of the Clergy.

This interpretation of revolutionary dynamics is in line with my finding of left-right polarization from the very beginnings of the National Assembly, but it does not take into account the fundamental unacceptability of the idea of opposition. The intense polarization in the National Assembly, resulting in part from the moderates' failure to cohere in the center, contributed to the attitude that opposition was illegitimate, even treasonous. Deputies on the right were so far apart from deputies on the left, whose numbers were great enough to allow them to dominate the drafting and passage of constitutional laws, that there was little common ground and almost no will to compromise. The very idea of legitimate opposition was rejected, a legacy from the days of royal absolutism. If I am correct that in 1789 the centrist deputies were held together by a belief in strong executive authority, it would have been impossible for them to defend their views and expand their numbers in the face of the king's recurring challenges to the Constitution-in-the-making, particularly after his delay in accepting the Declaration of the Rights of Man and of the Citizen, beginning in August, 1789.

The establishment of a legislature was one of the important legacies of the Revolution to future French politics. In 1789 the main arena of national political struggle started to shift from royal court to legislature. The failure to develop a belief in opposition as a legitimate political practice in the legislature established one of the main differences between French and English nation building and set precedents for such recurring political phenomena as acrimonious debate, extremes of polarization and stalemate, and regime instability.

An astute contemporary observer, the editor Loustallot, wrote in the May 1–8, 1790, issue of the radical journal *Révolutions de Paris* a trenchant analysis of polarization in the National Assembly, arguing that fear of abuses of executive power was eroding the center. He claimed that rejection of the absolute veto and the king's acceptance of the first constitutional decrees had curbed the political powers of aristocrats, some of whom had even joined the "forces of liberty," but others of whom were in search of new allies. In the spring of 1790 the constitutional issues that had come to the fore concerned executive prerogatives: judicial authority, the army, and the power to make war and peace. All of these had the potential to be used to destroy public liberty and tyrannize citizens. Those on the *côté noir* who were called "impartiaux" believed they had much to gain from royal and ministerial favors, such as ambassadorships, pensions, and honors; and the aristocrats were clever enough to work with them to regain special indemnities from executive power. Loustallot, himself a man of the left, feared the possibility of a new majority formed from those aiming to curry favor from ministers who exercised executive power.[19] Two months later he returned to the subject, this time emphasizing his concern that representatives were always potentially corruptible by special interests and recommending measures to increase popular control over legislators and to require national ratification of the Constitution.[20] Loustallot came to the same conclusion toward which my analysis of deputies' attitudes and alignments points: the breach between left and right widened and the center collapsed because of contention over the conduct of executive power.

Loustallot's analysis highlights the absence of trust among those engaged in legislative politics and their inability to accept opposition as a legitimate political stance that need not undercut liberty and destroy the Constitution. This interpretation illustrates one line of continuity from the centralized monarchy of the Old Regime into and beyond the Revolution. The legal and judicial structures of the Old Regime and the long period without a national deliberative institution allowed no precedent to develop for adversarial debate or the practice of legitimate opposition, and the links among deputies' alignments, political experience, and revolutionary roles foreclosed the possibility of developing new values and habits that might facilitate centripetal legislative politics.

At the same time, the unacceptability of opposition marked a revolutionary change when it became a feature of legislative and electoral politics—whole new arenas to be contrasted with court, parlements, provincial estates, and the like. Historians studying later revolutionary legislatures have emphasized the rejection of the legitimacy of opposition in their analyses of political dynamics. C. J. Mitchell used the seven roll-call votes held during the Legislative Assembly to determine that the largest number of

19. *Révolutions de Paris,* Vol. IV, No. 43 (May 1–8, 1790), 253–60.
20. *Ibid.,* Vol. IV, No. 52 (July 3–10, 1790), 732–35.

deputies actually occupied the center, but failed to identify themselves as a center party because they scorned the concept of competing political factions.[21] The long-running debate between Michael J. Sydenham and Alison Patrick over the nature of political alignments within the National Convention really turns on the point of disapproval of the idea of opposition. Sydenham's study of the Girondins, published thirty years ago, argued that the Jacobins were a fairly disciplined, coherent, and ambitious minority, whereas their opponents, the Girondins, were disunified and both ideologically and organizationally amorphous. It was only Jacobin propaganda that portrayed them as a large and effective party, and that propaganda was convincing to contemporaries because of the general distrust of parties.[22] Patrick's counterthesis is supported by her use of roll-call votes to classify the members of the National Convention. She contends that there were more Jacobin supporters, whom she labels Montagnards, than Sydenham believes—so many that they actually constituted a majority of 433 out of 730 total deputies by the middle of the summer of 1793; moreover, the Girondin supporters were more structured than the remainder of the Plain deputies and were ideologically distinct.[23] Focusing on conceptions of revolutionary government, Theodore Di Padova supports Patrick's interpretation with evidence that Girondin deputies shared opposition to Paris and a desire to consolidate the federalist gains of August 10, 1792, in a strong and autonomous Convention.[24] A further modification of this position finds the Girondins separating from other deputies of the Plain in April and May, 1793, but not on votes during the trial of the king the previous winter. No matter which way the party structure is delineated, the development of

21. C. J. Mitchell, "Political Divisions Within the Legislative Assembly of 1791," *French Historical Studies,* XIII (1984), 356–89, esp. 387.

22. Sydenham, *Girondins,* 198–206.

23. Alison Patrick, "Political Divisions in the French National Convention, 1792–93," *Journal of Modern History,* XLI (1969), 421–74. Her original categories are defined in Patrick, *Men of the First French Republic,* chap. 2. See also Michael J. Sydenham, "The Montagnards and Their Opponents: Some Considerations on a Recent Reassessment of the Conflicts in the French National Convention, 1792–93," *Journal of Modern History,* XLIII (1971), 287–93; Theodore A. Di Padova, "The Girondins and the Question of Revolutionary Government," *French Historical Studies,* IX (1976), 432–50.

24. Di Padova, "Girondins and the Question of Revolutionary Government," 432–50.

democratic legislative politics was ultimately blocked by the insistence that only one party could represent the general will, and therefore all opposing groups were inimical to the nation and illegitimate.[25] This illegitimacy became a hallmark of French legislative politics for generations—some would say until the Fifth Republic and the referendum of 1962 on direct election of the president.[26] It became a significant characteristic of the nationalization of politics from the Revolution forward through subsequent changes of constitution and regime, and it complicated the political absorption of new issues of contestation in the nineteenth and twentieth centuries.

Deputies' roles as leaders and followers were another important dimension of the Revolution's legacy to legislative politics. Parliamentary representation could not produce continuity from the Old Regime to the Revolution, since there had been no national deliberative or lawmaking body in France for 175 years. The roles that deputies invented for themselves beginning in May, 1789, created precedents for internal legislative politics in the future. The styles of being nonconciliatory, uncompromising, and ideological grew out of the first six weeks of struggle and stalemate, apprehension about forced dissolution, the pressures exerted by the radical patriots, and the Breton deputation's meetings to organize and coordinate their tactics. Pamphlet evidence attests to the deputies' perceptions of conflict, challenge, and nonconciliation, and to their disapproval of factions, coupled with their tendency to define their own roles as defenders of their groups' interests, rather than as conciliators.

Right from the beginning of the Estates General, certain political practices worked against a politics of compromise. As we saw, for example, imperative mandates were charged mostly to deputies from the two upper orders, and those with imperative mandates were more likely to see themselves as challengers. For another example, patriot nobles, who were sympathetic to the demands of the Third Estate in May and June, 1789, were not named as commissioners in the search for a resolution of the dispute over the method of voting in the Estates.

25. On this point see Lewis-Beck, Hildreth, and Spitzer, "Was There a Girondist Faction in the National Convention?" and Commentary, 537–48. See esp. Alison Patrick's commentary, p. 542.
26. Duverger, *La République des citoyens,* 41–56.

The leadership of the National Assembly was dominated by deputies from the Third Estate and by the patriot nobles. The two groups labeled leaders and dominant leaders had 65 percent of their members on the left, 11 percent in the center, and 24 percent on the right. This distribution of partisan strength must be interpreted with care. The left contributed the most leaders, but did not monopolize control of the National Assembly. Also, the partisan distribution overlapped with distribution by estate. Left-wing leaders were mostly from the Third Estate and were disproportionately Jacobin Club members. Some of the important left-wing leaders were patriot nobles, who contributed 36 percent of the presidents of the National Assembly. Right-wing leaders were drawn from leaders of the church and the old aristocracy, both of which had been reluctant to support the demands of the Third Estate in the Estates General. The thirty-five leaders classified in the center included a dozen nobles and clergy (two deputies from the middle ranks of the clergy, two curés, one robe noble, five sword nobles, and two other nobles) and twenty-three Third Estate deputies. These associations show once again the impact of estate on deputies' political careers and convictions, and thus on the structure of leadership of France's first constitutional convention.

In the deputies' political world, the probability of being elected a leader was greater for those who were members of political clubs, including not only the Jacobins but also clubs in the center and on the right. All club members across the political spectrum were disproportionately likely to be leaders. These extrainstitutional links with legislative politics worked against compromise and conciliation. Political clubs did not originate as electoral organizations or independent interest groups operating within legitimate political structures and employing conventional political strategies, but rather as forums to make the issues of the day conform to broad ideological perspectives and to deliver the votes of their deputy members in the desired direction. Their debates were usually combative and defensive, and all other clubs and competing points of view except their own were considered divisive, factional, unpatriotic, intolerable, and ultimately illegitimate.

In summary, France's first modern legislators were not setting down precedents for consensual politics and styles of bargaining and compromise but were continuing a tradition of the unacceptability of opposition characteristic of bureaucratic monarchy. The 29 percent of them who had had careers in the administrative and judicial institutions of the Old Regime may well have practiced a kind of democratic egalitarianism within their corps, but they also learned habits of opposition to those outside.[27] At the same time, their new institutions such as the National Assembly and political clubs and their innovative behavior such as constitution writing and national political debate were replacing court and provincial politics with a style and substance not conducive to representative government and limited monarchy.

In the conclusion to her study of political culture, Lynn Hunt noted that the members of the "revolutionary political class" had no experience with democratic sociability, since institutions for debate and for power sharing had either been eliminated or severely constricted after 1614.[28] My study offers some evidence that the limited opportunities that did exist for democratic sociability—or at least elite group politics—affected the opinions and actions of the men who experienced them. A strong case exists for the deputies with Masonic affiliation. The 244 deputies who were probably Freemasons were more likely than other deputies to have had experience in provincial assemblies, provincial estates, and the Assembly of Notables, and to have published pamphlets. Those who were nobles were disproportionately likely to support the patriot party by joining the National Assembly before the king ordered them to do so. Nearly a quarter of the Freemasons were members of the Société de 1789, the Club de Valois, or the Club Monarchique; 27 percent were Jacobins. Freemasons also played a very active role in the Assembly; 41 percent of the Masonic deputies were leaders or dominant leaders. They were disproportionately likely to sit on the left.

If we look at all the deputies with experience in a prerevolutionary assembly, whether or not they were Masons, we find that they tended to behave differently than their colleagues in the National Assembly. Only 16 percent of the deputies had sat in some kind of political assembly, but

27. This interpretation is an extension of the argument by David Bien in "Offices, Corps, and a System of State Credit," in *Political Culture of the Old Regime*, ed. Baker, esp. 111–12.

28. Hunt, *Politics, Culture, and Class in the French Revolution*, 215.

they were more likely to publish political pamphlets. Furthermore, the kind of experience they had had made a difference in their political opinions; those who had sat in provincial assemblies or in the estates of Dauphiné were more inclined than other deputies to support mobilizing the masses, to approve of factions, and to fear excessive authority. Also, deputies with experience in assemblies aligned differently, with those from the Assemblies of Notables on the right and those from the estates of Dauphiné in the center. Among the patriot nobles, 29 percent had had experience in some kind of assembly, 6 percent in one or both Assemblies of Notables, and the rest in Necker's assemblies, provincial estates, or the estates of Dauphiné. It is probable that the patriot nobles' involvement in these deliberative and debating bodies inclined them toward support for the demands of the Third Estate; this was certainly true of Mounier's noble colleagues in Dauphiné.

It would be logical to expect that these experiences in assemblies would shape future deputies into liberals, sharing Enlightenment values of individual achievement and egalitarian cooperation. But the missing ingredient was respect for the rights of those with minority opinions, one specific dimension of the damage Tocqueville believed that centralization had wrought in France, allowing no value to be put on compromise or conciliation, let alone on opposition as a legitimate political stance. Hatred of privilege and egalitarian convictions were insufficiently buttressed by these other cooperative values, necessary to consolidate liberal legislative politics in a constitutional monarchy.

The significance of estate as a predictor of the attitudes and actions of deputies can hardly be downplayed. More than any occupational, regional, or other institutional line of division among them, estate was consistently and firmly drawn. Taking into account the significant contributions of patriot nobles and curés, it was nonetheless the Third Estate that produced the National Assembly, determined most of the contents of the Constitution of 1791, and remained at various levels of political office until the Restoration. Many of the other political variables that proved of some importance were reflections of the political significance of estate, such as the differences between the Breton and the Dauphinois delegations. The political struggles of the first two and a half years of the Revolution were not a radical departure, not an unprecedented politicization of a formerly non-political world, but a continuation and deepening of political cleavages growing out of decades of royal reform attempts, the resurgence of privilege and prerogative, bishops against priests, the tax-privileged against the tax-burdened. When reforming ministers sought some kind of deliberative body to strengthen their efforts against powerful and entrenched opposition, they first convoked the Notables, only to discover that they had given yet another forum to their opponents. When next they dusted off the historical model of the Estates General, they solidified the distinctions between estates as they debated how to determine proportionate representation and the method of voting. This interpretation does not contradict the advocates of the converging-elites thesis, who agree that these issues divided the estates. Where my findings do depart from and modify that interpretation is in the demonstration of the roots, repercussions, and persistence of estate as a correlate of deputy alignment, roles, and careers after 1791.

As historians have shifted their attention away from social and economic explanations of the French Revolution and toward understanding it as a political struggle, they have tended to cite specific events as decisive moments forcing participants to take sides and making it next to impossible to remain neutral or uninvolved. For the deputies, such events included the night of August 4, 1789, the *journées* of October 5 and 6, the votes on clerical oaths in November, 1790, and the king's flight to Varennes in June, 1791. Plotting deputy alignment trajectories along the chronological line of these events is made extremely difficult by the lack of lists of roll-call votes; not every deputy can be assigned to an alignment category on a particular date. Evidence from the pamphlets in chapters 1 and 2 indicates that opinions on violence and on the king did consolidate in the summer of 1791, isolating most of the deputies from the aristocratic supporters of the king on the right and radical supporters of the Cordeliers and popular societies on the left. The analysis of alignment trajectories presented in chapter 4 suggests that many generalizations about politics in the National Assembly mask a very complicated process—really an experiment with parliamentary strategies such as forcing or delaying votes, using procedures to engage in struggles over substance, resigning and then sometimes returning to the Assembly, and selectively using nonparticipation in debate as an oppositional strategy. Allegedly massive numbers of resignations from the Assembly at the time of its relocation in Paris in October, 1789, were not actually so massive and in any event did not produce a permanent reduction in the total number voting after that date. Left-wing dominance of legislative outcomes was not assured in 1790 or after. Jacobin maneuvering and gallery intimidation did not totally silence right-wing debaters. Politics in the National Assembly were fluid much more than predetermined, and responsive much more than rigid.

Findings here do suggest two very important realities that should be highlighted: the central political importance of the liberal nobles in the National Assembly and the demonstrable impact of club membership on deputies' political careers. The liberal nobles who supported the patriot program in 1789—many of whom in fact had drawn it up in the Society of Thirty—were monarchists, but fewer than half of them shifted to the right during the two and a half years of the National Assembly. They were also disproportionately likely to be elected to leadership positions. Unfortunately for the future of the Constitution, they were not able to persuade other nobles to their point of view. Political clubs, mostly but certainly not exclusively the Jacobins, were key institutions for activist and powerful deputies. It would be an exaggeration to say that they ruled France or even that they could always deliver the votes of their members, but they were the most important institution for communication, coordination, and fraternity available to the deputies. The sociability that they fostered was conflictual, however; clubs contributed in a major way to factional and centrifugal politics and, by 1791, to downright enmity and hostility among political opponents.

Certain research directions might be taken in the future to answer some of the questions that this study suggests. I found that deputies' estate was associated with their published opinions before the formation of the National Assembly, with their initial experiences in public life, and with the circumstances of their election. These connections could fruitfully be probed further by looking back at public careers in the Old Regime, perhaps by reconstructing the roles of those future deputies who served in provincial assemblies or by tracing the public lives and occupational connections of fathers and grandfathers of the men who became deputies. Tracing career trajectories backward in time would illuminate the reasons behind the early, intense, and estate-related lines of demarcation in the National Assembly. Such studies could also further probe Tocqueville's interpretation of the negative political impact of centralization on political activities and on democratic sociability.[29]

Another extension of this work would be an analysis of the published opinions of deputies after the disbanding of the National Assembly in 1791. Given that the left-wing deputies had the greater likelihood of holding political office again in the future, such investigation would throw additional light on the question of elite convergence by placing the Revolution's first elected representatives along the spectrum of political beliefs as the Revolution radicalized into 1794 and then consolidated as a regime favoring property holders. My data show only that left-wing deputies remained more political than the others; they do not measure alignment beyond 1791.[30]

The knottiest analytical problem created by the lack of roll-call votes for the National Assembly is the impossibility of ranking all the deputies from left to right at any one time between May, 1789, and September, 1791. The measures I used in setting up the alignment scale date from the Jacobin Club membership list of December, 1790, to protest-list signatures from September, 1791. As we have seen, there is no reliable way to determine just how many deputies were in attendance at the National Assembly on any given day. This limitation makes it impossible to follow and compare deputies of different alignments as they lived through and reacted to the events of the Revolution. Those deputies who participated in debate would be traceable through the procès-verbal of the National Assembly, but those who did not debate at the time of the event in question would not present any record of their interpretation.[31] For the whole membership,

29. Models for such work include Dawson, *Provincial Magistrates;* Vivian R. Gruder, "Class and Politics in the Pre-Revolution: The Assembly of Notables of 1787," in *De l'Ancien Régime à la Révolution française: Recherches et perspectives,* ed. Albert Cremer (Göttingen, 1978), 207–32; and Egret, *Le Parlement de Dauphiné.*

30. Harvey Chisick has linked the publication of pamphlets to the printing of revolutionary journals in an interesting study of revolutionary propaganda, "Pamphlets and Journalism in the Early French Revolution: The Offices of the *Ami du Roi* of the Abbé Royou as a Center of Royalist Propaganda," *French Historical Studies,* XV (Fall, 1988), 623–45.

31. Tackett, "Nobles and Third Estate," 296. He relied mainly upon *mémoires* and letters from deputies to produce a list of 205 Jacobins and 292 "Capuchins" (signers of the "Déclaration d'une partie . . . 13 avril 1790") who dominated politics in the National Assembly beginning in spring, 1790.

including those who did not join clubs and did not sign protests, it is very difficult to gauge the impact of events on left-to-right alignment.

Much of the legislation passed between 1789 and 1791 transformed or abolished the institutions that had structured political relationships among members of the three estates in the Old Regime; such legislation included the refusal to declare a state religion, the requirement of clerical oaths, changes in the methods of appointing bishops and archbishops, and the abolition of nobility. Debate over these and related outcomes sharpened the conflicts among deputies along lines of estate—conflicts that otherwise would have become more muted as the material interests of a propertied elite converged. Analysis of these debates could not be done to include all the deputies, but the alignments of those who did intervene in debate could be reviewed systematically. Additionally, the structure and tone of the arguments might be analyzed to understand their scope and the changing logic of positions taken.

What I have tried to achieve in this book is not a full collective biography of 1,318 men, but a maplike delineation of their alignment and its relation to other aspects of their public careers, tracing the distribution of political influence within the body that was both a constitutional convention and the first modern French legislature. The customs, styles of conduct, and formal parliamentary procedures that the deputies established set precedents for their successors and laid down the rules of the game for legislative power politics in the future.

Recent analyses of revolutionary political culture by Lynn Hunt, Patrice Higonnet, and Norman Hampson have treated that culture as though it were uniform.[32] The political struggles during the period of the National Assembly produced what they variously label as democratic sociability, bourgeois universalism, and popular sovereignty. Their insights are built upon evidence that eroded the basis for a theory of class struggle while supporting a theory of power politics to account for the radical nature of

32. Hunt, *Politics, Culture, and Class,* esp. 213–16; Higonnet, *Class, Ideology, and the Rights of Nobles;* Hampson, *Prelude to Terror,* esp. 185–90. Hunt does delineate lines of division in the political class; however, she sees these as developing not among deputies but outside of legislatures altogether, among all politically aware and active Frenchmen (pp. 216–18).

the Revolution. The evidence presented here on the beliefs and behavior of 1,318 different individuals certainly depicts a power struggle, but suggests that that struggle was rooted in more than individual ambition. The men who drafted the Constitution of 1791 came from at least three broad political cultures—and in fact from many more, if we take into account the demonstrated differences between, for example, the ministerials and the consistent left, or the moderate right and the extreme right. These differences were ideological, and they were correlated with differences in political experience and background. Although we have a subtly different interpretation of revolutionary dynamics, my reading of the political cultures of the National Assembly is close to Timothy Tackett's argument that the understructure of political conflicts among the deputies rested upon differences in wealth, status, and previous political experience—and their subjective reactions to those differences.

I have provided a group portrait of the most critically important political elites in France from 1789 through 1791 as they built an institution that has been a major force in politics from the Revolution to the present. The deputies' attitudes and behaviors, constructed and restrained by factors analyzed here, shaped and reshaped a nation's political cultures in transition. These men's visions, strategies, and laws defined a political field of action that was admirably broad or hopelessly limited, depending on one's perspective, but very influential in the short run and in the long run. The deputies were positioned on the watershed of revolution. As elites who had risen to prominence in the Old Regime, they had perspectives on goals and power that had been set in place by their experiences within the institutions of monarchical government and with the politics of reform and reaction to reform. In this sense their alignments and behavior represent one form of continuity from Old Regime to Revolution and beyond. But they were also men who drafted France's first written Constitution that delineated and limited political power. They were part of the collectivity that abolished and transformed the institutions of public life in the Old Regime, and in this sense their alignments and behavior represent revolutionary change.

The seed of Terror that was planted in the National Assembly grew out of the failure to recognize the legitimacy of political opposition and the failure to achieve what I have called majoritarian politics that might have pulled deputies toward the center and away from extremes of right and left.

But there were also seeds of democratic politics in the National Assembly, both in parliamentary procedures and in the achievement of constitutional definitions of rights.

The deputies were insulated by experience, inclination, electoral regulations, and deliberate effort from the needs and demands of a very broad and extensively politicized group of largely unenfranchised men and women, mobilized within new local and neighborhood organizations, who were radically challenging high politics and making themselves part of the political nation. While the deputies were defining the exact conditions for the legitimacy of constitutional monarchy, these men and women were actually confronting the National Assembly with the sovereign nation in person—especially on October 5, 1789, and July 16, 1791.

After July, 1789, with the nullification of imperative mandates, the deputies had no delegated powers and no mechanisms through which they could be held politically responsible to their constituents. Viewing the world through a Manichean lens, they succeeded in transferring the legitimacy of a royal sovereign to a sovereign Assembly, but they failed to develop both the theories and the mechanisms of representation that would allow the creation of majoritarian politics: consensus on political responsibility, beneath which the idea of legitimate opposition could flourish. Believing that they could sweep away the old order and invent a wholly new politic by the acts of declaring the National Assembly and binding themselves by oath not to disband until they had given France a constitution, they developed a conception of sovereignty as an almost mystical unity of equal and isolated individuals whose interests were unmediated by any corporate structures. Their political cultures were adversarial but did not allow the admission of any opposition as legitimate. The National Assembly was instrumental in ending a long period of regime stability and introducing a long period of dramatic regime changes. The style of legislative politics that deputies introduced bequeathed to a long future the habit of confronting political crises by resorting to the constitutional drafting boards as the people took to the streets.

List of 1,318 Deputies by Alignment Categories

Consistent Right
(N = 108)

Allain
Angosse
Anterroche
Argenteuil
Artur de La Villarmois
Ayroles
Batz
Beauharnois, François, marquis
Belbeuf
Bengy de Puyvallée
Bernigaud de Grange
Bois
Bournazel de Buisson
Bouthillier de Beaujeu
Bouville
Castellas
Cauneille
Cayla de La Garde
Chabrol
Chalon

Clairmont d'Avranville
Clermont-Mont-Saint-Jean
Clermont-Tonnerre, A. A. J. (Châlons)
Colson
Cortois de Balore
Coster
Crussol d'Uzès, A. C. E.
Culant
David, Lucien
Depuch de Monbreton
Digoine du Palais
Ducastaing
Dufraisse Duchey
Dufresne
Duhart
Durget
Esponchés, de Leyris
Farochon
Faucigny de Lucinge
Folleville, A. C. G., marquis
Font

Foucauld Lardimalie
Fresnay (de Bailly), marquis
Gagnière
Gonnès
Goullard
Grandin
Gros, J. M.
Guilhem-Clermont-Lodève
Guilhermy
Hercé
Houdet
Irland de Bazôges
Iversay
Juigné, J. G. L., marquis
Juigné, L. M., comte
Lachastre, C., vicomte
LaLande, Jean Jacques
Lambert de Frondeville
Lambertye, J. E. A. F.
La Place
Laporte

Le Clerc, G. G. (*sic*)
Le Clerc de Lassigny de
    Juigné
Lefort (Geffrier)
Le François (Gabriel
    Sébastien)
Le Tellier
Levis-Mirepoix, M. A.,
    comte
Leymarye
Loynes
Lusignan, A., marquis
Madier de Montjau
Malartic
Malide
Malrieu
Martin, J. J.
Mascon
Maury
Mayet
Monstiers de Merinville
Mortemart, V. B. V.,
    marquis
Murinais
Ormesson de Noyseau
Peretti Della Rocca
Pierre de Bernis
Piffon
Plas de Tane
Pochet
Rafelis Broves
Reynaud de Montlosier
Rochebrune, A. de
    Brugier, baron
Rolin
Rouph de Varicourt
Royer, H. J.
Rozé
Ruffo, C. M.
Seurrat de Laboulaye

Simon, J. F.
Tailhardat de La
    Maisonneuve
Ternay, R. H. L. G.,
    comte
Thomas, M.
Vaneau
Vaudreuil, de Rigaud
Verthamon d'Ambloy
Villemort de Bouex,
    marquis
Villoutreix de Faye
Vincent de Panette
Virieu
Yvernault

Moderate Right (N = 315)

Achard
Aigalliers, de Brueys
Albignac
Alençon
Ambly
Andlau
Andlau de Hombourg
Antraigues
Argentré
Aurillac
Avaray
Avessens de Saint Rome
Ballidart
Bandy de Lachaud
Bannassat
Banyuls de Montferré
Barbotin
Barmond
Barrau

Beauchamps
Beaudrap de Sotteville
Beaupoil de Saint-
    Aulaire
Begouen Demeaux
Benoit
Berardier
Bergasse
Bernard, F. A.
Bertereau, Louis
Bertrand, Pierre
Bertrand de Montfort
Béthisy de Mézières
Bigot de Verniere
Blacons
Blaisel du Rieu
Blandin
Boisgelin de Cucé
Bois-Rouvraye, D. C.
    Pasquer
Boisse
Bonal
Bonnac
Bonnay, C. F.
Bonnegens
Bonnet, N. J.
Bottex
Boudart
Bousmard de Chantraine
Bouveiron
Bremond d'Ars, marquis
Breuvart
Burignot de Varenne
Burle
Buttafoco
Cairon
Chabanettes
Chabault
Chambors de la Boessière
Chambray

Charrier
Chatelet-Lomont
Chatrian
Chevreuil
Chevreux
Choiseul d'Aillecourt
Choiseul, duc de Praslin
Chopier
Clapiers-Collongues
Clermont-Tonnerre,
    S. M. A.
Cocherel
Coigny de Franquetot, duc
Coma Serra
Conzié
Cornus
Costel
Couturier
Crécy
Créniere, J. B.
Crussol d'Uzès,
    E. H. C., baron
Davin
Delage
Delfau
Delort (Puymalie)
Deschamps
Desvernay
Devoisins
Diot
Dortan, comte
Dubois
Dubuat
Dulau
Dupuis
Egmont Pignatelli,
    Casimir
Eprémesnil, du Val d'
Escars de Pérusse,
    L. F. M., comte

Escars de Pérusse,
    F. N. R., comte
Escouloubre, de
    Monstrou-Sauton
Estourmel, marquis
Eymar de Walchrétien
Failly
Fenis de Lacombe
Ferrieres
Flachat
Fleury, Jean
Fontanges
Forest de Masmoury
Fougere
Fournès (de Faret)
Fournetz
Fournier de la
    Pommeraye
Galbert
Gandolphe
Garnier, J. M.
Gaschet-Delisle
Gaultier, U. A. L. F. (de
    Tours)
Genetet
Girard, J. F.
Gleises de Lablanque
Godefroy
Gontier de Biran
Goubert, F.
Goze
Graimberg de Belleau
Grangier, P. J.
Gresolles de Gayardon
Griffon de Romagné
Grosbois
Gueidan
Guépin
Guingand de Saint-
    Mathieu

Guiraudez de Saint-
    Mezard
Guyon
Harchies
Hardy de la Largère
Hautoÿ
Hennet
Henry de Longuêve
Hingant
Hodicq de Courteville
Humblot
Hurault
Hutteau
Innocens de Maurens
Jacquemart
Jersé
Jouffroy de Gonssans
Joyeux
Juigné, A. E. L. L.,
    archbishop
LaBlache (de Falcoz)
La Boissiere
Laboreys de
    Chateaufavier
Labrousse de Beauregard
Lachastre, C. L., comte
Lachèse
La Fare
La Gallisonniere
Lagoille de
    Lochefontaine
La Linière
Lamy, M. L.
Lancosme
Landreau
Langon
Lannoy
Laqueuille
Larêne, Benoît (Combet
    de Peccat)

La Rochefoucauld,
   Dominique
La Rochefoucauld-
   Bayers, F. J.
La Rochefoucauld-
   Bayers, P. L.
La Rochefoucauld du
   Breuil, C. F.
La Roque de Mons
Lasalle
Laslier
Lasmartres
Lastic
Le Berthon
Le Carpentier de
   Chailloué
Lefebvre
Lefrançois
Le Lubois
Lemulier de Bressay
Le Rouvillois
Lespinasse
Le Tonnellier de Breteuil
Leveque
Levis, duc de
Levis-Mirepoix,
   C. P. M. G.
Loëdon de Keromen
Lolier
Loras
Lousmeau-Dupont
Loys
Lubersac, J. B. J.
Lucas, Julien
Ludiere
Ludre de Frolois
Luillier-Rouvenac
Luppé
Macaye
Machault

Malartie
Malateste de Beaufort
Malouet
Manhiaval
Marguerittes (Tessier)
Marsane Font Juliane
Martinet
Mathias
Maubec de Planelli
Mazancourt
Méchin
Melon de Pradoux
Menonville (Thibault de)
Mercy
Meric de Montgazin
Merigeaux
Mesgrigny
Milet de Mureau
   (Destouffe de)
Mirabeau, A. B. L.,
   vicomte
Miremont
Moncorps Duchesnoy
Montcalm-Gozon,
   L. P. M. G., comte
Mont d'Or
Montjoye-Vaufrey
Moutier, M. A.
Murat
Nedonchel, M. A. B.,
   baron
Novion
Paccard
Palmaert
Panat, F. L. d'Adhémar,
   vicomte
Panat, D. F. Brunet de
   Castels-Pers
Pegot
Pélisson de Gennes

Pellegrin
Perier, C. C.
Peyruchaud
Picquet
Piis
Pinneliere
Pison du Galland
Pleurre, marquis
Pons de Soulages
Pothée
Poulle
Pous
Pradt
Privat
Provançal de
   Fonchateau
Puységur
Quémy
Rastignac, de Chapt de
Rathier
Rathsamhausen
Redon
Revol
Rey
Ricard, L. E.
Richard de la Vergne
Rivière
Riviere, J. F.
Robecq, A. L. A.
Rocque
Rohan-Guéménée
Roquefort, J. de Lasalle
Roulhac, G. G.
Roussel
Roy
Roys, C. E. A., comte
Ruallem
Ruello
Ruffo de Bonneval
Ruillé, comte

Rully, P. G. de
  Montessus
Sabran
Saige
Saint-Albin
Sainte-Aldegonde
  d'Aimeries, comte
Saint-Esteven
Saint-Maurice
Saint-Sauveur
Saint-Simon, C. A.,
  marquis
Sales de Costebelle
Sallé de Chou
Samary
Ségur-Cabanac
Seignelay-Colbert de
  Castle-Hill
Serent
Symon
Talaru de Chalmazel
Talleyrand-Périgord,
  A. A. (Reims)
Terrats
Texier
Thiboutot, A. L.,
  marquis
Thirial
Thomas, J.
Tixedor
Toulouse Lautrec
Tournyol Duclos
Toustain Viray
Tridon
Trie Pillavoine
Usson, L. M. A.
Ustou-Saint-Michel,
  vicomte
Valerian-Duclau
Valete

Vassé, A. B. E., marquis
Vassy, L. M., comte
Verdet
Vialis
Villaret, J. F. A. I. de
Villebanois
Villeblanche, Levasseur
  de
Villeneuve Bargemon
Vogüé
Vrigny, marquis
Warel
Wolter de Neurbourg

Center Right
(N = 147)

Apchier de Châteauneuf
  Randon
Auvry
Auvynet
Badens, d'Upac de
Barbançon
Barbotan
Barbou
Barville
Bastien
Benazet
Bernard de Sassenay
Berthereau, Thomas
Biencourt
Billy
Bodineau
Boyer
Brousse
Burdelot
Cardon de Sandrans
Cartier

Castries de la Croix, duc
Causans
Caylus
Cazalez
Cesarges
Chaléon
Champion de Cicé,
  J. M. (Bordeaux)
Champion de Cicé,
  J. B. M. (Auxerre)
Chatizel
Chevallier, F.
Cipieres
Coiffier
Coulmiers
Cousin
Damas de Crux
Defrance
Delandine
Devillâs
Dolomieu
Douzon
Ducret
Dumont
Dumoustier Delafond
Durand, E.
Esclans
Eymar du Bignosc
Flachslanden, J. F. H.
Flachslanden, J. B. A.
Fournier, Charles
Fumel Monségur
Gaillon
Galland
Gayon
Gomer
Gossuin
Grand de Champrouet
Grieu
Guégan

Guillou
Harambure
Havré et de Croy
Héral
Huard
Hunault
La Bastide
La Baume de Montrevel
La Béviére de Garron
La Luzerne
Landenberg-
  Wagenbourg
Landrin
Lanusse
La Poype-Vertrieux
La Queüille
Larouziére
Latil
La Tour du Pin-
  Gouvernet
Launay, J. M.
Launey, J. B. G.
La Valette Parizot
Le Bigot de
  Beauregard
Le Borlhe de Grand'Pré
Le Clerc, C. G.
Le Clercq de Lannoy
Le Franc de Pompignan
Le Guillou de Kerincuff
Lemoyne de Bellisle
Lescurier de la Vergne
Lezay-Marnesia
Loaisel
Luxembourg, duc
Mailly,
  A. A. M. G. J. F.,
  marquis
Maisonneuve

Martin Dauch
Maulette
Mazurié de Pennach
Mercey (baron de Raclet)
Milhet de Belisle
Millet
Millot
Monspey, marquis
Monssinat
Montboissier, C. P. S.
  Beaufort-Canillac
Montboissier, P. C.
  Beaufort-Canillac,
  comte
Montcalm-Gozon,
  J. P. J. F., marquis
Montesson
Moreau
Morel, J. B.
Mortemart, V. J. B. M.
  Rochechouart
Naurissart
Nicolaï
Nompere de
  Champagny
Panat, A. J. S. E.
  Brunet Castels-Pers
Panetier
Paroy, G., Le Gentil,
  marquis
Perier, M. G. L. F.
Pinelle
Plaquet
Poissac
Poüilly, A. L., baron
Poupard
Rabin
Raby de Saint-Médard
Rennel

Richier de la
  Rochelongchamp
Rochegude
Rosé
Royère
Saint-Mexent
Satillieu (Dufaur de St.
  Silvestre)
Solliers
Surade
Talon
Tessé
Thebaudieres
Thévenot de Maroise
Thiebaut
Touzet
Tualt de la Bouvrie
Turkheim
Turpin
Vallet
Vanden Baviere
Vernin
Verny
Veytard
Villequier, d'Aumont
Wartel

Resigning Right
$(N = 51)$

Aguesseau
Bruet
Brun, G.
Bussi
Charrier de la Roche
Collinet
Croy (Solre) duc

Dabbaye
Damas d'Anlezy
Delettre, Claude
Desfossez, vicomte
Deulneau
Dode
Dourthe
Dupont, M. F.
Dupré de Ballay
Escourre de Peluzat
Escoutes
Escuret, Laborde
Espic
Gausserand
Gauville, L. H. C.
Helmstatt
Henryot
Lally-Tolendal
Langhac
Larchevesque-Thibaud
La Roche-Negly
La Tour-Maubourg
Lavie, M. D.
Le Brun, F., curé
Mailly, L. M., duc
Mayer
Milscent
Morges
Mounier
Moyon
Noÿelles, L. S.,
   baron
Pelauque Beraut
Pellerin
Pere d'Artassen
Picart de la Pointe
Poix
Robin de Morhery
Roussier

Royer, C. L. du
Sancy, J. B., père
Simon de Maibelle
Tillet
Toulongeon, J. R. H.,
   marquis
Viochot

Right Center
(N = 13)

Agoult
Bechant
Favre
Gerard, J. N.
Gibert
Guilloz
Hanoteau
Kÿtspotter
Laporterie
Leissegues de Rozaven
Marandat d'Olliveau
Mestre
Rolland

Contradictory
(N = 44)

Augier
Aury
Beaulieu
Bérenger
Binot
Bonneville
Bordeaux

Bruges, M. A. B.
Champeaux
Cheynet
Choiseul, comte de
   Praslin
Daude
Demandre
Du Pont de Nemours
Elbhecq, P. J. (Delbecq)
Faydel
Froment
Gantheret
Gidoin
Gounot
Guerin
Hauducoeur
Hebrard, Pierre
Jamier
La Borde
Lafargue
Laignier
Laipaud
Lavie, P. M. A.
Lenglier
LePeletier de Feumusson
Leroulx
Marsay
Melon
Merceret
Mesnard
Meusnier-Dubreuil
Monneron, C. C. A.
Montesquiou, F. X.
Nadal de Saintrac
Richard de
   Maisonneuve
Thoret, J.
Visme, de
Wimpffen

Unclassifiable (N = 173)

Afforty
Ailly
Albert
Allard
Allard du Plantier
Allarde
Andurand
Arberg
Arnoult
Arraing
Augier de La Sauzaye
Bailleul
Barbié
Baron
Béhin
Belzais de Courmenil
Berthier
Beviere
Beylié
Birotheau des Burondieres
Bizard
Blanc
Blanquart
Blin
Bluget
Boissonnot
Bonnefoy
Bordier
Bouchet
Bouchotte
Boulliotte
Boulouvard
Bourdeau
Bourdet
Bouvet
Bracq

Brassart
Briault
Brignon
Brocheton
Bucaille
Buffy
Chabert de Lachariere
Chenon de Beaumont
Cherfils
Chesnon de Baigneux
Choîzy
Cigongne Maupassant
Coquille
Crussol d'Uzès, A. E. F. G., marquis
Dabadie, J. M.
Davoust
Delaforge
Delambre
Dieusie, comte
Douchet
Druillon
Ducellier
Estagniol
Eude
Faulcon
Feraud
Filleau
Fleurÿ, C. S.
Fleurye, J. B.
Fos de Laborde
Francheteau de la Glaustière
Gabriel, René
Garat, Dominique (l'aîné)
Germain d'Orsanville
Germiot
Glezen

Gossin
Gouges Cartou
Gournay
Gouttes
Goyard
Grellet de Beauregard
Gros, Bernard
Guino
Guiot, Antoine
Harmand
Héliand
Herman
Jaillant
Janson
Jeannet d'Arcis, L. N.
Jenot
Joüye Desroches
Prudhomme de Kérangon
Labat, J. A.
Labat, Louis de
La Beste
Larreyre
Lartigue
Latour
Latteux
Lattre, F. P. (l'aîné)
Lattre de Batsaert, H. B.
Laurence (l'aîné)
Laurent, F. X.
Laviguerie
Laziroule
LeBrun, Léon Henri Eléonor
LeCesve
Lefort, Denis
Legros, C. J. F.
Le Guen
Lejeans, Louis
Le Moine (l'aîné)

Lenoir de la Roche
Leroux, C. F.
Le Sacher de La Palière
Lesergeant d'Isbergue
Lesure
Lienart
Lilia de Crose
Lindet
Liquier
Loison
Lomet
Lompré
Mans de Bourglevesque
Marchais
Margonne
Marie de la Forge
Maujean
Menu de Chomorceau
Meyer
Meyniel
Michaud
Michelon de Cheuzat
Millon de Montherlant
Missy
Monneron, P. A.
Montaudon
Montesquiou-Fezensac,
  A. P.
Montjallard
Mourot
Nairac
Nicodême
Noussitou
Pardieu
Pellissier
Perdry, J. C. A. J.
Perrigny, C. L. de
  Taillevis, marquis
Perrin de Rosier
Pinterel de Louverny

Pinteville
Poilloüe de Saint-Mars
Poultier
Pruche
Prugnon, P. J.
Puisaye, comte
Quatrefages de Laroquete
Raze
Regnard
Repoux
Reynaud de Villeverd
Richard, A. J.
Riche
Richond
Riquier
Robert
Rochechoüart, A. L. R.
Rousselet
Salm-Salm
Sarrazin
Sentetz
Sieyès La Baume
Thibaudeau, R. A. H.
  (l'aîné)
Toulongeon, F. E.,
  vicomte
Viefville des Essars

Ministerials,
Monarchical Left
(N = 184)

Adam de Verdonne
André
Ango
Anson
Aubert
Aubry

Aubry-Dubochet
Baco de la Chapelle
Beauperrey
Beauvais
Becherel
Besnard (Duchesne)
Biaille de Germon
Bidault
Bignan de Coyrol
Bion
Biron Lauzun, A. L.
  de Gontaut
Boëry
Bouchette
Boufflers
Boullé
Bourdon, P. J. N.
Bouron
Bourran
Bouteville-Dumetz
Briois de Beaumez
Bureaux de Pusy
Burnequez
Buschey des Noës
Campmas
Castellane, comte
Cavailhés
Chasset
Châtenay-Lanty
Chavoix
Cherrier
Chombart
Christin
Claude
Cochelet
Colaud de La Salcette
Colonna de Cesari-
  Rocca
Crillon, F. F. D. B.,
  comte

Crillon, L. P. N. F. B.,
    marquis
Croix
Cussy
Custine, A. P., comte
Darnaudat
Daubert
Dauchy
Defaÿ
Delacour d'Ambésieux
Delavigne
Delaville Le Roulx
Démeunier
Desmazieres
Despatys de Courteille
Dillon, Arthur
Dillon, Dominique
Dionis du Séjour
Dosfant
Drevon
Dufau
Dumaire
Dumas-Gonthier, Elie
Dumesnil-Desplanques
Duquesnoy
Durand, A.
Enjubault
Estin
Fisson-Jaubert
Flaust
Fontenay, P. N.
Francoville
Fréteau de Saint-Just
Fricot
Garat, Dominique-
    Joseph (le jeune)
Garésché
Garnier, J. B. E.
Gassendi

Gerard, Michel
Gillet de La
    Jaqueminière
Giraud-Duplessix
Graffan
Grenier
Guillotin
Guinebaud
Guyardin
Herwyn
Huguet
Jac
Jaume
Jessé
Joubert
Jourdan
Julien
Laclaverie
LaCoste de Messelière
Lalande
La Marck
Lambel
La Rade
La Rochefoucauld
    d'Enville, L. A.
Lasnon
Laterrade
Laurendeau
Lavenüe
Le Blanc, C. C.
Le Brun de Grillon
Le Couteulx de Canteleu
Le Gendre
Le Grand, Jérôme
Le Lay de Grantugen
Lemercier
Liancourt, A. F. F. de La
    Rochefoucauld, duc
Lombard Taradeau

Long
Luynes
Luze Letang
Luzignem
Maillot
Martineau
Maupetit
Merle
Mollien
Monnel
Montmorency-Laval,
    comte
Morel, J. C. A.
Morin
Mortier
Mougins de Roquefort,
    A. B.
Mougins de Roquefort,
    J. J.
Nau de Belislle
Neuville
Pain
Palasne de
    Champeaux
Parent de Chassy
Paÿen
Payen Boisneuf
Peloux
Perés de Lagesse
Pernel
Perrée Duhamel
Petiot
Petit
Pezous
Phelines
Poncet-Delpech
Poncin
Pougeard Dulimbert
Pouret de Roquerie

Poutrain
Quéru de Lacoste
Rangeard
Ratier de Montguyon
Regnaud de Saint-Jean-
    d'Angely
Regnauld d'Epercy
Regneault de Lunéville
Ricard, J. P.
Roca
Rodat d'Olemps
Rostaing,
    J. A. H. M. G.,
    marquis
Rousselot
Roussillou
Salomon de La Saugerie
Schmits
Schwendt
Seze
Simon, P. M.
Sinety de Puylon,
    comte
Talleyrand-Périgord,
    C. M. (Autun)
Target
Tellier
Thouret, J. G.
Tracy
Treilhard
Tronchet
Troüillet
Ulry
Valentin-Bernard
Verguet
Viard
Volfius
Volney, C. F. Chassebeuf
    de

Shifting Left
(N = 176)

Aiguillon
Alquier
Andrieu
Anthoine
Aoust
Armand
Audier-Massillon
Babey
Baillot
Barere de Vieuzac
Barnave
Basquiat de Mugriet
Baudoüin de
    Maisonblanche
Bazin
Beauharnois, A. F. M.,
    vicomte
Benoist
Billette
Blancard
Boislandry
Boissy d'Anglas
Bonnet, P. F. D.
Bouche, C. F.
Bouche, P. F. B.
Boussion
Boutaric
Bouvier
Branche
Brevet de Beaujour
Broglie
Brostaret
Brulart de Sillery
Brunet de Latuque
Carondelet
Castaignede

Castelanet
Chabroud
Chaillon
Chambon de la Tour
Châteauneuf-Randon du
    Tournel
Chevalier, E.
Claye
Clerget
Cochard
Cochon de Lapparent
Cottin
Couppé
Cretot (Decretot)
Creuzé de Latouche
Darche
Davost
Defermon des
    Chapelières
Delarevelliere Delépeaux
Delay d'Agier
Desandrouin
Dinochau
Dubois de Crancé
Du Port
Dupré
Duval de Grandpré
Emmery
Expilly
Fouquier d'Heroüel
François, Jean
Fricaud
Frochot
Gallot
Gaultier de Biauzat
Gauthier des Orcières
Geoffroy
Gerard, J. B.
Dom Gerle, C. A.

Girerd
Girod de Chevry (le jeune)
Girot de Pouzol
Gobel
Goudard
Goupil de Prefelne
Goupilleau
Gouy d'Arsy
Grégoire
Grenot
Guillaume, L. M.
Guittard, J. B.
Hell
Hernoux, C.
Huot de Goncourt
Jary
Kauffmann
Laborde de Méréville
Lacharmie (Fournier de)
Lafayette
Lameth, C. M. F., comte
Lameth, A. T. V., chevalier
La Methérie-Sorbier
Lancelot Dubourg
Lanjuinais
Lapoule
La Touche-Levassor, L. R. M. (Treville)
Latyl
Le Breton, J. P.
Le Carlier
Le Chapelier
Le Déan
Le Deist de Botidoux
Le Floch, Corantin
Le Goazre de Kervelegan
Le Guen de Kerengall

L'Eleu de La Ville aux Bois
Lemarechal
Lepoutre
Lesterpt (l'aîné)
Lesterpt de Beauvais
Livré
Lofficial
Lucas de Bourgerel
Malès
Marquis
Martin, F.
Massieu
Maupassant
Mauriet de Flory
Mênager
Menard de La Groye
Menou
Merlin
Meurinne
Mévolhon
Meynier de Salinelles
Millanois
Millet de Lamambre
Moreau de Saint-Méry
Moyot
Muguet de Nanthou
Nioche
Noailles, L. M., vicomte
Nolf
Orléans, L. P. J., duc
Oudot
Pampelone (Guyon de Geis de)
Papin
Parisot
Pelerin de La Buxière
Pemartin
Pérez
Perisse du Luc

Pervinquiere de La Baudinière
Petitmengin
Pflieger
Pilastre de la Brardière
Pincepré de Buire
Populus, M. E.
Poulain de Boutancourt
Poulain de Corbion
Prevost
Prieur
Rabaut de Saint-Etienne
Regnier
Renaut, Roch
Reubell
Riberolles de Martinanches
Ricard de Sealt, G. J. X.
Roger
Saliceti
Salle
Sieyès
Soustelle
Thibault, A. A. M.
Trehot de Clermont
Vadier
Varin de La Brunelière
Verchère de Reffye
Vernier
Vieillard, P. J. (fils)
Viellart, R. L. M.
Vimal Flouvat
Voulland

Consistent Left
(N = 107)

Agier
Arriveur

Aucler des Cottes
Bailly, Charles Maximin
Bailly, Jean Silvain
Ballard
Baucheton
Bazoche
Berthomier de Lavillette
Besse
Bonet de Treiches
Bonnemant
Boucher
Bourdon, A.
Bourgeois
Boyer de Gris
Brillat-Savarin
Brouillet
Buzot
Camus
Camusat de Belombre
Chantaire
Chouvet
Colombel de Bois au
    Lard
Cornilleau
Corroller du Moustoir
Couderc
Coupard
Curt
Debourge
Delacour
Delahaye de Launay
Dubois-Maurin
Dubuisson
Dumas
Dumouchel
Dupont, P. C. F.

Durand de Maillane
Dusers
Dutrou de Bornier
Duvivier
Ferté
Gagon du Chenay
Gardiol
George
Gillon
Girod de Thoiry (l'aîné)
Gombert
Gourdan
Guiot, Florent
Hebrard, Dominique
Heurtault de Lamerville
Jallet
Janny
Jeannet Le Jeune, F. L.
Laloy
Lamarque
Lasnier de Vaussenay
Le Boys Desguays
Leclerc, J. B.
LeFebvre de Chailly
Legolias
Le Maignan
Lemoine de La Giraudais
Lepeletier de Saint-
    Fargeau
Lereffait
Lucas, J. B. J.
Mangin
Marolle
Mathieu de Rondeville
Meifrund
Mirabeau, G. H., comte

Monneron, J. L.
Mougeotte de Vignes
Moutier, G. N. P.
Ogé
Oudaille
Paulhiac de La Sauvetat
Paultre des Epinettes
Perret de Tregadoret
Pétion de Villeneuve
Pilat
Pocheron
Poignot
Poulain de Beauchène
Poya de Lherbay
Prez de Crassier
Ramel Nogaret
Rancourt de Villiers
Raux
Renaut, P. L. J.
Rigouard
Robespierre
Roederer
Royer, J. B.
Saint-Martin
Sancy, C. (fils)
Saurine
Scheppers
Terme
Vaillant
Verdollin
Vignon
Viguier
Voidel
Vyau de Baudreuille

Bibliography

The works given here were the major sources consulted for biographical information that I used in constructing quantitative measures of the deputies' political careers.

The point of departure was the list of names of the 1,318 deputies who sat in the Estates General/National Assembly at any point between May 5, 1789, and September 30, 1791. The names are listed in Armand Brette, *Recueil de documents relatifs à la convocation des Etats généraux de 1789* (4 vols.; Paris, 1894–1911), II, 35–333. This list was also the source for deputies' estates, electoral circumscriptions, and occupations. In the interest of consistency, I have followed Brette for all spellings and order of names and titles, even where these may no longer be the standard modern spellings. This book was completed before the publication of Edna Lemay's fine biographical dictionary, which will be a boon to students of the National Assembly: Edna Hindie Lemay, *Dictionnaire des Constituants, 1789–1791* (2 vols.; Paris, 1991).

The following additional sources supplied information on the public careers of the deputies: Michel Prevost *et al.*, *Dictionnaire de biographie française* (Paris, 1933–), and Adolphe Robert, Edgar Bourlotin, and Gaston Cougny, *Dictionnaires de parlementaires françaises* (5 vols.; Paris, 1891–95). For the Breton deputies, two indispensable sources were René Kerviler, *Cent Ans de représentation bretonne: Galerie de tous les députés envoyés par la Bretagne aux diverses législateurs qui se sont succédées depuis 1789 jusqu'à nos jours* (Paris, 1889–91), and Kerviler, *Répertoire général de bio-bibliographie bretonne* (16 vols.; Rennes, 1886–1906).

Sources for deputies' roles within the National Assembly included *Archives parlementaires de 1787 à 1860* (34 vols.; Paris, 1867–90); *Procès-verbal de l'Assemblée nationale* (77 vols.; Paris, 1789–91); and *Réimpression de l'Ancien Moniteur universel* (32 vols.; Paris, 1840–45). For the first six weeks of the Estates General, the sessions are detailed in Georges Lefebvre and Anne Terroine, eds., *Recueil de documents relatifs aux séances des Etats généraux, mai–juin 1789,* Tome I (2 vols.; Paris, 1953), and Olga Ilovaïsky, ed., *ibid.,* Tome 2, *Les Séances de la Noblesse, 6 mai–6 juillet* (2 vols.; Paris, 1974).

For prerevolutionary provincial assemblies, I used the following: *Procès-verbaux: Assemblée des trois ordres de la province de Dauphiné et très respectueuses représentations des trois ordres de la province de Dauphiné, du 21 juillet 1788* (Grenoble, 1788); *Procés-verbal de l'assemblée provinciale du Berri* (3 vols.; Bourges and Paris, 1787); *Procès-verbal des séances de l'assemblée provinciale de l'Isle de France, tenue à Melun, novembre et décembre 1787* (Paris, 1788); *Procès-verbal des séances de l'assemblée provinciale de l'Orléanais tenue à Orléans aux mois de novembre et décembre 1787* (Orléans, 1787); *Procès-verbaux des assemblées générales des trois ordres et des états du Dauphiné tenus à Romans en 1788* (Lyon, 1888).

Documents on electoral assemblies came from *Archives nationales,* Series C 16/36; 17/50; 18/68; 71; 19/79, 82, 84, 142; 21/108, 109, 111; 22/115, 117, 125; 23/132; 24/145, 146, 161; 25/168; 30/252 bis; Series Ba 25, 26, 43, 44, 53, 84; Series B III/97.

I also used *Procès-verbal de l'assemblée générale des trois ordres du ressort de la sénéchaussée du Bourbonnais, à Moulins, du 16 mars 1789, in Bulletin de la Société d'émulation du département de l'Allier,* II (1846–50), 196–216, 309–32, and *Procès-verbal de l'assemblée générale du clergé, ibid.,* III (1851–55), 58–68; *noblesse,* 69–82; *Tiers état,* 83–94.

I used the following lists as the sources of information to create the alignment scales that rank deputies from left to right: "Déclaration de 293 députés sur les décrets qui suspendent l'exercice de l'authorité royale et qui portent atteinte à l'inviolabilité de la personne sacrée du roi," *Archives parlementaires,* XXVIII, 3d Annex (July 9, 1791), 91–96; *Déclaration d'une partie de l'Assemblée nationale sure le décret rendu le 13 avril 1790, concernant la religion* (Paris, 1790); Jean Jacques du Val d'Eprémesnil, *Déclaration d'une partie des députés aux Etats-Généraux, touchant l'Acte constitutionnel et l'état du Royaume* (Paris, 1791): *Liste de MM. les archevêques, évêques, curés, et autres membres ecclésiastiques de l'Assemblée nationale qui ont adopté le 4 janvier la for-*

mule de serment qui avait été proposée par M. l'évêque de Clermont (Paris, 1791); *Liste par lettres alphabétiques des députés du côté droit, aux Etats généraux, au mois de septembre 1791* (Paris, 1791); *Liste par ordre alphabétique de bailliage et sénéchaussée de MM. les députés de la majorité de l'Assemblée nationale, vulgairement appelés le côté gauche ou les enragés* (Paris, 1791); *Le Véritable Portrait de nos législateurs; ou, Galerie des tableaux exposés à la vue du public depuis le 5 mai 1789, jusqu'au 1ᵉʳ octobre 1791* (Paris, 1792); James Murphy and Patrice Higonnet, "Les Députés de la noblesse aux Etats généraux de 1789," *Revue d'histoire moderne et contemporaine,* XX (1973), 230–47.

For deputies who were members of the Jacobin Club, I consulted F. A. Aulard, *La Société des Jacobins: Recueil de documents pour l'histoire du club des Jacobins de Paris* (6 vols.; Paris, 1889–97). For members of other clubs, I used Augustin Challamel, *Les Clubs contre-révolutionnaires, cercles, comités, sociétés, salons, réunions, cafés, restaurants, et librairies* (1895; rpr. New York, 1974). The names of deputies who were members of Masonic lodges came from Pierre Lamarque, *Les Francs-Maçons aux Etats généraux de 1789 et à l'Assemblée nationale* (Paris, 1981).

The rest of the works consulted for this book are listed alphabetically.

Books and Articles

Albert, David. "Messire Chevreuil." *Bulletin diocésain d'histoire et d'archéologie, diocèse de Quimper et de Léon* (1934), 282–88.

Applewhite, Harriet B. "Political Legitimacy in Revolutionary France." *Journal of Interdisciplinary History,* IX (1978), 245–73.

Aulard, F. A. "La Formation du parti républicain, 1790–1791." *La Révolution française,* XXXV (1898), 296–347.

———. "La Fuite à Varennes et le mouvement républicain." *La Révolution française,* XXXV (1898), 385–436.

———. "Patrie, patriotisme au début de la Révolution française." *La Révolution française,* LXVIII (1915), 415–48, 481–525; LXIX (1916), 35–59.

———. "Patrie, patriotisme avant 1789." *La Révolution française,* LXVIII (1915), 193–224.

———. "Patrie, patriotisme sous Louis XVI et dans les cahiers." *La Révolution française,* LXVIII (1915), 301–39.

————. "Le Programme royal aux élections de 1789." *La Révolution française,* XVI (1889), 289–300.

————. "Relation sommaire, fidèle, et véritable de ce qui s'est passé dans l'Assemblée du clergé de Paris, intra muros." Attributed to Pierre Brugière. *La Révolution française,* XXVI (1894), 57–87.

————. "Les Républicains et les Démocrates depuis le massacre du Champ de Mars jusqu'à la Journée du 20 juin 1792." *La Révolution française,* XXXV (1898), 485–529.

Bailly, Jean Silvain. *Mémoires de Bailly avec une notice sur sa vie.* 3 vols. Paris, 1821–22.

Baker, Keith Michael. *Inventing the French Revolution: Essays on French Political Culture in the Eighteenth Century.* Cambridge, Eng., 1990.

————. "On the Problem of the Ideological Origins of the French Revolution." In *Modern European Intellectual History: Reappraisals and New Perspectives,* edited by Dominick La Capra and Steven L. Kaplan. Ithaca, 1982.

————, ed. *The Political Culture of the Old Regime.* New York, 1987. Vol. I of *The French Revolution and the Creation of Modern Political Culture.* 3 vols.

Baldensperger, Fernand. *Le Mouvement des idées dans l'Emigration française.* 2 vols. Paris, 1924.

Barbier, Antoine Alexandre. *Dictionnaire des ouvrages anonymes et pseudonymes.* 2d ed. Paris, 1822–27.

Barnave, Antoine Pierre Joseph Marie. *Introduction à la Révolution française.* Edited by Fernand Rude. Paris, 1960.

Barruel, Augustin. *Mémoires pour servir à l'histoire du Jacobinisme.* Hamburg, 1798.

Bastid, Paul. *L'Assemblée nationale de 1789 à 1791.* Paris, 1964–65.

————. *Sieyès et sa pensée.* Paris, 1939.

Behrens, Catherine Betty Abigail. "Nobles, Privileges, and Taxes in France at the End of the Ancien Régime." *Economic History Review,* XV (1963), 451–75.

Bellevue, M. D. "Tualt de La Bouvrie, dernier sénéchal de la sénéchaussée de Ploërmel, député aux Etats-Généraux." *Association bretonne,* 3d ser., XXVIII (1910), 10–21.

Bergasse, Louis. "La Déclaration des droits de l'homme et du citoyen à la Constituante." *La Réforme sociale,* L (1905), 473–96.

Berlanstein, Lenard R. *The Barristers of Toulouse in the Eighteenth Century, 1740–1793.* Baltimore, 1986.

Berthe, Léon-Noël. *Dictionnaire des correspondants de l'Académie d'Arras au temps de Robespierre.* Arras, 1969.

Beylié, J. de. "Barnave avocat." *Bulletin de l'Académie delphinale,* ser. 5, XI (1917), 138–262.

Bien, David D. "François Furet, the Terror, and 1789." *French Historical Studies,* XVI (1990), 777–83.

Biernawski, Louis. *Un Département sous la Révolution française: L'Allier de 1789 à l'an III.* Moulins, 1909.

Biographie moderne, du dictionnaire biographique de tous les hommes morts et vivants qui ont marqué à la fin du XVIIIe siècle et au commencement de celui-ci. 2d ed. 4 vols. Breslau, 1806.

Birembaut, Arthur. "La Jeunesse et les Dernières Années du constituant Phélines." *Annales historiques de la Révolution française,* XXIX (1957), 265–67.

Bizardel, Paul Emile Robert. *L'Assemblée provinciale du Nivernais.* Bordeaux, 1913.

Blanchard, Marcel. "Une Campagne de brochures dans l'agitation dauphinoise de l'été 1788." *La Révolution française,* LXV (1913), 225–41.

Bluche, François. *Les magistrats du parlement de Paris au XVIIIe siècle, 1715–1771.* Besançon, 1960.

Bollème, Geneviève, *et al. Livre et société dans la France du XVIIIe siècle.* 2 vols. Paris, 1965, 1970.

Bonnardot, François. "Essai historique sur le régime municipal à Orléans d'après les documents conservés aux archives de la ville." *Mémoires de la Société archéologique et historique de l'Orléanais,* XVIII (1881), 113–60.

Bordes, Maurice. *La Réforme municipale du Contrôleur-Général Laverdy et son application, 1764–1771.* Toulouse, 1968.

Bosher, J. F., ed. *French Government and Society, 1500–1850.* London, 1973.

Bouchary, Jean. "Sur Lanjuinais." *Annales historiques de la Révolution française,* XVIII (1946), 164.

Boudet. "Les Prêtres (136) originaires de Dreux jusqu'à la Révolution." *Mémoires de la Société archéologique d'Eure-et-Loir,* XVI (1923–36), 347–69.

Bouloiseau, Marc. "Elections de 1789 et communautés rurales." *Annales historiques de la Révolution française,* XXVIII (1956), 29–47.

Bourne, Henry E. "American Constitutional Precedents in the French National Assembly." *American Historical Review,* VIII (1902–1903), 466–90.

Bouvier. "Orléans de 1760 à 1790." *Mémoires de la Société d'agriculture, sciences, belles-lettres, et arts d'Orléans,* LIX (1911), 190–241.

Brainne, Charles. *Les Hommes illustres de l'Orléanais: Biographie générale des trois départements du Loiret, d'Eure-et-Loir, et de Loir-et-Cher.* Orléans, 1852.

Bredin, Jean-Denis. *Sieyès: La Clé de la Révolution française.* Paris, 1988.

Brette, Armand. "Les Cahiers de 1789 considérés comme mandats impératifs." *La Révolution française,* XXXI (1896), 123–47.

———. "La Vérification des pouvoirs à l'Assemblée constituante." *La Révolution française,* XXV (1893), 413–36, 504–26, XXVI (1894), 26–52.

Britsch, Amedée. "Philippe-Egalité avant la Révolution." *Revue des études historiques* (Société des études historiques), LXX (1904), 337–63, 478–504.

Brucker, Gene A. *Jean-Sylvain Bailly: Revolutionary Mayor of Paris.* Westport, Conn., 1984.

Brun-Durand, Justin. *Dictionnaire biographique et biblio-iconographique de la Drôme.* 2 vols. Grenoble, 1900–1901.

Bruneau, Marcel. *Les Débuts de la Révolution dans les départements du Cher et de l'Indre, 1787–1791.* Paris, 1902.

————. "Les Elections et les cahiers du Tiers état de la ville de Bourges en 1789." *Bulletin de la Société historique, littéraire, artistique, et scientifique du Cher,* XIII (1889), 265–380.

Bryant, Lawrence M. "Royal Ceremony and the Revolutionary Strategies of the Third Estate." *Eighteenth-Century Studies,* XXII (1989), 413–50.

Burguière, A. "Société et culture à Reims à la fin du XVIIIᵉ siècle: La Diffusion des Lumières analysée à travers les cahiers de doléances." *Annales: Economies, Sociétés, Civilisations,* XXII (1967), 303–33.

Calan, de. "Le Recrutement régional des partis politiques de 1789 à 1914: Un Pays de la gauche, la Champagne." *Revue des sciences politiques,* XXXVII (1917), 266–94.

————. "Un Pays de droite conservatrice: La Guyenne." *Revue des sciences politiques,* XXXVIII (1917), 266–94.

————. "Un Pays d'extrême-gauche: La Provence." *Revue des sciences politiques,* XL (1918), 216–46.

Caron, Pierre. *Manuel pratique pour l'étude de la Révolution française.* Paris, 1947.

Carré, Henri. *La Fin des parlements, 1788–1790.* Paris, 1912.

Catalogue de l'histoire de France. 11 vols. Paris, 1855–95.

Censer, Jack R. "The Coming of a New Interpretation of the French Revolution." *Journal of Social History,* XXI (1987), 295–309.

Censer, Jack R., and Jeremy D. Popkin. *Press and Politics in Pre-Revolutionary France.* Berkeley, 1987.

Chabrand, Dr. "Briançon pendant la Révolution, 1788–1789." *Bulletin de la Société d'études des Hautes Alpes,* IX (1890), 376–84, X (1891), 61–75, 146–56, 255–65, 365–80, XI (1892), 21–33.

————. "La Noblesse et la Bourgeoisie à Briançon avant 1789." *Bulletin de la Société d'études des Hautes Alpes,* III (1884), 69–83.

Chaillou des Barres. "Les Anciennes Sociétés savantes d'Auxerre." *Bulletin de la Société des sciences historiques et naturelles de l'Yonne,* V (1851), 177–205.

Challe, A. *Historie de l'Auxerrois, son territoire, etc.* Auxerre, 1878.

Champion, Edmé. "La Conversion de la noblesse en 1789." *La Révolution française,* XXVIII (1895), 5–14.

————. "L'Unité nationale et la Révolution." *La Révolution française,* XIX (1890), 6–26.

Chartier, Roger. *The Cultural Origins of the French Revolution.* Translated by Lydia G. Cochrane. Durham, N.C., 1991.

Chassin, Charles L. *Les Elections et les cahiers de Paris en 1789.* 4 vols. Paris, 1888–89.

Chaussinand-Nogaret, Guy. "Aux origines de la Révolution: Noblesse et bourgeoisie." *Annales: Economies, Sociétés, Civilisations,* XXX (1975), 265–78.

————. *La Noblesse au XVIIIᵉ siècle: De la Féodalité aux Lumières.* Paris, 1976.

Chenavaz, O. *La Journée des Tuiles à Grenoble, 7 juin 1788: Documents contemporains en grande partie inédits, recueillis et publiés par un vieux bibliophile dauphinois.* Grenoble, 1881.

Chevalier, Jean Jacques. *Barnave; ou, Les Deux Faces de la Révolution, 1761–1793.* Paris, 1936.

Chevalier, Jules. "L'Eglise constitutionnelle du département de la Drôme, 1790–1801." *Bulletin de la Société d'archéologie et de statistique de la Drôme,* XLVIII (1914), 17–39, 143–66, 281–308; XLIX (1915), 17–37, 113–44, 225–55; L (1916), 50–82, 213–50, 297–330.

————. *L'Eglise constitutionelle et le persécution religieuse dans le département de la Drôme pendant la Révolution, 1790–1801.* Valence, 1919.

Chisick, Harvey. "Pamphlets and Journalism in the Early French Revolution: The Offices of the *Ami du Roi* of the Abbé Royou as a Center of Royalist Propaganda." *French Historical Studies,* XV (1988), 623–45.

Christophe, Paul. *Les Choix du Clergé dans les révolutions de 1789, 1830, et 1848.* Vol. I of 2 vols. Lille, 1975–76.

Christophelsmeier, Carl. "The First Revolutionary Step: June 17, 1789." *University Studies* (University of Nebraska), IX (1909), 1–87.

Clairefond, Marius. "Notice sur les députations de la province du Bourbonnais et du département de l'Allier aux grandes assemblées nationales de 1413–1814." *Bulletin de la Société d'émulation du département de l'Allier,* I (1846–50), 242–65.

Clapham, John Harold. *Abbé Sieyès: An Essay in the Politics of the French Revolution,* London, 1912.

"Le Clergé du diocèse de Saint-Brieuc avant et pendant la Révolution." *Mémoires de la Société archéologique et historique des Côtes-du-Nord,* Ser. 2, Vol. III (1889), 85–363.

Cobb, Richard C. *The Police and the People: French Popular Protest, 1789–1820.* New York, 1970.

Cobban, Alfred. *The Myth of the French Revolution.* London, 1955.

————. *The Social Interpretation of the French Revolution.* Cambridge, Eng., 1964.

Cochin, Augustin. "Comment furent élus les députés aux Etats généraux?" *Société d'histoire contemporaine,* XXII (1912), 24–39.

———. *Les Sociétés de pensée et la démocratie.* Paris, 1921.

———. *Les Sociétés de pensée et la révolution en Bretagne, 1788–1789.* 2 vols. Paris, 1925.

Coiffier de Moret, H. L. de. *Dictionnaire biographique et historique des hommes marquans de la fin du dix-huitième siècle.* London, 1800.

Cornillon, J. "Cahier du Tiers-état du bailliage royal de Cusset, lors des élections des députés aux Etats-Généraux en 1789." *Notre Bourbonnais: Bulletin de la Société des études locales,* Nos. 13–16 (1926), 37–42, 55–59.

Corvisier, André. *L'Armée française de la fin du XVIIe siècle au ministère de Choiseul: Le Soldat.* 2 vols. Paris, 1964.

Costa de Beauregard, M. C. A. *Le Roman d'un royaliste sous la Révolution: Souvenirs du comte de Virieu.* Paris, 1892.

Courtaut. "Etudes sur l'esprit public du Tiers état du bailliage d'Auxerre en 1789." *Bulletin de la Société des sciences historiques et naturelles de l'Yonne,* IV (1850), 265–368.

Creuzé-Latouche, Jacques Antoine. *Journal des Etats-Généraux et du début de l'Assemblée nationale, 18 mai–29 juillet 1789.* Edited by Jean Marchand. Paris, 1946.

Crozet, R. *Histoire de l'Orléanais.* Paris, 1936.

Darnton, Robert. "What Was Revolutionary About the French Revolution?" *New York Review of Books,* January 19, 1989, pp. 3–10.

Daumard, A., and François Furet. *Structures et relations sociales à Paris au milieu du XVIIIe siècle.* Paris, 1961.

Dawson, Philip. "The *Bourgeoisie de Robe* in 1789." *French Historical Studies,* IV (1965), 1–21.

———. *Provincial Magistrates and Revolutionary Politics in France, 1789–1795.* Cambridge, Mass., 1972.

———. "Le Sixième Bureau de l'Assemblée nationale et son projet de Déclaration des droits de l'homme." *Annales historiques de la Révolution française,* L (1978), 161–79.

Dawson, Philip, and Gilbert Shapiro. "Social Mobility and Political Radicalism: The Case of the French Revolution of 1789." In *The Dimensions of Quantitative Research in History,* edited by Robert Fogel. Princeton, 1972.

Delarc, A. *L'Eglise de Paris pendant la Révolution française.* Paris, n.d.

Delbèke, Baron Francis. *L'Action politique et sociale des avocats du dix-huitième siècle: Leur Part dans la préparation de la Révolution française.* Louvain, 1927.

Del Vecchio, Giorgio. *La Déclaration des droits de l'homme et du citoyen dans la Révolution française.* Paris, 1968.

Demay, Charles. "L'Evêque d'Auxerre et le chapitre cathédral au XVIIIe siècle."

Bulletin de la Société des sciences historiques et naturelles de l'Yonne, LII (1898), 5–226.

Des Cilleuls, A. "L'Accession aux emplois publics avant et depuis la Révolution." *La Réforme sociale: Bulletin de la Société d'économie sociale,* LXI (1911), 56–69.

Desmé de Chavigny, O. "Histoire de Saumur pendant la Révolution." *Revue historique de l'Ouest,* VII (1891), 415–57, 541–78, 703–53.

Di Padova, Theodore A. "The Girondins and the Question of Revolutionary Government." *French Historical Studies,* IX (1976), 432–50.

Douarche, A. *Les Tribunaux civiles de Paris pendant la Révolution.* 2 vols. Paris, 1907.

Doyle, William. *Origins of the French Revolution.* New York, 1980.

———. *The Oxford History of the French Revolution.* New York, 1989.

———. "The Parlements of France and the Breakdown of the Old Regime." *French Historical Studies,* VI (1970), 415–58.

Doyle, William, *et al.* "The Origins of the French Revolution: A Debate." *French Historical Studies,* XVI (1990), 741–65.

Dubreuil, Léon. "Le Clergé de Bretagne aux Etats généraux." *La Révolution française,* LXX (1917), 481–503.

Du Bus, Charles. *Stanislas de Clermont-Tonnerre et l'échec de la Révolution monarchique, 1757–1792.* Paris, 1931.

Du Châtelier, A. "Essai de monographie électorale pour les années 1790–1792," *Bulletin de la Société académique de Brest,* Ser. 2, Vol. X (1884–85), 253–98.

Duclos, Pierre. *La Notion de constitution dans l'oeuvre de l'Assemblée constituante.* Paris, 1932.

Dufayard. "La Journée des Tuiles à Grenoble, le 7 juin 1788." *Revue historique,* XXXVIII (1888), 305–45.

Dugour, Antoine Jeudy. *Collection de pièces intéressantes sur les grands événements de l'histoire de France, 1789–1791.* 12 vols. Paris, 1801.

Duguit, Léon. "La Séparation des pouvoirs et l'Assemblée nationale de 1789." *Revue d'économie politique,* VII (1893), 92–132, 336–72, 567–615.

Duguit, Léon, and Henri Monnier. *Les Constitutions et les principales lois politiques de la France depuis 1789.* Paris, 1943.

Dumont, Etienne. *Souvenirs sur Mirabeau et sur les deux premiers assemblées législatives.* Paris, 1951.

d'Unrug, Marie-Christine. *Analyse de contenu et acte de parole: De l'énoncé à l'énonciation.* Paris, 1974.

Duquesnoy, Adrien Cyprien. *Journal d'Adrien Duquesnoy, député du Tiers état de Bar-Le-Duc, sur l'Assemblée Constituante (3 mai 1789–3 avril 1790),* ed. Robert de Crèvecoeur. 2 vols. Paris, 1894.

Dutil, Léon. "D'où est venue l'idée du doublement du Tiers aux Etats généraux de 1789?" *La Révolution française,* LXXXII (1929), 48–58.

Duverger, Maurice. *La République des citoyens*. Paris, 1982.

Dye, Thomas R. "Taxing, Spending, and Economic Growth in the American States." *Journal of Politics*, XLII (1980), 1085–1107.

Edmonds, Bill. "Successes and Excesses of Revisionist Writing About the French Revolution." *European History Quarterly*, XVII (1987), 195–217.

Egret, Jean. "L'Aristocratie parlementaire française à la fin de l'Ancien Régime." *Revue historique*, CCVIII (1952), 1–14.

————. *Les Derniers Etats de Dauphiné: Romans, septembre 1788–janvier 1789*. Grenoble, 1942.

————. "Les Origines de la Révolution en Bretagne, 1788–1789." In *New Perspectives on the Revolution in France*, edited by Jeffry Kaplow. New York, 1965.

————. *Le Parlement de Dauphiné et les affaires publiques dans la deuxième moitié du XVIIIᵉ siècle*. 2 vols. Grenoble, 1942.

————. *La Pré-Révolution française, 1787–1788*. Paris, 1962.

————. *La Révolution des Notables: Mounier et les monarchiens, 1789*. Paris, 1950.

————. "La Seconde Assemblée des Notables." *Annales historiques de la Révolution française*, XXI (1949), 193–228.

Eisenstein, Elizabeth L. "Who Intervened in 1788? A Commentary on *The Coming of the French Revolution*." *American Historical Review*, LXXI (1965), 77–103.

Esquieu, L., and L. Delourmel. "Brest pendant la Révolution: Correspondance de la municipalité avec les députés de Brest aux Etats généraux, 1789–1791." *Bulletin de la Société académique de Brest*, XXXII (1906–1907), 87–242; XXXIII (1907–1908), 9–140.

Ferrières, Charles Elie, marquis de. *Correspondance inédite (1789, 1790, 1791)*. Edited by Henri Carré. Paris, 1932.

————. *Mémoires du marquis de Ferrières*. 3 vols. Paris, 1821–22.

Fitzsimmons, Michael P. "Privilege and the Polity in France, 1786–1791." *American Historical Review*, XCII (1987), 269–95.

Flammermont, Jules. *Remontrances du Parlement de Paris au dix-huitième siècle*. 3 vols. Paris, 1888–98.

Fling, Fred Morrow. "The Oath of the Tennis Court." *University Studies* (University of Nebraska), II (1902), 1–10.

Ford, Franklin L. "The Revolutionary and Napoleonic Era: How Much of a Watershed?" *American Historical Review*, LXIX (1963), 18–29.

————. *Robe and Sword: The Regrouping of the French Aristocracy After Louis XIV*. Cambridge, Mass., 1953.

Forsyth, Murray. *Reason and Revolution: The Political Thought of the Abbé Sieyès*. New York, 1987.

Fortescue, G. K. *List of the Contents of the Three Collections in the British Museum Relating to the French Revolution*. London, 1899.

Freddi, Fabio. "La Presse parisienne et la nuit du 4 août." *Annales historiques de la Révolution française,* LVII (1985), 46–59.

Frederiksen, Oliver J. "The Bureaus of the French Constituent Assembly of 1789: An Early Experiment in the Group-Conference Method." *Political Science Quarterly,* LI (1936), 418–37.

Fréville, Henri. *L'Intendance de Bretagne, 1689–1790.* 3 vols. Rennes, 1953.

Fromont, Henry. *Essai sur l'administration de l'Assemblée provinciale de la Généralité d'Orléans.* Paris, 1907.

Furet, François. "A Commentary: François Furet's Interpretation of the French Revolution." *French Historical Studies,* XVI (1990), 792–802.

———. *Interpreting the French Revolution.* Translated by Elborg Forster. New York and Cambridge, 1981.

———, and Mona Ozouf, eds. *The Transformation of Political Culture, 1789–1848.* New York, 1989. Vol. III of *The French Revolution and the Creation of Modern Political Culture.* 3 vols.

Furet, François, and Ran Halévi, eds. *Les Constituants.* Paris, 1990. Volume I of *Orateurs de la Révolution française* (ongoing).

Furet, François, and Denis Richet. *The French Revolution.* Translated by Stephen Hardman. London, 1970.

Gandilhon, ed. *Bibliographie générale des travaux historiques et archéologiques, 1910–1940.* Paris, 1944.

Garrett, Mitchell B. "The Call for Information Concerning the States-General in 1788." *American Historical Review,* XXXVII (1932), 506–14.

———. *The Estates General of 1789.* New York, 1935.

Garsonnin, Maurice. *Histoire de la Communauté des notaires au Châtelet d'Orléans, 1303–1791.* Orléans, 1922.

Gaston-Martin, René. "La Préparation de la Révolution: Les Chambres littéraires de Nantes." *La Révolution française,* LXXV (1939), 103–20.

Gauville, Louis Henri Charles de. *Journal de baron de Gauville, député de l'ordre de la noblesse aux Etats généraux depuis le 4 mars 1789 jusqu'au 1er juillet 1790.* Paris, 1864.

Gerbner, George, *et al.,* eds. *The Analysis of Communication Content.* New York, 1969.

Gibert, François. "L'Amiral Latouche-Tréville, député à Montargis, aux Etats-Généraux." *Bulletin de la Société d'émulation de Montargis,* I (1922), 10, 11.

Gillis, John R. "Political Decay and the European Revolutions, 1789–1848." *World Politics,* XXII (1970), 344–70.

Godechot, Jacques. *La Prise de la Bastille.* Paris, 1965.

Gojat, Georges. "Les Corps intermédiaires de la décentralisation dans l'oeuvre de

Tocqueville." In *Libéralism, traditionalisme, décentralisation,* edited by Robert Pelloux. Paris, 1952.

Goodwin, Albert. "Calonne, the Assembly of the French Notables of 1787, and the Origins of the 'Révolte Nobiliaire.'" *English Historical Review,* LXI (1946), 202–34, 329–77.

Gordon, Daniel. "'Public Opinion' and the Civilizing Process in France: The Example of Morellet." *Eighteenth-Century Studies,* XXII (1989), 302–28.

Goubert, Pierre. *La Société.* Paris, 1969. and *La Politique.* Paris, 1970. Vols. I and II of Goubert, *L'Ancien Régime.* 2 vols.

———. *Mil sept cent quatre-vingt-neuf: Les Français ont la parole; cahiers de doléances des Etats généraux, présentés par Pierre Goubert et Michel Denis.* Paris, 1964.

Goulemot, Jean Marie. "Le Mot 'Révolution' et la formation du concept de Révolution politique, fin XVIIᵉ siècle." *Annales historiques de la Révolution française,* XXXIX (1967), 417–44.

Grange, Henri. *Les Idées de Necker.* Paris, 1974.

———. "Necker et Mounier devant le problème politique." *Annales historiques de la Révolution française,* XLI (1969), 588–605.

Greenlaw, Ralph W. "Pamphlet Literature in France During the Period of the Aristocratic Revolt." *Journal of Modern History,* XXIX (1957), 349–54.

Greer, Donald. *The Incidence of the Emigration During the French Revolution.* Cambridge, Mass., 1951.

———. *The Incidence of the Terror During the French Revolution.* Cambridge, Mass., 1935.

Grellet de Beauregard, Jean Baptiste. "Lettres de 12 juin 1789–19 avril 1791," edited by Abbé Dardy. *Mémoires de la Société des sciences naturelles et archéologique de la Creuse,* Ser. 2, Vol. VII (1899), 53–117.

Griffiths, Robert Howell. *Le Centre perdu: Malouet et les "monarchiens" dans la Révolution française.* Grenoble, 1988.

Gruder, Vivian R. "Class and Politics in the Pre-Revolution: The Assembly of Notables of 1787." In *De l'Ancien Régime à la Révolution française: Recherches et Perspectives,* edited by Albert Cremer. Göttingen, 1978.

———. "A Mutation in Elite Political Culture: The French Notables and the Defense of Property and Participation, 1787." *Journal of Modern History,* LVI (1984), 598–634.

———. *The Royal Provincial Intendants: A Governing Elite in Eighteenth-Century France.* Ithaca, 1968.

Guillaume, Paul. "Documents relatifs à la vie économique et sociale de la Révolution. Election de Grenoble, partie comprise dans le département des Hautes-Alpes. Le Champsaur et le Valgaudemar en 1789." *Bulletin de la Société d'études des Hautes-Alpes,* XXXI (1912), 1–40, 103–50, 294–335.

————. *Recueil des réponses faites par les communautés de l'élection de Gap au question-naire envoyé par la commission intermédiaire des états du Dauphiné.* Paris, 1908.

Guillet. "Quéru de la Coste, 1742–1805." *Bulletin et Mémoires de la Société archéo-logique d'Ille-et-Vilaine,* LX (1934), procès-verbaux, XVI.

Guillois, Antoine. *Le Salon de Mme. Helvétius: Cabanis et les idéologues.* Part 3: De Stutt de Tracy. Paris, 1894.

Halévi, Ran. *Les Loges maçonniques dans la France d'Ancien Régime aux origines de la sociabilité démocratique.* Paris, 1984.

Hampson, Norman. *Prelude to Terror: The Constituent Assembly and the Failure of Consensus, 1789–1791.* London, 1988.

————. *Will and Circumstance: Montesquieu, Rousseau, and the French Revolution.* London, 1983.

Hardy, James D., John H. Jensen, and Martin Wolfe. *The Maclure Collection of French Revolutionary Materials.* Philadelphia, 1966.

Hayden, Horace E., ed. *French Revolutionary Pamphlets: A Check List of the Talleyrand and Other Collections.* New York, 1945.

Hémon, Pierre. *Documents sur l'histoire de la Révolution en Bretagne: Carhaix et le district de Carhaix pendant la Révolution.* Nantes, 1912.

————. "Les Prêtres assermentés dans les Côtes-du-Nord." *Annales de Bretagne,* XII (1897), 622–62.

————. *La Révolution en Bretagne: Notes et documents.* Saint-Brieuc, 1903.

Herr, Richard. *Tocqueville and the Old Regime.* Princeton, 1965.

Higonnet, Patrice. *Class, Ideology, and the Rights of Nobles During the French Revolu-tion.* New York, 1981.

————. *Sister Republics: The Origins of French and American Republicanism.* Cam-bridge, Mass., 1988.

Holsti, Ole R. *Content Analysis for the Social Sciences and Humanities.* Reading, Mass., 1969.

Houtin, Albert. *Les Manuscrits relatifs à l'histoire de la Révolution et de l'Empire dans les bibliothèques publiques des départements.* Paris, 1913.

————. *Les Séances des députés du Clergé aux Etats généraux de 1789: Journaux du curé Thibault et du chanoine Coster.* Paris, 1916.

Hunt, Lynn. "Commentary on the Origins of the French Revolution: A Debate." *French Historical Studies,* XVI (1990), 761–63.

————. "French History in the Last Twenty Years: The Rise and Fall of the *An-nales* Paradigm." *Journal of Contemporary History,* XXI (1986), 209–24.

————. *Politics, Culture, and Class in the French Revolution.* Berkeley, 1984.

————, ed. "The French Revolution in Culture." Special Issue, *Eighteenth-Century Studies,* XXII (Spring, 1989).

Hunt, Lynn, David Lansky, and Paul Hanson. "The Failure of the Liberal Republic in France, 1795–1799: The Road to Brumaire." *Journal of Modern History,* LI (1979), 734–59.

Hutt, M. G. "The Curés and the Third Estate: The Ideas of Reform in the Pamphlets of the French Lower Clergy in the Period 1787–1789." *Journal of Ecclesiastical History,* VIII (1957), 74–92.

———. "The Role of the Curés in the Estates-General." *Journal of Ecclesiastical History,* VI (1955), 190–220.

Hyslop, Beatrice Fry. *L'Apanage de Philippe-Egalité, duc d'Orléans, 1785–1791.* Paris, 1965.

———. *A Guide to the General Cahiers of 1789.* New York, 1936.

Jean, Le P. Armand, S.J. *Les Evêques et archevêques de France depuis 1682 jusqu'à 1801.* Paris, 1891.

Jordan, David P. "Economics Versus Culture: Two Views of the French Revolution." *Eighteenth Century,* XXVIII (1987), 83–90.

———. *The Revolutionary Career of Maximilien Robespierre.* New York, 1985.

Kaplan, Steven L. *Bread, Politics, and Political Economy.* 2 vols. The Hague, 1976.

Kaplow, Jeffry, ed. *New Perspectives on the Revolution in France.* New York, 1965.

Kelly, George Armstrong. "Bailly and the Champ de Mars Massacre." *Journal of Modern History,* On-Demand Supplement, LII (1980), D1021–D1046.

Kennedy, Michael L. *The Jacobin Clubs in the French Revolution: The First Years.* Princeton, 1982.

Kerviler, René. "Recherches et notices sur les députés de la Bretagne aux Etats généraux." *Revue historique de l'Ouest,* I (1885), 484–92.

———. "Recherches et notices sur les députés de la Bretagne aux Etats-Généraux et à l'Assemblée Constituante de 1789." *Revue historique de l'Ouest,* I (1886), 45–60, 95–127, 265–84, 338–62, 466–505; II (1886), 60–83, 129–41, 177–201, 315–43, 421–41; III (1887), 63–84, 108–29, 326–45, 427–43; IV (1888), 43–55, 128–67, 281–94, 343–73, 417–65, 569–92; V (1889), 5–29, 133–60, 325–50, 417–39, 573–90.

Kessel, Patrick. *La Nuit du 4 août 1789.* Paris, 1969.

Kientz, Albert. *Pour analyser les média: L'Analyse de contenu.* Tours, 1971.

Kuhlmann, Charles, "Influence of the Breton Deputation and the Breton Club in the Revolution, April–October, 1789." *University Studies* (University of Nebraska), II (1902), 207–98.

———. "Relation of the Jacobins to the Army and Lafayette." *University Studies* (University of Nebraska), VI (1906), 153–92.

Kuscinski, Auguste. *Dictionnaire des conventionnels.* Paris, 1916–19.

La Capra, Dominick, and Steven L. Kaplan, eds. *Modern European Intellectual History: Reappraisals and New Perspectives.* Ithaca, 1982.

Lachaze, Lucien. *Les Etats provinciaux de l'ancienne France et la question des états provinciaux aux XVIIᵉ et XVIIIᵉ siècles.* Paris, 1909.

Lallié, Alfred. "Le Clergé du diocèse de Nantes en 1791." *Revue historique de l'Ouest,* VI (1890), 378–417.

Lamarque, Pierre. *Les Francs-Maçons aux Etats généraux de 1789 et à l'Assemblée nationale.* Paris, 1981.

Langlois, Claude, David D. Bien, Donald Sutherland, and François Furet. "Forum: François Furet's Interpretation of the French Revolution." *French Historical Studies,* XVI (1990), 766–802.

Lasteyrie, Robert de, ed. *Bibliographie générale des travaux historiques et archéologiques publiés par les sociétés savantes de la France.* Paris, 1888.

Laurent, Gustave. "La Faculté de droit de Reims et les hommes de la Révolution." *Annales historiques de la Révolution française,* VI (1929), 329–58.

Lebègue, Ernest. *La Vie et l'Oeuvre d'un constituant: Thouret.* Paris, 1910.

Lefebvre, Georges. "Les Bureaux de l'Assemblée nationale en 1789." *Annales historiques de la Révolution française,* XXII (1950), 134–40.

———. *Etudes orléanaises.* Paris, 1962.

———. *The French Revolution from Its Origins to 1793.* Translated by Elizabeth Moss Evanson. London, 1962.

———. "Le Mythe de la Révolution française." *Annales historiques de la Révolution française,* LVII (1985), 1–7.

Leguai, André. *Histoire du Bourbonnais.* Paris, 1960.

Lemaire, Jacques. *Les Origines françaises de l'antimaçonnisme: 1744–1797.* Brussels, 1985.

Lemarchand, Guy. "L'Eglise, appareil idéologique d'état dans la France d'Ancien Régime (XVIᵉ–XVIIIᵉ siècles)." *Annales historiques de la Révolution française,* LI (April–June, 1979), 250–79.

Lemas, Thomas. *Etudes sur le Cher pendant la Révolution.* Paris. 1887.

———. "Les Assemblées électorales du département des Hautes-Alpes pendant la Révolution." *Bulletin de la Société d'études des Hautes-Alpes,* VIII (1889), 274–88; IX (1890), 43–60, 201–209.

Lemay, Edna Hindie. "La Composition de l'Assemblée nationale constituante: Les hommes de la continuité?" *Revue d'histoire moderne et contemporaine,* XXIV (1977), 341–63.

———. *La Vie quotidienne des députés aux Etats généraux, 1789.* Paris, 1987.

———. "Une Voix dissonante à l'Assemblée constituante: Le Prosélytisme de Robespierre." *Annales historiques de la Révolution française,* LIII (July–September, 1981), 390–404.

Lepeletier, Félix. *Oeuvres de Le Peletier de Saint-Fargeau, précédées de sa vie, suivies de documents historiques relatifs à sa personne, à sa sort, et à l'époque.* Brussels, 1826.

Lesueur, F. "L'Assemblée de département de Blois et Romorantin et son bureau intermédiaire, 1787–1790." *Mémoires de la Société des sciences et lettres de Loir-et-Cher,* XXI (1910), 1–385.

Le Téo, Ch. "Le Club Breton et les origines du Club des Jacobins." *La Révolution française,* XXXVI (1899), 385–95.

Leusse, Paul de. "Notes sur l'émigration du baron de Montboissier et de sa famille." *Bulletin de la Société Dunoise,* XVI (1932–35), 337–83.

Levy, Darline Gay. *The Ideas and Careers of Simon Nicolas Henri Linguet.* Urbana, 1980.

Levy, Darline Gay, Harriet B. Applewhite, and Mary D. Johnson. *Women in Revolutionary Paris.* Urbana, 1979.

Lewis-Beck, Michael S., Anne Hildreth, and Alan B. Spitzer. "Was There a Girondist Faction in the National Convention, 1792–1793?" *French Historical Studies,* XV (1988), 519–36.

Lucas, Colin. "Nobles, Bourgeois, and the Origins of the French Revolution." *Past and Present,* August, 1973, pp. 84–126.

———, ed. *The Political Culture of the French Revolution.* New York, 1989. Vol. II of *The French Revolution and the Creation of Modern Political Culture.* 3 vols.

Maier, Charles S., ed. *Changing Boundaries of the Political: Essays on the Evolving Balance Between the State and Society, Public and Private in Europe.* Cambridge, Eng., 1987.

Malouet, Pierre Victor. *Mémoires de Malouet.* Edited by le baron Malouet. 2 vols. Paris, 1874.

Margerison, Kenneth. "History, Representative Institutions, and Political Rights in the French Pre-Revolution (1787–1789)." *French Historical Studies,* XV (1987), 68–98.

Marion, Marcel. *La Bretagne et le duc d'Aiguillon, 1753–1770.* Paris, 1898.

———. *Histoire du Berry et du Bourbonnais.* Paris, 1933.

Markoff, John, and Gilbert Shapiro. "Consensus and Conflict at the Onset of Revolution: A Quantitative Study of France in 1789." *American Journal of Sociology,* XCI (1985), 28–53.

Martin, André, and Gérard Walter. *Catalogue de l'histoire de la Révolution française.* 3 vols. Paris, 1936.

Masclet, Jean-Claude. *Le Rôle du député et ses attaches institutionnelles sous la Ve République.* Paris, 1979.

Mathiez, Albert. *Le Club des Cordeliers pendant la crise de Varennes et le massacre du Champ de Mars.* 1910; rpr. Geneva, 1975.

———. *Les Grandes Journées de la Constituante, 1789–1791.* Paris, 1913.

Mazauric, Claude. "France révolutionnaire, France révolutionnée, France en Révolution: Pour une clarification des rhythmes et des concepts." *Annales historiques de la Révolution française,* LX (1988), 127–50.

McManners, John. *French Ecclesiastical Society in the Old Regime.* Manchester, Eng., 1960.

————. *The French Revolution and the Church.* London, 1969.

Mège, Francisque, ed. *Gaultier de Biauzat.* 2 vols. Paris, 1890.

Meyer, Jean. *La Noblesse bretonne au dix-huitième siècle.* 2 vols. Paris, 1966.

Michon, Georges. *Essai sur l'histoire du parti Feuillant: Adrien Duport.* Paris, 1924.

Mirkine-Guetzévitch, B. "L'Abbé Sieyès." *La Révolution française,* LXXXIX (1936), 229–36.

————. "Etudes constitutionnelles de la Révolution." *La Révolution française,* XXXIII (1897), 5–22.

Mitchell, C. J. "Political Divisions Within the Legislative Assembly of 1791." *French Historical Studies,* XIII (1984), 356–89.

Monceaux, Henri. "La Révolution dans le département de l'Yonne, essai bibliographique, 1783–1800." *Bulletin de la Société des sciences historiques et naturelles de l'Yonne,* XLIII (1889), 45–288, 343–586; XLIV (1890), 17–262.

Monin, Hippolyte. *L'Etat de Paris en 1789: Études et documents sur l'Ancien Régime à Paris.* Paris, 1889.

Montier, A., ed. *Correspondance de Thomas Lindet pendant la Constituante et la Législative (1789–1792).* Paris, 1889.

Mousnier, Roland E. *The Organs of State and Society.* Translated by Arthur Goldhammer. Chicago, 1984. Vol. II of Mousnier, *The Institutions of France Under the Absolute Monarchy, 1598–1789.* 2 vols.

————. "La Participation des gouvernés à l'activité des gouvernants dans la France des XVIIᵉ et XVIIIᵉ siècles." *Recueils de la Société Jean Bodin pour l'histoire comparative des institutions,* XXIV (1966), 235–97.

Murphy, James, Bernard Higonnet, and Patrice Higonnet. "Notes sur la composition de l'Assemblée constituante." *Annales historiques de la Révolution française,* XLVI (1974), 321–26.

Murphy, James, and Patrice Higonnet. "Les Députés de la noblesse aux Etats généraux de 1789." *Revue d'histoire moderne et contemporaine,* XX (1973), 230–47.

Necheles, Ruth F. "The Curés in the Estates-General of 1789." *Journal of Modern History,* XLVI (1974), 425–44.

Neton, Albéric. *Sieyès d'après des documents inédits.* Paris, 1900.

Palmer, R. R. *The Challenge.* Princeton, 1959. *The Struggle.* Princeton, 1964. Vols. I and II of Palmer, *The Age of the Democratic Revolution.* 2 vols.

————. *Catholics and Unbelievers in Eighteenth-Century France.* Princeton, 1939.

————. *The Improvement of Humanity: Education and the French Revolution.* Princeton, 1985.

————. "Sur la composition sociale de la gauche à la Constituante." *Annales historiques de la Révolution française,* XXXI (1959), 154–56.

————. *The Two Tocquevilles, Father and Son: Hervé and Alexis de Tocqueville on the Coming of the French Revolution.* Princeton, 1987.

Pariset, E. "Guillotin, à propos d'une récente thèse allemande." *La Révolution française,* XXV (1893), 437–62.

Pascal, Jean. *Les Députés bretons de 1789 à 1983.* Paris, 1983.

Patrick, Alison. *The Men of the First French Republic.* Baltimore, 1972.

————. "Political Divisions in the French National Convention, 1792–93." *Journal of Modern History,* XLI (1969), 421–74.

Péronnet, Michel. "L'Assemblée du Clergé de France tenue en 1788." *Annales historiques de la Révolution française,* LX (1988), 227–46.

Perroissier, Cyprien. "Lettre de J. B. Veyrenc, notaire à Grignan, à M. Bignan de Coyrol, député à l'Assemblée nationale, sur les événements du pays en 1790." *Bulletin de la Société d'archéologie et de statistique de la Drôme,* XXXIV (1900), 97.

Pertué, Michel. "Remarques sur les listes des Conventionnels." *Annales historiques de la Révolution française,* LIII (1981), 366–78.

Peyron, P. "Les Confesseurs de la foi, victimes de la Révolution française, dans le Finistère." *Bulletin diocésain d'histoire et d'archéologie, diocèse de Quimper et de Léon* (1918), 28–32, 62–80, 113–28, 160–76, 209–23, 264–70.

Pilven, J. M. "Le Premier Evêque constitutionnel: Expilly, évêque du Finistère." *Bulletin diocésain d'histoire et d'archéologie, diocèse de Quimper et de Léon* (1911), 5–12, 33–40, 65–74, 97–106, 129–38, 161–70, 257–68, 321–34, 361–74.

Pisani, Paul. *Répertoire biographique de l'épiscopat constitutionnel, 1791–1802.* Paris, 1907.

Pocquet, Barthélemy. *Le Pouvoir absolu et l'esprit provincial: Le Duc d'Aiguillon et La Chalotais.* 3 vols. Paris, 1900–1901.

————. *Les Origines de la Révolution en Bretagne.* 2 vols. Paris, 1885.

Pommeret, H. *L'Esprit public dans la département des Côtes-du-Nord pendant la Révolution, 1789–1799.* Saint-Brieuc, 1921.

Poncet-Delpech, J. B. *La Première Année de la Révolution vue par un témoin.* Edited by Daniel Ligou. Paris, 1961.

Porée, Charles, "Mémoires du chanoine Frappier sur le clergé d'Auxerre, pendant la Révolution de 1789 à l'an IV." *Bulletin de la Société des sciences historiques et naturelles de l'Yonne,* LXXVII (1923), 101–42.

Porset, Charles. "Les Francs-Maçons et la Révolution (autour de la 'Machine' de Cochin)." *Annales historiques de la Révolution française,* LXII (1990), 14–31.

[Rangeard, Jacques]. *Procès-verbal historique des actes du Clergé par un député à l'Assemblée des Etats généraux des années 1789 et 1790.* Paris, 1791.

Ravitch, Norman. "Robe and Sword in the Recruitment of French Bishops." *Catholic Historical Review*, L (1965), 494–508.

———. *Sword and Mitre: Government and Episcopate in France and England in the Age of Aristocracy*. Paris, 1966.

Raynal, Louis Hector Chaudru de. *Histoire du Berry depuis les temps les plus anciens jusqu'en 1789*. 4 vols. Bourges, 1844–47.

———, and Rénouard, eds. *Le Tribunal de la cour de cassation: Notices sur le personnel, 1791–1879*. Paris, 1879.

Rébillon, Armand. *Les Etats de Bretagne de 1661 à 1789*. Rennes, 1932.

Reinhard, Marcel. "Elite et noblesse dans la seconde moitié du XVIIIᵉ siècle." *Revue d'histoire moderne et contemporaine*, III (1956), 5–37.

Renouvin, Pierre. *Les Assemblées provinciales de 1787*. Paris, 1921.

Rétat, Pierre. "Forme et discours d'un journal révolutionnaire: Les *Révolutions de Paris* en 1789." In *L'Instrument périodique: La Fonction de la presse au XVIIIᵉ siècle*. Edited by Claude Labrosse, Pierre Rétat, and Henri Duranton. Lyon, 1986.

Révolutions de Paris, Vol. IV, No. 43 (May 1–8, 1790), No. 52 (July 3–10, 1790).

Richard, Guy. "A propos de la noblesse commerçante de Lyon au XVIIIᵉ siècle." *L'Information historique*, IV (1957), 156–61.

———. "Les Corporations et la noblesse commerçante en France au XVIIIᵉ siècle." *L'Information historique*, IV (1957): 185–89.

———. "Un Essai d'adaptation sociale à une nouvelle structure économique: La Noblesse de France et les sociétés par actions à la fin du XVIIIᵉ siècle." *Revue d'histoire économique et sociale*, XLI (1962), 484–523.

———. "La Noblesse commerçante à Bordeaux et à Nantes au XVIIIᵉ siècle." *L'Information historique*, V (1958), 185–90.

Ricommard, Julien. "Les Subdélégués des intendants jusqu'à leur érection en titre d'office." In *Etudes sur l'histoire administrative et sociale de l'Ancien Régime*, edited by Georges Pagès. Paris, 1938.

Robiquet, Paul. *Le Personnel municipal de Paris pendant la Révolution*. Paris, 1890.

Rochas, Adolphe. *Biographie du Dauphiné, contenant l'histoire des hommes nés dans cette province*. 2 vols. Paris, 1856–60.

Roels, Jean. "La Notion de représentation chez les Révolutionnaires français." *Commission internationale pour l'histoire des Assemblées d'états*, XXVII (1965), entire issue.

———. "Le Concept de représentation politique au XVIIIᵉ siècle français." *Anciens Pays et assemblées d'états*, XLV (1968–69), entire issue.

Rose, Robert Barrie. *The Making of the Sans-Culottes*. Manchester, Eng., 1983.

Rouanet, Gustave. "La Correspondance de Bretagne." *Annales révolutionnaires*, X (1918), 542–49.

————. "Les Débuts du parlementarisme française." *Annales révolutionnaires,* VIII (1916), 173–211.

————. "Les Premiers Leaders parlementaires en France." *Annales révolutionnaires,* VIII (1916), 480–503, 612–25; IX (1917), 12–33, 610–28.

————. "Les Séances de la Constituante après le 14 juillet 1789." *Annales révolutionnaires,* IX (1917), 433–55.

Ruault, Nicolas. *Gazette d'un Parisien sous la Révolution: Lettres à son frère, 1783–1796.* Paris, 1976.

Rudé, George. *The Crowd in the French Revolution.* New York, 1959.

Sagnac, Philippe. "La Composition des Etats généraux et de l'Assemblée nationale de 1789." *Revue historique,* CCV (1951), 8–28.

————. "Le Clergé constitutionnel et le clergé réfractaire en 1791." *La Révolution française,* LIII (1907), 403–21.

————. "Les Curés et le patriotisme pendant la Révolution, 1789–1792." *La Révolution française,* LXXV (1939), 166–77.

————. "L'Eglise de France et le serment à la Constitution civile du Clergé, 1790–1791." *La Révolution française,* LIII (1907), 317–41.

————. "Les Grands Courants d'idées et de sentiments en France vers 1789." *Revue d'histoire politique et constitutionnelle,* II (1938), 317–41.

Saluden, Louis. "Le Protégé de Robespierre, l'abbé Denis Bérardier." *Bulletin diocésain d'histoire et d'archéologie, diocèse de Quimper et de Léon* (1928), 109–14.

Saricks, Ambrose. *A Bibliography of the Frank E. Melvin Collection of Pamphlets of the French Revolution in the University of Kansas Libraries.* 2 vols. Lawrence, Kans., 1960.

Saulnier de la Pinelais, Gustave. *Les Gens du roi au Parlement de Bretagne, 1553–1790.* Paris, 1902.

Schama, Simon. *Citizens: A Chronicle of the French Revolution.* New York, 1989.

Sentou, Jean. *Fortunes et groups sociaux à Toulouse sous la Révolution (1789–1799): Essai d'histoire statistique.* Toulouse, 1969.

Sepet, M. "Le Serment du Jeu de Paume et la déclaration du 23 juin." *Revue des questions historiques,* XLIX (1891), 491–546.

Sewell, William H., Jr. "Ideologies and Social Revolutions: Reflexions on the French Case." *Journal of Modern History,* LVII (1985), 57–85.

Shafer, Boyd C. "Bourgeois Nationalism in the Pamphlets on the Eve of the French Revolution." *Journal of Modern History,* X (1938), 31–50.

Shennan, J. H. *The Parlement of Paris.* Ithaca, 1968.

Six, Georges. *Dictionnaire biographique des généraux et amiraux français de la Révolution et de l'Empire, 1792–1814.* 2 vols. Paris, 1943.

Skocpol, Theda. "Cultural Idioms and Political Ideologies in the Revolutionary

Reconstruction of State Power: A Rejoinder to Sewell." *Journal of Modern History,* LVII (1985), 86–96.

Souchet, Jean Baptiste. *Histoire du diocèse et de la ville de Chartres.* 4 vols. Chartres, 1866–73.

Stewart, John Hall. *A Documentary Survey of the French Revolution.* New York, 1951.

———. *France, 1715–1815: A Guide to Materials in Cleveland.* Cleveland, 1942.

Stone, Philip J., *et al. The General Inquirer: A Computer Approach to Content Analysis.* Cambridge, Mass., 1966.

Sutherland, Donald M. G. "An Assessment of the Writings of François Furet." *French Historical Studies,* XVI (1990), 784–91.

———. *France, 1789–1815: Revolution and Counter-revolution.* New York, 1986.

Sydenham, Michael John. *The Girondins.* London, 1961.

———. "The Montagnards and Their Opponents: Some Considerations on a Recent Reassessment of the Conflicts in the French National Convention." *Journal of Modern History,* XLIII (1971), 287–93.

Tackett, Timothy. "Nobles and Third Estate in the Revolutionary Dynamic of the National Assembly, 1789–1790." *American Historical Review,* XCIV (1989), 271–301.

———. *Priest and Paris in Eighteenth-Century France.* Princeton, 1977.

Tanguy, E. "L'Emigration dans l'Ille-et-Vilaine et la vente des biens nationaux de deuxième origine." *Annales de Bretagne,* XXI (1905–1906), 160–65.

Taylor, George V. "Revolutionary and Nonrevolutionary Content in the *Cahiers* of 1789: An Interim Report." *French Historical Studies,* VII (1972), 479–502.

Tempier, D. "Correspondance des députés des Côtes-du-Nord aux Etats-Généraux et l'Assemblée nationale constituante." *Bulletins et mémoires de la Société d'émulation des Côtes-du-Nord,* XXVI (1888), 210–63.

Thénard, J. F. "L'Abbé Sieyès, électeur et élu, 1789." *La Révolution française,* IV (1888), 1083–89.

Thibault, Adrien. "L'Abbé Michel Chabault, député aux Etats-Généraux de 1789." *Mémoires de la Société des sciences et lettres de Loir-et-Cher,* XIV (1900), 37–44.

Thompson, Eric. *Popular Sovereignty and the French Constituent Assembly, 1789–1791.* Manchester, Eng., 1952.

Thompson, James M. *The French Revolution.* Oxford, Eng., 1964.

———. *Leaders of the French Revolution.* Oxford, Eng., 1929.

Tilly, Charles. *The Contentious French.* Cambridge, Eng., 1986.

Tocqueville, Alexis de. *L'Ancien Régime et la Révolution.* Edited by J. P. Mayer and André Jardin. Paris, 1951. Vol. II of Tocqueville, *Oeuvres, papiers, et correspondances.* 13 vols. Available in English as *The Old Regime and the French Revolution.* Translated by Stuart Gilbert. New York, 1955.

Toulongeon, François Emmanuel, vicomte de. *Eloge historique de A. G. Camus, membre de l'Institut national.* Paris, 1806.

Tourneux, Maurice. *Bibliographie de l'histoire de Paris pendant la Révolution française.* 5 vols. Paris, 1890–1913.

Treilhard, Jean. *Jean-Baptiste Treilhard, ministre plénipotentiaire de la République au congrès de Rastadt.* Gaillon, 1939.

Tuetey, Alexandre. *Les Papiers des assemblées révolutionnaires aux Archives nationales: Inventaire de la série C.: Constituante.* Paris, 1908.

————. *Répertoire de l'histoire de la Révolution française.* Paris, 1890–1914.

Vallon. "Notice biographique sur Dinochau." *Mémoires de la Société des sciences et lettres de Loir-et-Cher,* II (1836), 259–79.

Van Kley, Dale. *The Damiens Affair and the Unraveling of the Ancien Régime, 1750–1770.* Princeton, 1984.

————. "The Jansenist Constitutional Legacy in the French Pre-Revolution." *Historical Reflections/Réflexions historiques,* XIII (1986), 393–453.

Vayssière, A. *Les Etats du Bourbonnais, notes et documents.* Moulins, 1890.

Vellein, G. "Quelques événements de la vie de Guy Allard: Ses Démêlés avec la justice." *Petite Revue des bibliophiles dauphinois,* II (1908–10), 162–79.

Vermale, F. "Les Complots monarchiens de Mounier après les 5 et 6 octobre 1789." *Bulletin de l'Académie delphinale,* LXXIII (1936), 33–67.

Vidalenc, Jean. *Les Emigrés français, 1789–1825.* Caen, 1963.

Villers, Robert, *L'Organisation du Parlement de Paris et des Conseils supérieurs d'après la réforme de Maupeou, 1771–1774.* Paris, 1937.

Viple, Joseph. "François Xavier Laurent, député à l'Assemblée constituante, évêque constitutionnel du département de l'Allier, 1744–1821." *Bulletin de la Société d'émulation du Bourbonnais,* XXIII (1920), 11–63.

Vovelle, Michel. "L'Historiographie de la Révolution française à la veille du Bicentenaire." *Annales historiques de la Révolution française,* LIX (1988), 113–26.

————. "Structure et répartition de la fortune foncière et de la fortune mobilière d'un ensemble urbain: Chartres de la fin de l'Ancien Régime à la Réstauration." *Revue d'histoire économique et sociale,* IV (1958), 385–98.

Walter, Gérard. *Répertoire de l'histoire de la Révolution française.* Paris, 1941.

White, Andrew Dickson. *Catalogue of the Historical Library of Andrew Dickson White* (Vol. II: The French Revolution). Ithaca, 1894.

White, Louise G, with Robert P. Clark. *Political Analysis: Technique and Practice,* 2d ed. Pacific Grove, Calif., 1990.

Wick, Daniel L. *A Conspiracy of Well-Intentioned Men: The Society of Thirty and the French Revolution.* New York, 1987.

————. "The Court Nobility and the French Revolution: The Example of the Society of Thirty." *Eighteenth-Century Studies,* XIII (1980), 263–84.

Pamphlets

Allarde, Pierre Gilbert Leroy, baron d'. *Opinion . . . sur l'éligibilité à l'électorat.* Paris, 1791.

Anson, Pierre Hubert. *A. M. l'abbé Maury.* Paris, 1790.

————. *Discours . . . sur l'organisation du ministère.* Paris, 1791.

————. *Note sur l'opinion de M. l'abbé Maury concernant la dette publique.* Paris, 1790.

————. *Rapport fait à l'Assemblée nationale le 31 décembre 1790: Comité des finances.* Paris, 1791.

Baco de La Chapelle, René Gaston. *Copie de la lettre à MM. les électeurs du département de la Loire inférieure, 12 septembre 1791.* Nantes, 1791.

————. *Opinion sur le project des comités de constitution et de la législation criminelle.* Paris, 1790.

————. *Réponse à l'adresse à l'Assemblée nationale de Directoire du district, du Conseil général de la commune, et des sociétés des Amis de la Constitution de Nantes.* Paris, 1791.

Bailly, Jean Silvain. *Compte rendu à l'Assemblée nationale par les députés du bureau de la ville de Paris, 10 mars 1790.* Paris, 1790.

————. *Délibération de l'Assemblée nationale du mercredi 17 juin 1789.* Paris, 1789.

————. *Discours . . . à l'Assemblée nationale sur les prisonniers.* Paris, 1790.

————. *Discours de M. le maire de Paris à l'Assemblée nationale.* Paris, 1790.

————. *Discours de la Commune de Paris à l'Assemblée nationale.* Paris, 1790.

————. *Extrait du registre des délibérations du corps municipal du dimanche 17 juillet 1791.* Paris, 1791.

————. *Lettre . . . à M. le Feuvre d'Arles, commandant du bataillon des Petits-Augustins, sur la liberté du culte religieux.* Paris, 1791.

————. *Lettre de . . . , maire de Paris, à messieurs des districts.* Paris, 1789.

————. *Mémoires, ou Avant-Moniteur: Des 8 premiers mois de la Révolution française.* Paris, 1805.

Bailly, Jean Silvain, Armand Gaston Camus, and Alexis François Pison du Galland. *Récit de ce qui s'est passé à l'Assemblée nationale le 17 juin 1789.* Versailles, 1789.

Barnave, Antoine Pierre Joseph Marie. *Coup d'oeil sur la lettre de M. Calonne.* Grenoble, 1789.

————. *Esprit des édits enregistrés militairement au Parlement de Grenoble.* Grenoble, 1788.

————. *Grand discours au roi, à l'entrevue des commissaires de l'Assemblée nationale, le 21 juin 1791.* Paris, 1791.

————. *Lettre d'un campagnard dauphinois, à M. son subdélégué.* N.p., 1788.

————. "Lettre du 30 juin 1790 à la société des Amis de la Constitution de Grenoble." Published by J. de Beylié in *Bulletin historique et philologique,* 1899 (Paris, 1900), 407–16.

————. *Lettres inédites de Barnave sur la prise de la Bastille et sur les journées des 5 et 6 octobre.* Published by J. de Beylié. Grenoble, 1906.

————. *Opinions de M. Barnave et Salle sur les événemens du 21 juin 1791, prononcés à la séance du 15 juillet.* Châlons, 1791.

————. "Pensées diverses: Séparation des ordres." Communication faite à l'Académie delphinale par J. de Beylié. *Bulletin de l'Académie delphinale,* Ser. 4, Vol. XII (1899), 1–24.

————. *Profession de foi d'un militaire: Discours prononcé dans un conseil militaire.* N.P., 1788.

————. *Rapport fait à l'Assemblée nationale le 8 mars 1790 au nom du comité des colonies.* Paris, 1790.

————. *Rapport sur les colonies et décret, 28 septembre 1791.* Paris, 1791.

Baudoüin de Maisonblanche, Jean Marie, and Gabriel Hyacinthe Couppé. Letters to Correspondence Committee, August 13, 1790–September 17, 1791. *Mémoires de la Société d'émulation des Côtes-du-Nord,* XXVII (1889), 21–63.

Beauharnais [Beauharnois], Alexandre François Marie, vicomte de. *L'Assemblée nationale aux François: Proclamation décrétée dans la séance du 22 juin 1791.* Paris, 1791.

Bengy de Puyvallée, Philippe Jacques de. *Opinion sur la question du droit de la guerre et de la paix, prononcée à la séance du 21 mai 1790.* Paris, 1790.

————. *Seconde Opinion sur les principes naturels et politiques de la représentation nationale, séance du 17 novembre 1789.* Paris, 1789.

Berardier, Denis François Joseph. *Les Principes de la foi sur le gouvernement de l'église, en opposition avec la Constitution civile du Clergé, ou réfutation du développement de l'opinion de M. Camus.* Paris, 1791.

Bevière, Jean Baptiste Pierre. *De la necessité de la suppression du contrôle des actes des notaires et des moyens d'en remplacer le produit.* Paris, 1790.

Blandin, Liphard Daniel. *Apologie du clergé de France; ou, Commentaire raisonné sur l'instruction pastorale de l'Assemblée nationale concernant l'organisation civile du clergé.* Paris, 1791.

Blin, François Pierre. *Lettre à M. Mounier, député du Dauphiné, sur l'ouvrage intitulé "Considérations sur les gouvernemens, et principalement sur celui qui convient à la France."* Paris, 1789.

————. *Opinion sur la motion de M. le comte de Mirabeau, relative à l'admission des ministres dans l'Assemblée nationale, 6 novembre 1789.* Paris, 1789.

————. *Réflexions sur les colonies.* Paris, 1791.

Bonnay, Charles François, marquis de. *La Prise des Annonciades: Epitre sur la Révolution.* N.p., 1790.

Boullé, Jean Pierre. *Discours prononcé le 3 août 1791 à la Garde-nationale de Douai assemblée . . . pour prêter . . . le serment prescrit par la Loi du 22 juin.* Douai, 1891.

————. Series of letters, May 1–October 30, 1789. Edited by Albert Macé. *Revue de la Révolution,* X (1887), Documents, 161–71; XI (1888) Documents, 11–20, 45–53, 113–20; XII (1888), Documents, 7–14, 34–42, 49–58, 109–12; XIII (1888), Documents, 11–17, 65–79; XIV (1889), Documents, 26–32, 42–51, 82–92, 114–23; XV (1889), Documents, 13–28, 99–120; XVI (1889), Documents, 15–29, 45–84.

————. *Lettre de Boullé, lire à la séance du 7 septembre 1791.* Paris, 1791.

————. *Rapport sur la situation de la frontière et de l'armée du nord, 25 septembre 1791.* Paris, 1791.

Bouthillier de Beaujeau, Charles Léon, marquis de. *Motion sur la vente des biens ecclésiastiques, et les assignats.* N.p., 1790.

————. *Premier Rapport fait au nom du comité militaire à l'Assemblée nationale, 19 novembre 1789.* Paris, 1789.

Camus, Armand Gaston. *Développement de la motion de . . . relativement a l'Ordre de Malte, 4 janvier 1790.* Paris, 1790.

————. *Développement de l'opinion de . . . dans la séance du samedi 27 novembre 1790 sur l'exécution des Lois, concernant la Constitution du Clergé.* Paris, 1790.

————. *Histoire abrégée des travaux de l'Assemblée nationale constituante.* Paris, 1791.

————. *Observations sur deux brefs du pape en date du 10 mars et du 13 avril 1791.* Paris, 1791.

————. *Opinion . . . sur la motion faite par D. Gerle relativement à la religion Catholique.* Paris, 1790.

————. *Réponse . . . au mémoire adressé par M. Necker à l'Assemblée nationale, le premier août 1790.* Paris, 1790.

Césarges, Jean Baptiste Florimond Joseph. *Coup d'oeil rapide sur l'affaire des Quinze-Vingts.* Paris, n.d.

————. *Opinion . . . sur la motion de M. Lavenue tendante à imposer les rentiers dans la proportion des rentes dont ils jouissent.* Paris, 1790.

Chabroud, Jean Baptiste Charles. *Un Echantillon de leur méchanceté, aux honnêtes gens.* Paris, 1791.

————. *Opinion . . . et motion sur le jugement des appels, 20 juillet 1790.* Paris, 1790.

————. *Opinion sur l'ordre judiciaire, 30 mars, 1790.* Paris, 1790.

Chaillon, Etienne. *Aux bons patriotes, salut.* N.p., n.d. [Rennes, 1788].

————. *Extrait du tribut de la Société des Neuf Soeurs, 14 novembre 1790.* Paris, 1790.

————. *Moyens de prévenir la disette des grains et d'assurer la subsistance du peuple à un prix uniforme et moderé dans toute l'étendue du royaume.* Paris, 1790.

Champion de Cicé, Jean Baptiste Marie. *Discours prononcé . . . le 23 mars 1789, dans l'assemblée des trois ordres réunis du bailliage d'Auxerre et imprimés sur leur demande.* N.p., 1789.

Chevallier, François. "Histoire philosophique de la Révolution française." Excerpts from manuscript in René Kerviler, "Recherches et notices sur les députés de la Bretagne aux Etats généraux." *Revue historique de l'Ouest,* I (1885), 484–92.

Clermont-Tonnerre, Stanislas Marie Adélaïde, comte de. *Analyse raisonnée de la Constitution française décrétée par l'Assemblée nationale.* Paris, 1791.

————. *Au peuple de Paris par un membre de l'Assemblée nationale.* N.p., 1789.

————. *Compte rendu à ses concitoyens, de ce qui s'est passé de relatif à lui, à l'occasion du Club des Amis de la Constitution Monarchique.* Paris, 1791.

————. *Déclaration . . . remise à M. le président de l'Assemblée, le 5 juillet 1791.* N.p., 1791.

————. *Dernière Opinion sur l'affaire d'Avignon.* N.p., 1791.

————. *Le Secret de la coalition des ennemis de la Révolution française.* N.p., 1791.

————. *Lettre . . . à M. Duval Désprémenil.* N.p., 1790.

————. *L'Ouvrage intitulé "A Bonne interpellation, mauvaise réponse de C.T.," par C. F. Bouche.* N.p., 1791.

————. *Nouvelles Observations sur les comités des recherches.* Paris, 1790.

————. *Opinion . . . du lundi 13 juillet 1789.* Paris, 1789.

————. *Opinion sur l'affaire d'Avignon, 20 novembre 1790.* N.p., 1790.

————. *Opinion . . . sur le propriété des biens du clergé.* Paris, 1789.

————. *Pièce très-importante dans l'affaire d'Avignon.* N.p., 1791.

————. *Translation of a Speech by Him on Admitting Non-Catholics, Comedians, and Jews to Privilege of Citizens According to the Declaration of Rights.* London, 1790.

Corroller du Moustoir, Louis Jacques Hippolyte. *Adresse au peuple breton des villes et campagnes, de la part de leurs députés à l'Assemblée nationale.* Paris, 1789.

Cottin, Jacques Edme. *Arrêté des officiers municipaux de la ville de Nantes, du 4 novembre 1788; suivi de la Requête du tiers-état et de l'Arrêté du 6 du même mois.* N.p., 1788.

Couppé, Gabriel Hyacinthe. *See* Baudoüin de Maisonblanche.

Créniere, Jean Baptiste. *De la sanction royale, 3 september 1789.* N.p., 1789.

Delay d'Agier, Claude Pierre de. *Rapport sur la vente de ces biens.* Paris, 1790.

Defermon des Chapelières, Jacques Joseph. *Décret sur l'organisation des Gardes nationales.* Paris, 1791.

Delavigne, Jacques. *Discours à M. Necker lors de son arrivé à l'Assemblée des electeurs de la ville de Paris.* N.p., 1789.

————. *Discours au roi prononcée à l'arrivée de Sa Majesté à Paris, à la barrière de la conférence, le 17 juillet 1789*. Paris, 1789.

Delaville Le Roulx, Joseph. Letters of May 19, June 7, July 14, and August 5, 1789, to his correspondence committee. Quoted in René Kerviler, "Recherches et notices sur les députés de la Bretagne aux Etats généraux." *Revue historique de l'Ouest*, II (1886–87), 320, 321, 323, 327–29, 332.

————. *Opinion . . . sur le système de deux chambres*. Paris, 1789.

Démeunier, Jean Nicolas. *Des conditions nécessaires à la legalité des Etats-Généraux*. N.p., 1788.

————. *Rapport sur la convocation de la première législature, fait au nom du comité de Constitution*. Paris, 1791.

————. *Rapport sur les dispositions qui doivent compléter l'organisation des corps administratifs, fait au nom du comité de Constitution*. Paris, 1791.

————. *Rapport sur les municipalités par cantons, fait au nom du comité de Constitution*. Paris, 1791.

————. *Rapport sur l'organisation du ministère, fait au nom du comité de Constitution*. Paris, 1791.

Dosfant, Jean Antoine. *Opinion . . . sur le contrôle des actes*. Paris, 1790.

Dumouchel, Jean Baptiste. *Discours . . . au sujet de la prestation du serment prescrit par le Décret de l'Assemblée nationale du 27 novembre, accepté par le roi*. Paris, 1790.

————. *Discours prononcé à l'Assemblée nationale, à la séance du 8 janvier 1791 . . . à la tête des députés de ce corps, lors de leur prestation de serment ordonné par la Loi du 26 décembre, sur le Décret du 27 novembre 1790*. Besançon, 1791.

————. *Lettre pastorale de M. l'évêque du département du Gard*. Paris and Nismes [*sic*], 1791.

————. *Observations pour l'Université de Paris, au sujet de la prochaine Assemblée des Etats généraux de royaume*. Paris, 1788.

Du Port, Adrien Jean François. *Discours sur la rééligibilité des membres du corps législatif*. Paris, 1791.

————. *Observations sur le réglement de la convocation de Paris, faites au Parlement, par M. D. P. T.* Paris, 1788.

————. *Opinion . . . prononcée à la séance du matin 14 juillet*. Paris, 1791.

————. *Projet d'une Déclaration des Droits et des Principes fondamentaux du Gouvernement*. Versailles, 1789.

————. *Rapport fait au nom des comités de constitution et de jurisprudence criminelle, de la loi sur la Police de Sûreté, la Justice criminelle, et l'Institution des Jurés*. Paris, 1790.

Dusers, Charles Guillaume. *Opinion . . . sur le remplacement de plusieurs impôts indirects, supprimés ou supprimables*. Paris, 1790.

Expilly, Louis Alexandre. *Lettre écrite au pape par . . . nouvel évêque du Finistère, conformément à l'article 19 du titre 2 de la Constitution Civile de Clergé.* Paris, 1791.

————. *Lettre pastorale de M. l'évêque du Finistère.* Paris, 1791.

Fournier de la Pommeraye, Jean François. "Lettre à sa femme, Versailles, 6 mai 1789." *Revue de la Révolution,* I (1883), Documents, 119–21.

Gagon [du Chenay], Marie Toussaint. *Observations relatives au droit féodal de la province de Bretagne.* N.p., 1790.

Garnier, Jean Baptiste Etienne. *Moyens d'établir un ordre propre à consigner . . . les noms de familles.* N.p., 1789.

Gauville, Louis Henry Charles de. *Journal de baron de Gauville, député de l'ordre de la noblesse aux Etats généraux depuis le 4 mars 1789 jusqu'au 1er juillet 1790.* Paris, 1864.

Germain d'Orsanville, Ambroise François. *Opinion . . . sur les petits assignats de 5 livres.* Paris, 1791.

Gillet de La Jacqueminière, Louis Charles. *Projet de décret sur les droits de péage, minage, hallage, étalonnage.* Paris, 1790.

Glezen, Jacques Marie. *Lettre d'un homme à huit cents soixante-quatre nobles bretons, 2 février 1789.* N.p., 1789.

Grellet de Beauregard, Jean Baptiste. *Lettres aux Etats généraux.* Published by Abbé Dardy. Guéret, 1899.

Gros, Joseph Marie. *Extrait du procès-verbal de l'assemblée générale du district de Saint-Nicolas du Chardonnet du 17 mai 1790.* N.p., 1790.

Guillotin, Joseph Ignace. *Motion pour l'établissement d'un comité de santé.* N.p., 1790.

————. *Pétition des citoyens domiciliés à Paris, 8 décembre 1788.* Paris, 1788.

————. *Projet de décret sur l'enseignement et l'exercise de l'art de guérir, présenté au nom du comité du salubrité.* Paris, 1791.

Guillou, René Marie. *Réponse . . . aux protestations données par deux personnes respectables, et lues à la Chambre de l'Eglise, par M. le cardinal, le lundi 18 mai 1789.* Reprinted in Léon Dubreuil, "Les origines de la Chouannerie dans le département des Côtes-du-Nord," *La Révolution française,* LXVIII (1915), 135–37.

Henry de Longuêve, Jean Louis. *Observations . . . sur la partie du Rapport de M. Chabroud qui lui est personnelle.* Paris, 1790.

————. *Rapport fait à l'Assemblée nationale au nom du comité des rapports le 14 août 1790 sur les nouveaux troubles de la ville de Schelestat, en Alsace.* Paris, 1790.

Heurtault de Lamerville, Jean Marie, vicomte de. *Décret de l'Assemblée nationale du 3 février 1791 précédé du rapport . . . sur la découverte physique de M. de Trouville.* Paris, 1791.

————. *Discours prononcé à l'Assemblée de la noblesse de la vicomté de Paris, le 28 avril 1789.* N.p., 1789.

————. *Discours sur la propriété des mines.* Paris, 1791.

Jary, François Joseph. *Rapport fait au nom du comité de l'imposition sur la contribution personnelle.* Paris, 1790.

Juigné, Antoine Eléonor Léon Leclerc de. *L'Archevêque de Paris à ses diocésains.* Paris, 1789.

————. *Lettre pastorale de M. l'archevêque de Paris au clergé séculier et régulier et aux fidèles de son diocèse.* Paris, 1791.

————. *Lettre pastorale de monseigneur l'archevêque de Paris pour le soulagement des pauvres pendant les rigueurs de cet hiver.* Paris, 1789.

————. *Mandement de monseigneur l'archevêque de Paris qui ordonne des prières publiques dans tout son diocèse pour les Etats généraux du royaume.* Paris, 1789.

————. *Mandement de monseigneur l'archevêque de Paris qui ordonne une quête générale dans la ville et le diocèse de Paris en faveur des paroisses du diocèse qui ont été ravagées par la grèle du 13 de ce mois.* Paris, 1788.

————. *Mandement de monseigneur l'archevêque de Paris pour le Saint Tems de Carême qui permet l'usage des oeufs.* Paris, 1789.

————. *Mandement de monseigneur l'archevêque de Paris qui ordonne des prières publiques dans toutes les églises de son diocèse, conformément aux intentions du roi, exprimées dans la lettre de Sa Majesté, en date du deux de ce mois.* Paris, 1789.

————. *Mandement . . . qui ordonne des prières publiques dans tout son diocèse, pour les Etats généraux du royaume.* Paris, 1789.

————. *Mandement . . . qui ordonne que le Te Deum sera chanté dans toutes les églises de son diocèse, à l'occasion des délibérations prises dans l'Assemblée nationale, le quatre de ce mois.* Paris, 1789.

————. *Ordonnance de M. l'archevêque de Paris au sujet de l'élection faite le 13 mars 1791, de M. l'évêque de Lydda, par MM. les électeurs du département de Paris, en qualité d'évêque métropolitain dudit département.* Paris, 1791.

Lablache, Alexandre Joseph de Falcoz, comte de. *Opinion . . . contre l'émission des assignats.* Paris, 1790.

Lachastre, Claude Louis, comte de. *Lettre . . . à M. le comte de Guibert, le 1er avril 1789.* Paris, 1789.

————. *Précis de ce qui s'est passé à son égard à l'Assemblée de Berri, 25 mars 1789.* N.p., 1789.

Lally-Tolendal, Trophime Gérard, comte de. *Adresse aux amis de la liberté.* N.p., 1790.

————. *De l'influence de la Révolution sur la ville de Paris.* Geneva, 1791.

————. *Extrait d'une lettre . . . à Mme. la comtesse de ———— pour servir à sa justification.* N.p., 1789.

————. *Lettre du comte . . . au président de l'Assemblée nationale, 10 octobre 1789.* N.p., 1789.

————. *Lettre écrite au très-honorable Edmund Burke, membre du Parlement d'Angleterre.* Geneva, 1791.

————. *Le Tulerunt; ou, Récit pour servir de suite du discours de M. le Comte de Lally-Tolendal à ses co-députés sur l'insurrection de la ville de Paris contre le roi.* Paris, 1789.

————. *Mémoire; ou, Seconde lettre à ses commettans.* Paris, 1789.

————. *Motion . . . à l'assemblée générale des trois ordres du bailliage de Dourdans, 17 mars 1789.* Paris, 1789.

————. *Observations sur la lettre écrite par M. le comte de Mirabeau au comité des recherches, contre M. le comte de Saint-Priest, ministre d'état.* Paris, 1789.

————. *Pièces justificatives, contenant différentes motions de M. le comte de Lally-Tolendal.* N.p., 1789.

————. *Post scriptum d'une lettre . . . à M. Burke.* N.p., 1791.

————. *Quintius Capitolinus aux Romans: Extrait du troisième livre de Tite-Live.* Geneva, 1790.

Lancelot (Dubourg), Joseph Joachim François Esmé Jean Emmanuel. *Lettre à un de ses confrères au sujet du serment civique, 9 février 1791.* Paris, 1791.

Lanjuinais, Jean Denis. *Rapport fait au nom du comité ecclésiastique sur les vicaires des églises supprimées.* Paris, 1791.

————. *Réflexions patriotiques, sur l'arrêté de quelques nobles de Bretagne, du 25 octobre 1788.* N.p., 1788.

La Rochefoucauld, Louis Alexandre, duc de. *Discours . . . au nom du comité de l'imposition sur la contribution foncière.* Paris, 1790.

————. *Lettre à un membre de l'Assemblée nationale législative, sur l'état du travail des contributions publiques lors de la clôture de l'Assemblée nationale constituante; par un membre du comité des contributions publiques.* Paris, 1791.

————. *Opinion . . . sur les assignats-monnoie, le 15 avril 1790.* Paris, 1790.

————. *Opinions . . . sur les biens ecclésiastiques et sur les parlemens des 31 octobre et 3 novembre 1789.* Paris, 1789.

La Touche, Louis René Madeleine Levassor, comte de. *Discours prononcé le 16 mars 1789 à l'ouverture de l'Assemblée des trois ordres réunis du bailliage de Montargis-le-France. . . .* N.p., 1789.

Latyl, Jean Paul Marie Anne. *Discours prononcé à l'Assemblée électorale du district de Paris, le 30 mars 1791 . . . lors de sa proclamation à le curé de Saint Thomas d'Aquin.* N.p., 1791.

Launay, Jean Marie de. *L'Innocence outragée; ou, Pièces concernant les accusations, calomnies, et détention de l'abbé de Launay dans les prisons de la Tour-le-Bat à Rennes, mêlées de réflexions politico-morales, relatives aux décrets de l'Assemblée nationale.* N.p., 1789.

Laurent, François Xavier. *Déclaration d'un curé sur la Constitution du Clergé*. Paris, 1790.

―――. *Lettre de . . . à ses paroissiens*. N.p., 1791.

Le Breton, Jean Pierre. *Lettre à MM. les ecclésiastiques du département du Morbihan*. Paris, 1791.

Le Brun (de Grillon), Charles François. *La Voix du citoyen*. Paris, 1789.

―――. *Opinion sur la propriété des biens des églises, 30 octobre 1789*. Paris, 1789.

Le Chapelier, Issac René Guy. *Discours de M. le président au roi du 13 août 1789*. Paris, 1789.

―――. *Lettre adressée à messieurs les citoyens de la ville de Rennes, 12 septembre 1789*. Rennes, 1789.

―――. *Discours de M. Le Chapelier . . . sur la conduite de la chambre des vacations de Bretagne*. Paris, 1790.

―――. *Projet de loi et rapport sur la résidence des fonctionnaires publics, fait au nom du comité de Constitution*. Paris, 1791.

―――. *Rapport fait . . . au nom du comité de Constitution, sur la pétition des auteurs dramatiques, dans la séance du jeudi 13 janvier 1791*. Paris, 1791.

Le Deist de Botidoux, Jean François. *Opinion . . . sur les assignats, prononcée le 5 septembre 1790*. N.p., 1790.

Le Franc de Pompignan, Jean Georges. *Lettre pastorale de Mgr. l'archevêque de Vienne, aux curés de son diocèse, 15 juillet 1788*. N.p., 1788.

―――. *Réponse des députés de la province de Dauphiné aux Etats généraux au nouveau mémoire intitulé: "Mémoire pour une partie du clergé, et de la noblesse de Dauphiné."* Paris, 1789.

Le Gendre, Laurent-François. "Correspondance, 28 avril 1789 à 30 décembre 1791." Edited by A. Corre and Delourmel. *La Révolution française*, XXXIX (1900), 515–58; XL (1901), 46–78.

Legros, Charles Jean François. *Examen du systême politique de M. Necker*. N.p., 1789.

Le Guen de Kerangall, Guy Gabriel François Marie. *Lettre circulaire à mes commettans et aux membres des directoires des quatre districts de la partie du nord du département de Finistère*. Paris, 1790.

―――. *Neuvième Lettre à MM. les administrateurs du département de Finistère, avec instruction sur la nécessité de réunir les deux districts de Landernau et de Lesneven*. Paris, 1790.

Le Guillou de Kerincuff, Joseph Jean Marie. *A l'Assemblée nationale: Observations du district de Quimper, sur l'établissement du cheflieu du département de Finistère*. Quimper, 1790.

Le Lay de Grantugen, Guillaume. *Motion presentée à l'Assemblée nationale*. N.p., 1789.

————. *Opinions servans de préambule à son projet de décret.* Paris, 1791.

Lepeletier de Saint-Fargeau, Louis Michel. *Réponse à un écrit intitulé: "Bulletin de la grande assemblée du Club des Jacobins."* Paris, 1789.

Levis-Mirepoix, Charles Philibert Marie Gaston, comte de. *Protestation contre le décret du 19 juin 1790.* N.p., 1790.

Lubersac, Jean Baptiste Joseph de. *Discours prononcé . . . à l'Assemblée du principal bailliage de Tulles . . . le 16 mars 1789.* N.p., 1789.

Marsane Font Juliane, Jean Louis Charles François, comte de. *Motion faite à l'Assemblée nationale. . . .* Paris, 1790.

Martineau, Louis Simon. *Voeu d'un bon citoyen en forme de pétition à l'Assemblée nationale pour un établissement public en faveur des accusés absous, et des pauvres qui n'ont pas le moyen de défendre leurs droits en justice.* Paris, 1790.

Millet, Noël Charles. *Lettre à un de ses amis.* N.p., 1790.

Montboissier, Charles Philippe Simon de Montboissier-Beaufort-Canillac, baron de. *Opinion à la séance du soir, le 17 septembre 1789.* Versailles, 1789.

Montesquiou, François Xavier de. *Lettre adressée à M. le syndic-général du clergé du diocèse du Mans . . . à l'occasion des Etats-Généraux.* N.p., 1789.

Montesquiou-Fezensac, Anne Pierre, marquis de. *Adresse aux provinces; ou, Examen des opérations de l'Assemblée nationale.* N.p., 1789.

————. *Aux trois ordres de la nation.* N.p., [1789].

————. *Lettre . . . à M. ————.* Paris, 1790.

————. *Lettre . . . à M. Garet le jeune, rédacteur de l'article "Assemblée nationale, du 'Journal de Paris,'" à Paris, 16 juillet 1791.* Paris, 1791.

————. *Mémoires sur les finances du royaume, présentés à l'Assemblée nationale à la séance du 9 september 1791.* Paris, 1791.

————. *Opinion . . . à l'Assemblée nationale sur la liquidation de la dette publique.* Paris, 1790.

————. *Opinion sur les assignats-monnoie.* Paris, 1790.

————. *Plan de travail présenté à l'Assemblée nationale au nom du comité des finances.* Paris, 1790.

————. *Rapport des commissaires de l'Assemblée nationale envoyés dans les départements de la Meuse, etc.* Paris, 1791.

————. *Rapport fait à l'Assemblée nationaie au nom du comité des finances sur la demande faite par le municipalité de Paris d'une avance de fonds.* Paris, 1791.

————. *Réponse . . . à la réplique de M. Bergasse.* Paris, 1791.

————. *Réponse à MM. Bergasse, Maury, etc.* Paris, 1791.

Mounier, Jean Joseph. *Appel au tribunal de l'opinion publique.* Geneva, 1790.

————. *Aux Dauphinois.* N.p., [1790].

————. *Avis aux gens de toute profession: science, arts, commerce et métiers: composant l'ordre du Tiers-état de la province de Bretagne, par un propriétaire, en ladite province.* N.p., [1788].

———. *Considération sur les gouvernements, et principalement sur celui qui convient à la France.* Paris, 1789.

———. *Déclaration* [made to M. Sartoris, officer of the Republic of Geneva, July 10, 1790]. In "Mounier, président de la Constituante, et les journées des 5 et 6 octobre 1789," edited by Edouard Chapuisat. *La Révolution française,* LXXXVII (1934), 210–21.

———. *Délibération de la ville de Grenoble, 14 juin 1788.* N.p., 1788.

———. *Exposé de la conduite de . . . dans l'Assemblée nationale et des motifs de son retour en Dauphiné.* Paris, 1789.

———. *Extrait des registres des Etats de Dauphiné assemblés à Romans, 9 décembre 1788.* N.p., 1788.

———. *Extrait du procès-verbal de la commission intermédiaire des Etats de Dauphiné, 24 et 25 mars 1789.* N.p., 1789.

———. *Faits relatifs à la dernière insurrection.* N.p., 1789.

———. *Lettre de MM. du clergé, de la noblesse, et autres notables citoyens de Grenoble au roi.* N.p., 1788.

———. *Lettre écrite au roi par les trois ordres de la province de Dauphiné sur les Etats généraux.* N.p., 1788.

———. *Lettre écrite par plusieurs citoyens du clergé, de la noblesse, et des communes de Dauphiné, à messieurs les syndics-généraux des Etats de Béarn.* N.p., 1788.

———. *Nouvelles Observations sur les Etats-Généraux de France.* N.p., 1788.

———. *Observations sur les principes que j'ai soutenus dans l'Assemblée nationale.* N.p., [1789].

———. *Rapport de. . . .* N.p., [1789].

———. *Rapport du comité chargé du travail sur la Constitution.* Paris, 1789.

———. *Réponse des négocians de la ville de Grenoble à MM. les juges-consuls de Montauban et à la chambre de commerce de Picardie.* N.p., 1788.

———. *Très-respectueuses Représentations au roi des trois ordres de la province de Dauphiné.* N.p., 1788.

Moutier, Marc Antoine. *Réflexions sur le projet du Comité des dîmes adressés à l'Assemblée nationale par . . . député de bailliage d'Orléans.* Paris, 1790.

Palasne de Champeaux, Julien François, and Jean François Pierre Poulain de Corbion. "Correspondance des députés des Côtes-du-Nord." Edited by D. Tempier. *Mémoires de la Société d'émulation des Côtes-du-Nord,* XXVI (1888), 210–63.

Pelerin de La Buxière, Louis Jean. *Réflexions sur l'inutilité et le danger des états provinciaux ou des assemblées provinciales.* Versailles, 1789.

Pellerin, Joseph Michel. *Discours d'un citoyen pour être prononcé à l'Assemblée de la Commune, le 15 décembre 1788: A mes concitoyens nantais.* N.p., 1788.

———. *Mémoire historique sur la constitution des Etats de Bretagne, addressée aux gentilshommes bretons.* N.p., 1788.

———. *Mémoire justificatif pour . . . détenu au Château de Nantes.* N.p., 1791.

Perrotin de Barmond, l'abbé Charles François. *Procès complet de. . . .* Paris, [1790].

Pétion de Villeneuve, Jérôme. *Avis aux François sur le salut de la patrie.* Paris, 1788.

———. *Discours prononcé dans l'assemblée de la Société des Amis de la Constitution de Paris, séante aux Jacobins.* Paris, 1791.

———. "Discours sur la liberté de la presse." In Pétion de Villeneuve, *Oeuvres.* Vol. II of 4 vols. Paris, 1792–93. Pp. 352–90.

———. *Discours sur la réunion d'Avignon à la France.* Paris, 1790.

———. *Discours sur les conventions nationales.* In Pétion de Villeneuve, *Oeuvres.* Vol. II of 4 vols. Paris, 1792–93. Pp. 298–349.

———. *Lettre . . . à ses commettans sur les circonstances actuelles, 18 juillet 1791.* In Pétion de Villeneuve, *Oeuvres.* Vol. III of 4 vols. Paris, 1792–93. Pp. 419–33.

———. *Lettre d'un citoyen de l'ordre du Tiers, à l'Assemblée des Notables, servant de réponse aux observations du Parlement* [October, 1788]. In Pétion de Villeneuve, *Oeuvres.* Vol. I of 4 vols. Paris, 1792–93. Pp. 7–35.

———. *Opinion sur un conseil d'exécution électif et national* [1791]. In Pétion de Villeneuve, *Oeuvres.* Vol. III of 4 vols. Paris, 1792–93. Pp. 399–415.

———. *Petit mot d'un Marseillois sur le mémoire des princes.* N.p., 1789.

———. *Ultimatum d'un citoyen du Tiers-état au mémoire des princes, présenté au roi: Fin Mot d'un Marseillois.* N.p., 1789.

Phélines, Louis Jacques de. *Rapport de . . . commissaire de l'Assemblée nationale envoyé dans les départements du Haut et du Bas-Rhin: Prononcé dans la séance du 19 août 1791.* Paris, 1791.

Pison du Galland, Alexis François. *Déclaration des droits de l'homme et du citoyen.* Versailles, 1789.

———. *Opinion . . . sur l'organisation politique du royaume, imprimée par ordre de l'Assemblée, 10 novembre 1789.* Paris, 1789.

Poignot, Jean Louis. *Opinion . . . sur le parti à prendre par l'Assemblée nationale pour le rétablissment provisoire des finances.* Paris, 1789.

Poulain de Corbion, Jean François Pierre. *La Poule au pot; ou, Première cause du bonheur public, suivie des contradictions qu'il éprouve.* N.p., 1789.

———, and Julien François Palasne de Champeaux. *See* Palasne de Champeaux.

Puységur, Jean Auguste de Chastenet de. *Lettre de M. l'archevêque de Bourges à MM. les électeurs du département du Cher.* Paris, 1791.

Quéru de Lacoste, Pierre. *Lettre de MM. les recteurs de Saint-Jean de Rennes et de Retiers à leurs confrères, messieurs les recteurs, curés, et autres ecclésiastiques du diocèse de Rennes.* Paris, 1790.

Rastignac, Armand Anne Auguste Antonin Sicaire de Chapt de. *Lettre à messieurs du Tiers-état.* Paris, 1789.

————. *Questions sur la propriété des biens fonds ecclésiastiques en France.* Paris, 1789.

Richard, Antoine Joseph. *Compte rendu par . . . à leurs concitoyens, de leurs opérations pendant leur séjour à Paris, et de ce qui s'y est passé relativement à l'affaire d'Avignon.* Lille, 1791.

Ruffo de Bonneval, Sixte Louis Constant. *Déclaration de M. l'abbé de Bonneval aux Etats-Généraux.* N.p., 1791.

————. *Déclaration . . . aux Etats-Généraux.* Paris, 1791.

————. *Opinion et réclamation de M. l'abbé de Bonneval sur le projet de décret proposé par le comité des dîmes tendant à prononcer l'expropriation des églises et des titulaires des bénéfices.* N.p., 1790.

————. *Opinion sur le décret à rendre pour le rétablissement de la tranquillité publique.* N.p., 1790.

————. *Troisième Lettre . . . à ses commettans, suivie de sa protestation contre l'acte constitutionnel.* N.p., 1791.

Sallé de Chou, Etienne François Xavier. *Plan sur la gabelle . . . proposé à la séance du 16 septembre 1789.* Versailles, 1789.

————. *Projet de déclaration des droits de l'homme en société.* Versailles, 1789.

Sarrazin, Gilbert, comte de. *Adresse à l'Assemblée nationale et au département des Bouches du Rhône portant plainte en diffamation contre le sieur Blanc-Gilli, administrateur audit département; suivie d'une analyse des écrits diffamatoires dudit sieur.* Marseille, 1790.

————. *Le Jugement Dernier, allégoire réprésentée par une groupe de figures que le sieur Renaud, sculpteur, a composé pour couronner la Fontaine des Allées de Meilhan.* Marseille, 1790.

Sérent, Armand Sigismond Félicité Marie, comte de. *Exposition des objets discutés dans les Etats-Généraux de France, depuis l'origine de la monarchie.* Londres [Paris?], 1789.

Seurrat de Laboulaye, Jacques Isaac. *Motion sur le droit de Grurie faite par lui.* Paris, 1790.

Sieyès, Emmanuel Joseph. *Déclaration des droits du citoyen françois, détachée du Préliminaire de la Constitution.* Paris, 1789.

————. *Délibérations à prendre pour les assemblées de bailliages.* N.p., 1789.

————. *Dire de . . . sur la question du veto royal: à la séance du 7 septembre 1789.* Paris, 1789.

————. *Essai sur les privilèges.* Paris, 1789.

————. *Motion faite par . . . du 10 juin 1789 suivie de l'arrêté des communes du même jour.* Paris, 1789.

————. *Observations sommaires sur les biens ecclésiastiques du 10 août 1789.* Paris, 1789.

————. *Opinion de . . . le 7 mai 1791 en réponse à la dénonciation de l'arrêté du département de Paris, sur 11 avril précédent, sur les édifices religieux et la liberté générale des cultes.* Paris, 1791.

————. *Quelques Idées de constitution, applicables à la ville de Paris en juillet 1789.* Versailles, 1789.

————. *Qu'est-ce que le Tiers-état?* Paris, 1789.

————. *Réflexions sur les pouvoirs à donner aux députés aux Etats-généraux.* Paris, 1789.

————. *Vues sur les moyens d'exécution dont les représentans de la France pourront disposer en 1789.* N.p., 1789.

Talon, Antoine Omer. *Discours prononcé à l'Assemblée nationale, par monsieur le lieutenant-civil.* N.p., 1790.

————. *Discours prononcé par M. le lieutenant-civil, à la séance du 26 mai 1790.* Paris, 1790.

Thoret, Jacques. *Projet de déclaration des droits de l'homme et du citoyen.* Paris, 1789.

Tracy, Antoine Louis Claude de Stutt, comte de. *M. de Tracy à M. Burke.* Paris, [1791].

————. *Opinion sur les affaires de Saint-Domingue, en septembre 1791.* Paris, 1791.

Treilhard, Jean Baptiste. *Lettre . . . aux auteurs de la Feuille qui a pour titre "L'Ami du Roi, des François, de l'Ordre, et surtout de la Verité."* Paris, 1790.

————. *Résumé de l'opinion sur l'administration des biens ecclésiastiques, et sur le remplacement des dîmes.* Paris, 1790.

Tridon, Pierre. *Réponse à la déclaration d'un curé . . . sur la Constitution du Clergé.* Paris, 1790.

Tronchet, François Denis. *Opinion . . . à la séance du 5 janvier 1791 sur la question de savoir si la procédure devant le Jury de jugement doit être écrite ou non.* Paris, 1791.

————. *Seconde Opinion . . . à la séance du 5 janvier 1791 sur la question de savoir si la procédure devant le Jury de jugement sera écrite ou non.* Paris, 1791.

Vallet, Claude Benjamin. *Mémoire présenté à l'Assemblée nationale, 25 juin 1789.* N.p., 1789.

————. "Souvenirs." *Nouvelle Revue rétrospective,* XVI (1901), 219–40, 313–35, 385–408.

Varin de La Brunelière, Pierre Vincent. *Rapport fait à l'Assemblée nationale au nom de son comité des rapports dans l'affaire de M. Toulouse-Latrec.* Paris, 1790.

Verguet, Claude François, dom. *Observations de Dom Verguet, député de Bretagne, sur le rapport du comité ecclésiastique, concernant les ordres religieux*. Paris, 1790.

―――. *Opinion . . . sur le traitement des ordres religieux, en case de suppression*. Paris, 1789.

Villebanois, François. *Dire de . . . sur la motion faite le 13 février 1790, par M. l'évêque de Nancy*. Paris, 1790.

Virieu, François Henri, comte de. *Esprit des opérations des trois ordres du Dauphiné, depuis le 10 mai 1788 jusqu'à ce jour, le 1 octobre 1788*. N.p., 1788.

Yvernault, Sylvain. *Observations sur le résumé de M. Treillard {sic} relativement à l'administration des biens ecclésiastiques*. Paris, 1790.

Index